Marian Cox

Cambridge IGCSE®
First Language English

Teacher's Resource

Fifth edition

CAMBRIDGE
UNIVERSITY PRESS

CAMBRIDGE
UNIVERSITY PRESS

Shaftesbury Road, Cambridge CB2 8EA, United Kingdom

One Liberty Plaza, 20th Floor, New York, NY 10006, USA

477 Williamstown Road, Port Melbourne, VIC 3207, Australia

314–321, 3rd Floor, Plot 3, Splendor Forum, Jasola District Centre, New Delhi – 110025, India

103 Penang Road, #05-06/07, Visioncrest Commercial, Singapore 238467

Cambridge University Press is part of the University of Cambridge.

It furthers the University's mission by disseminating knowledge in the pursuit of education, learning and research at the highest international levels of excellence.

www.cambridge.org
Information on this title: www.cambridge.org/9781108438940

© Cambridge University Press & Assessment 2010, 2014, 2018

This publication is in copyright. Subject to statutory exception and to the provisions of relevant collective licensing agreements, no reproduction of any part may take place without the written permission of Cambridge University Press.

First published 2010
Fourth edition 2014
Fifth edition 2018

20 19 18 17 16 15 14 13 12 11 10 9 8 7

Printed in Great Britain by CPI Group (UK) Ltd, Croydon CR0 4YY

A catalogue record for this publication is available from the British Library

ISBN 978-1-108-43894-0 Paperback with Cambridge with Digital Access Teacher's Resource

Cambridge University Press has no responsibility for the persistence or accuracy of URLs for external or third-party internet websites referred to in this publication, and does not guarantee that any content on such websites is, or will remain, accurate or appropriate. Information regarding prices, travel timetables, and other factual information given in this work is correct at the time of first printing but Cambridge University Press does not guarantee the accuracy of such information thereafter.

*IGCSE is a registered trademark

All sample answers in this title were written by the author.
In examinations, the way marks are awarded may be different.

....

NOTICE TO TEACHERS IN THE UK
It is illegal to reproduce any part of this work in material form (including photocopying and electronic storage) except under the following circumstances:
(i) where you are abiding by a licence granted to your school or institution by the Copyright Licensing Agency;
(ii) where no such licence exists, or where you wish to exceed the terms of a licence, and you have gained the written permission of Cambridge University Press;
(iii) where you are allowed to reproduce without permission under the provisions of Chapter 3 of the Copyright, Designs and Patents Act 1988, which covers, for example, the reproduction of short passages within certain types of educational anthology and reproduction for the purposes of setting examination questions.

Cambridge IGCSE First Language English

Contents

Introduction   v
About the Teacher's Resource   v
Using the resource   vi
Notes   vii

Skills grid   viii

READING

Part 1   Comprehension and Summary   1

Unit 1	A matter of time	1
Unit 2	The gentle touch	11
Unit 3	To board or not to board	18
Unit 4	Virtual existence	24

Part 2   Comprehension and Writers' Effects   28

Unit 5	Colourful characters	28
Unit 6	Hide-and-seek	34
Unit 7	Same difference	41
Unit 8	Dislocation	48

Part 3   Response to Reading   55

Unit 9	Missing persons	55
Unit 10	Home-and-away	59
Unit 11	Of sharks and whales	64
Unit 12	Marital misery	72

WRITING

Part 4   Directed Writing and Coursework 1   77

Unit 13	Fur and against	77
Unit 14	Caught in the web	83
Unit 15	Praise or blame?	90
Unit 16	Community spirit	94

© Cambridge University Press 2018

Part 5 Descriptive Composition and Coursework 2   100

Unit 17	Close observation	100
Unit 18	Seeing the future	108
Unit 19	Nightmare journeys	114
Unit 20	City portraits	121

Part 6 Narrative Composition and Coursework 3   128

Unit 21	Crucial decisions	128
Unit 22	Incredible tales	133
Unit 23	Framed	142
Unit 24	Just walking	149

Handouts   154

Argument writing structure	154
Aspects of narrative	155
Descriptive writing structure	157
Formal letter structure	158
Formal report structure	159
Journal content	160
Magazine article structure	161
Narrative writing structure	162
News report structure	163
Rhetorical devices	164
Success criteria	165
Summary writing process	167
Writers' effects process	168

Answers to coursebook questions   169

Acknowledgements   224

Cambridge IGCSE First Language English

Introduction

About the Teacher's Resource

This Teacher's Resource has been produced to support teachers with the delivery of the Cambridge IGCSE and IGCSE (9–1) First Language English syllabuses 0500 and 0990. It covers everything which is relevant – skills, materials, approaches, tasks, answers, advice – to the teaching of an English Language curriculum at this level. The pages are all photocopiable for classroom use and they can also be downloaded from your Cambridge Elevate Teacher's Resource.

This Teacher's Resource is part of the Cambridge IGCSE First Language English suite by the same author, consisting of a Coursebook and a Language and Skills Practice Book (both fifth edition 2018), and is most effectively used in conjunction with the other products in the suite. Specifically designed for the busy, inexperienced or resource-challenged teacher, this publication is unique in that it provides all of the following:

- 24 detailed lesson plans with suggested tasks, timings and groupings
- a range of topic-linked reading passages and writing models
- worksheets and handouts for students
- suggested answers (where appropriate)
- task tips and response guidance in lesson plans and answers
- answers to the coursebook questions
- progress check tasks and mark schemes for Units 1–12 in the coursebook.

Success in the Cambridge IGCSE First Language English course depends on skills development, adequate preparation for the different types of question, familiarity with the way responses are assessed, coverage of the syllabus, and careful lesson planning by teachers to ensure maximum focus, motivation and production by students. All of these criteria are satisfied by the Teacher's Resource, and because it provides teaching ideas as well as the necessary resources, the teacher has only to concentrate on effective delivery of the lesson. The various genres of reading passages or writing tasks that may be set in an examination are all included (letter, formal report, news report, magazine article, journal, speech script, interview), as are the types of writing likely to be encountered during assessment or for a Coursework portfolio: argumentative, discursive, descriptive, narrative, analytical and evaluative. Informative texts provide practice for summary questions, and literary texts for stylistic analysis and writers' effects responses, as well as for modelling good narrative and descriptive writing.

The resource reinforces the skills of skim-reading for gist, scan-reading for data identification, selecting, modifying, developing, paraphrasing, structuring, sequencing, and supporting. It also stresses throughout the importance of the Reading skills of understanding implicit as well as explicit meaning, tested by a range of short answer questions, and of the Writing skills of considering voice, audience, register and purpose, the adoption of an appropriate style, and accuracy of expression.

Each unit gives practice in all or most of the five Assessment Objectives for Reading, Writing, and Speaking and Listening, so that there is continual practice and reinforcement of these objectives across a range of tasks and topics. Every unit contains integrated speaking and listening tasks, some of which are relevant to the optional test. It is at the teacher's discretion which tasks could be considered suitable for formative feedback and which for summative assessment, depending on the stage of the course, the level of the students and the components being prepared for. At least two written responses designed to reflect the style and length of responses that students would be asked to produce in examination – and more if the additional tasks are also set – are produced in each unit.

Using the resource

The Teacher's Resource is divided into six parts to support each main type of examination question for the three components: reading paper, writing paper and coursework. In addition to the general skill of comprehension, the specific assessment reading skills practised are summary, writers' effects and response to reading; the writing genres covered are argument, descriptive and narrative.

The book contains **24 units**, each providing enough classwork for one double lesson of 90 minutes, plus homework and optional additional tasks. The units are not progressive and can be completed in any order according to the syllabus options selected (Paper 2 writing or Component 3 coursework portfolio) and/or the centre's departmental scheme of work. Used in conjunction with the Coursebook and Practice Book, this resource provides more than enough material for a two-year (five-term) course.

At the start of each unit is a content and skills list indicating the focus and resources for that unit. Asterisks denote responses to tasks set in the **additional tasks** section of the lesson plan. There are also opportunities throughout to practise, revisit and reinforce the specific language elements of style, sentence structure, vocabulary extension and mechanical accuracy.

Every unit has a complete **lesson plan** for the teacher with detailed and sequenced **tasks** for the students. There is an average of 12 tasks per unit, ensuring a variety of resources, groupings, feedback methods and outcomes. The plan includes advice on how the tasks should be completed (as an individual, pair, small group or whole class), the form of the feedback (spoken or written, volunteered or requested), and how it should be assessed (self, peer, class or teacher).

The lesson plan is followed by the **texts** (for teacher and students), typically either two or three per unit, some of which may be visual or in verse. Some units also include **worksheets** or **handouts** for the students (and there is a Success Criteria check list for use by students before and after producing extended responses.) At the end of each unit are **answers** (for the teacher), indicating the kind of response to be expected for those tasks for which it is possible to give specific or predicted answers.

The texts in each unit are linked by topic and aim to reflect the style and length of passages in examinations. These passages cover a range of genres to provide breadth of reading experience, to reflect the types of text likely to be used during assessment, and to supply models for the different types of writing response required. The texts have a variety of international settings and are on subjects relevant and of interest to young people.

The **timings** in the lesson plans (in brackets in multiples of five minutes) are necessarily approximate, since they will be affected by the number of students in the class, the pace of work, and the amount of discussion. A 90-minute lesson can easily be divided into two or three singles rather than one double if shorter lessons are required, or extended to two hours by setting the **additional task**, or by starting the **homework task** within the lesson. It is often possible to borrow time from one task to give to another, or to leave out some tasks completely if time is short. The longer writing tasks, providing the main exam-type practice, are set for homework as they require up to an hour to complete, depending on type, and should be done independently by the student. The additional tasks can be used as extension activities for individual students who finish the other tasks early or who need to be stretched. Thus the lesson plans are flexible and adaptable, enabling the teacher to tailor them to the size, ability and working speed of the class, and to give them the focus required for a particular task, discussion or feedback session.

It is hoped that the Teacher's Resource will be inspirational to both teachers and students in the range and abundance of its topics and tasks. Its focus on the fundamental skills that students need to become competent users of English, as well as its attention to the assessment criteria, should make it an invaluable aid to good teaching and learning.

Cambridge IGCSE First Language English

Notes

- Where texts are of American origin, the original spelling has been retained. Students may use either British or American spelling in their writing, provided that they are consistent.
- It is assumed that teachers will provide students with the generic mark scheme grids, as advised by most examination boards, so that assessment comments can include phrases from the descriptors and enable students to become familiar with what is required for each part of their examination, and how the Assessment Objectives relate to the tasks and their marking criteria. Generic mark schemes for Cambridge IGCSE First Language English are available at www.cambridgeinternational.org.
- Students are advised in the lesson plans to use highlighters – sometimes in two different colours – to annotate passages for text-based questions, as an aid to close focus on reading and easy selection of material for planning. It is good practice to annotate and to be encouraged throughout the course as well as in the examination.
- Lesson tasks are addressed to the teacher using the self-instructional style commonly used in lesson plans, whereas the homework tasks are in a form which enables them to be set for students without modification, either orally or in writing on the board.

Skills grid

	Reading skills	Writing skills	Reading text types	Writing text types	Writing purposes	Speaking and listening
Unit 1: A matter of time	Comprehension Writers' effects Summarising Comparing*	Sentence structure Discursive style	Article Novel Poem	Magazine article*	Persuading*	
Unit 2: The gentle touch	Comprehension Summarising	Summary style	Article	Interview Magazine article Letter*	Explaining Persuading*	
Unit 3: To board or not to board	Comprehension Summarising Paraphrasing Evaluating Writers' effects	Argumentative style	Magazine article	Speech Dialogue Letter Leaflet*	Arguing	Dialogue
Unit 4: Virtual existence	Comprehension Summarising Comparing Collating	Sentence structure Sequence Summary style Formal writing	Blog	Blog Letter Speech*	Evaluation	
Unit 5: Colourful characters	Comprehension Writers' effects Selecting	Punctuation	Memoir	Composition*	Descriptive*	
Unit 6: Hide and seek	Comprehension Writers' effects Inference	Sentence structure Narrative style Narrative structure	Short story Poem	Composition	Narrative	
Unit 7: Same difference	Comprehension Inference Writers' effects Summarising Comparing Style analysis	Summary style Narrative style	Article Short story	Encyclopedia entry Short story	Informative Narrative*	
Unit 8: Dislocation	Writers' effects	Descriptive style Descriptive structure	Novel	Composition	Descriptive	Talk*

Cambridge IGCSE First Language English

	Reading skills	Writing skills	Reading text types	Writing text types	Writing purposes	Speaking and listening
Unit 9: Missing persons	Inference Selecting Paraphrasing	Sequence Informative style Sentence structure	Informative article Memoir	News report Formal report Synopsis	Informative	Dialogue*
Unit 10: Home and away	Writers' effects Selecting Summarising Style analysis	Informative style Sentence structure	Monologue Novel	Dialogue News report Journal entry Speech*	Informative	Dialogue
Unit 11: Of sharks and whales	Selecting Collating Summarising Writers' effects	Summary style Sentence structure	Internet news article Fact sheet Novel	Dialogue News report Letter Journal entry* Interview*		
Unit 12: Marital discord	Selecting Inference Writers' effects	Sentence structure	Novel	Dialogue Journal entry Letter Composition*	Narrative*	Dialogue Discussion
Unit 13: Fur and against	Selecting Summarising Paraphrasing Comparing	Sequence Interview style Formal letter style Argumentative style	Magazine article Interview	Formal letter	Persuading	Debate*
Unit 14: Caught in the web	Evaluating Selecting Summarising Comprehension Style analysis	Punctuation Summary style Sentence structure Argumentative structure	Blog Internet magazine article	Blog Letter Magazine article*	Discursive	
Unit 15: Praise or blame?	Style analysis Comparing Selecting	Interview style Persuasive devices Sequence	Magazine article Newspaper article	Interview Letter Magazine article*	Evaluation Argument Persuading	Interview
Unit 16: Community spirit	Selecting Summarising Inference Collating Comparing	Interview style Persuasive devices Formal style Summary writing	Memoir News article	Interview Speech Formal report Personal letter* Internet article*	Persuading	Interview Speech

© Cambridge University Press 2018

Skills grid ix

Cambridge IGCSE First Language English

	Reading skills	Writing skills	Reading text types	Writing text types	Writing purposes	Speaking and listening
Unit 17: Close observation	Writers' effects Inference	Descriptive style	Novel Visual	Composition	Descriptive	Talk*
Unit 18: Seeing the future	Inference	Descriptive style Argumentative style	Visual Short story	Blog	Descriptive	Discussion*
Unit 19: Bad dreams	Writers' effects	Descriptive style Descriptive structure	Novel	Composition	Descriptive	
Unit 20: City portraits	Writers' effects	Informative style	Magazine travel article Travel blog Tourist guide	Guide book entry Blog*	Descriptive Persuading*	
Unit 21: Crucial decisions	Writers' effects	Narrative style Narrative structure	Memoir	Composition	Narrative Informative	
Unit 22: Incredible tales	Inference Summarising	Punctuation Narrative devices Narrative structure Sentence structure Informative style	Short story	Synopsis Composition News report* Dialogue*	Narrative Informative*	
Unit 23: Framed	Writers' effects Inference	Informative style Narrative structure Descriptive style	Short story Novel	News report Short story	Informative Narrative Descriptive	
Unit 24: Just walking	Writers' effects Inference	Narrative structure	Short story	Composition Journal entry*	Narrative	

Note: * indicates activities set as additional (and therefore optional) tasks.

Unit ? **Unit title** © Cambridge University Press 2018

Part 1: Comprehension and Summary

Unit 1: A matter of time

Topic outline

- **Main skills:** comprehension; summary; writers' effects
- **Secondary skills:** persuasive language; selecting material; complex sentences
- **Outcome:** summary; *magazine article; *comparison of texts
- **Materials:** argumentative article; novel extract; poem; Worksheet and answers for Text 1C; Summary writing process handout
- **Texts:** Text 1A: Time management; Text 1B: Time travel; Text 1C: Time

Lesson plan

1. Ask students to contribute to the creation of a class mindmap on the board for the topic of 'Time'. (5)
2. Ask students to read Text 1A and give definitions for the five verbs in bold. (10)
3. Ask students to work in pairs to identify and list the characteristics of argumentative language in Text 1A, and feed back to class. (10)
4. Give students the Summary writing process handout for them to refer to. Ask them to identify and list the points in Text 1A to use in a summary of 'recommended strategies for improving time management'. (There are 15.) (10)
5. Ask students to read Text 1B. Ask them to identify / highlight relevant points for a two-paragraph summary of a) what the time-traveller observed on the journey in the machine and b) what the time-traveller observed after the machine landed. Ask students to list the points in their own words. Check that the right points have been selected. (15)
6. Ask students to work in pairs a) to identify effective language in the description of the crabs in Text 1B, paragraph 5, and b) to provide explanations for their choices and how they contribute to an overall atmosphere. (10)
7. Go through the responses as a class, discussing why each choice is effective (or not). (10)
8. Ask students to read Text 1C aloud around the class. Ask them to complete the worksheet for Text 1C. (15)
9. Go through the worksheet and discuss answers. (5)

Homework task

Write the two summaries, using your points from Task 4 and Task 5, in not more than 120 words each, in complex sentences. Check your work for accuracy, clarity and concision of expression before submitting it. You will be marked out of 10 for content and out of 5 for style.

Additional tasks

a. Ask students to plan and write a magazine article called 'Passing time' which includes and develops ideas from the three texts in this unit, and the mindmap created in Task 1.

b. Ask students to write a comparison of Texts 1A and 1B, with attention to the differences of voice, structure and style.

Text 1A

Time management

How well do you manage your time? Do you feel overloaded, pressured by deadlines, as though you should be in two places at once? Do you rush things, half-finish things, leave things to the last minute?

The most successful and productive people are those who control time rather than let it control them. Many of us would like to be better time managers but have fallen into bad habits or lack effective strategies. If we could only avoid common pitfalls and adopt common-sense practices, we could change our lives overnight.

One of the main failures is to not keep a to-do list, so that, by the end of each day there will be things we should have done but didn't, because we forgot about them or didn't organise our time well enough to fit them in. Of course, having a list does no good if you don't look at it, or if it has an impossible number of items on it (so that they have to be moved on to the next day, and the next …), or if you actually have no intention of doing those things.

It's tempting to **procrastinate** and repeatedly put off a job we don't want to do, but this just creates guilt, which spoils pleasure in doing other things, and panic, later, when we realise we haven't left enough time to make a decent job of it. Just making a start on a dreaded task makes you feel so much better than trying to avoid doing it, and then it's easy to come back to and continue with it or complete it the next time. Often it turns out not to be as bad as you thought it would be!

Knowing how to **optimise** scheduling is another time management strategy: some of us work better early in the morning, some in the afternoon, and others in the evenings, or even late at night. Make sure your daily to-do list takes account of this. You also need to accept what is possible; some people take on too much, out of fear or a desire to please, or because they don't know how to say 'No'. It would be much better to **negotiate** a less demanding task or a longer time frame in which to do it than to let people down when you fail to deliver, or damage yourself with stress and overwork. Sometimes it's appropriate to **delegate** rather than micro-manage or believe that you are the only person capable of doing a job properly. This doesn't mean getting your elder sibling to do your homework for you; it does mean letting your project partner do their fair share of the research. People often say that they like to be busy and that they are afraid of being bored, but being frantic over a long period, especially if eating and sleeping are neglected, can lead to burnout or poor performance. Think quality not quantity!

It's essential that the items on your list are precise: 'learn Italian' is not going to be helpful, but 'read Chapter 5 of the Italian coursebook' is. And you have to **prioritise** according to what needs to be done sooner, not what is more important: that way you won't feel the pressure of urgency and time running out. Of course, you must be flexible enough to put aside the list if an unforeseeable emergency arises, and you shouldn't spend so long writing your to-do list each day that you are taking up time that could be spent actually doing the things on it!

The lists and short-term tasks need to be part of long-term goals: what do you want to have achieved by the end of the week, the month, the year? Without goals you won't be able to decide what's worth spending your time on or have the motivation to work towards the destination without distractions. It is so easy to wander off-track and spend time doing something trivial and unproductive but pleasant, such as reading personal emails instead of writing an essay, and then realise with a shock that several hours have passed with nothing to show for them. Successful work happens when we are totally absorbed, firing on all cylinders, and this cannot happen if we allow interruptions or flit from one task to another. Many people call this multi-tasking and believe it to be a useful skill, but it normally means making mistakes and doing jobs 20–40% less efficiently than doing them in sequence with full concentration.

Which is not to say that you can't take a break! Taking breaks is a crucial aspect of time management. No-one can keep working indefinitely at maximum output and efficiency. Students studying for exams, for instance, are advised to take a short break every two hours, preferably one involving physical movement from the work station, and thus return refreshed with a better focus. A break is especially necessary if you feel you've got a blockage or have reached a dead end and can't think of a solution to a problem. A rested brain will often produce the elusive answer and prove the value of a little down-time.

Text 1B

Time travel

'I HAVE already told you of the sickness and confusion that comes with time travelling. And this time I was not seated properly in the saddle, but sideways and in an unstable fashion. For an indefinite time I clung to the machine as it swayed and vibrated, quite unheeding how I went, and when I brought myself to look at the dials again I was amazed to find where I had arrived. One dial records days, and another thousands of days, another millions of days, and another thousands of millions. Now, instead of reversing the levers, I had pulled them over so as to go forward with them, and when I came to look at these indicators I found that the thousands hand was sweeping round as fast as the seconds hand of a watch—into futurity.

'As I drove on, a peculiar change crept over the appearance of things. The palpitating greyness grew darker; then—though I was still travelling with prodigious velocity—the blinking succession of day and night, which was usually indicative of a slower pace, returned, and grew more and more marked. This puzzled me very much at first. The alternations of night and day grew slower and slower, and so did the passage of the sun across the sky, until they seemed to stretch through centuries. At last a steady twilight brooded over the Earth, a twilight only broken now and then when a comet glared across the darkling sky. The band of light that had indicated the sun had long since disappeared; for the sun had ceased to set—it simply rose and fell in the west, and grew ever broader and more red. All trace of the moon had vanished. The circling of the stars, growing slower and slower, had given place to creeping points of light. At last, some time before I stopped, the sun, red and very large, halted motionless upon the horizon, a vast dome glowing with a dull heat, and now and then suffering a momentary extinction. At one time it had for a little while glowed more brilliantly again, but it speedily reverted to its sullen red heat. I perceived by this slowing down of its rising and setting that the work of the tidal drag was done. The earth had come to rest with one face to the sun, even as in our own time the moon faces the earth. Very cautiously, for I remembered my former headlong fall, I began to reverse my motion. Slower and slower went the circling hands until the thousands one seemed motionless and the daily one was no longer a mere mist upon its scale. Still slower, until the dim outlines of a desolate beach grew visible.

'I stopped very gently and sat upon the Time Machine, looking round. The sky was no longer blue. North-eastward it was inky black, and out of the blackness shone brightly and steadily the pale white stars. Overhead it was a deep Indian red and starless, and south-eastward it grew brighter to a glowing scarlet where, cut by the horizon, lay the huge hull of the sun, red and motionless. The rocks about me were of a harsh reddish colour, and all the trace of life that I could see at first was the intensely green vegetation that covered every projecting point on their south-eastern face. It was the same rich green that one sees on forest moss or on the lichen in caves: plants which like these grow in a perpetual twilight.

'The machine was standing on a sloping beach. The sea stretched away to the south-west, to rise into a sharp bright horizon against the wan sky. There were no breakers and no waves, for not a breath of wind was stirring. Only a slight oily swell rose and fell like a gentle breathing, and showed that the eternal sea was still moving and living. And along the margin where the water sometimes broke was a thick incrustation of salt—pink under the lurid sky. There was a sense of oppression in my head, and I noticed that I was breathing very fast. The sensation reminded me of my only experience of mountaineering, and from that I judged the air to be more rarefied than it is now.

'Far away up the desolate slope I heard a harsh scream, and saw a thing like a huge white butterfly go slanting and flittering up into the sky and, circling, disappear over some low hillocks beyond. The sound of its voice was so dismal that I shivered and seated myself more firmly upon the machine. Looking round me again, I saw that, quite near, what I had taken to be a reddish mass of rock was moving slowly towards me. Then I saw the thing was really a monstrous crab-like creature. Can you imagine a crab as large as yonder table, with its many legs moving slowly and uncertainly, its big claws swaying, its long antennæ, like carters' whips, waving and feeling, and its stalked eyes gleaming at you on either side of its metallic front? Its back was corrugated and ornamented with ungainly *bosses*, and a greenish incrustation blotched it here and there. I could see the many palps of its complicated mouth flickering and feeling as it moved.

'As I stared at this sinister apparition crawling towards me, I felt a tickling on my cheek as though a fly had lighted there. I tried to brush it away with my hand, but in a moment it returned, and almost immediately came another by my ear. I struck at this, and caught something threadlike. It was drawn swiftly out of my hand. With a frightful qualm, I turned, and I saw that I had grasped the antenna of another monster crab that stood just behind me. Its evil eyes were wriggling on their stalks, its mouth was all alive with appetite, and its vast ungainly claws, smeared with an algal slime, were descending upon me. In a moment my hand was on the lever, and I had placed a month between myself and these monsters. But I was still on the same beach, and I saw them distinctly now as soon as I stopped. Dozens of them seemed to be crawling here and there, in the sombre light, among the foliated sheets of intense green.

'I cannot convey the sense of abominable desolation that hung over the world. The red eastern sky, the northward blackness, the salt Dead Sea, the stony beach crawling with these foul, slow-stirring monsters, the uniform poisonous-looking green of the lichenous plants, the thin air that hurts one's lungs: all contributed to an appalling effect. I moved on a hundred years, and there was the same red sun—a little larger, a little duller—the same dying sea, the same chill air, and the same crowd of earthy crustacea creeping in and out among the green weed and the red rocks. And in the westward sky, I saw a curved pale line like a vast new moon.'

From *The Time Machine,* by H.G. Wells.

VOCABULARY

bosses: protruding features

Text 1C

Time

I am the nor'west air nosing among the pines
I am the water-race and the rust on railway lines
I am the mileage recorded on the yellow signs.

I am dust, I am distance, I am lupins back of the beach
I am the sums the sole-charge teachers teach
I am cows called to milking and the magpie's screech.

I am nine o'clock in the morning when the office is clean
I am the slap of the belting and the smell of the machine
I am the place in the park where the lovers were seen.

I am recurrent music the children hear
I am level noises in the remembering ear
I am the sawmill and the passionate second gear.

I, Time, am all these, yet these exist
Among my mountainous fabrics like a mist,
So do they the measurable world resist.

I, Time, call down, condense, confer
On the willing memory the shapes these were:
I, more than your conscious carrier,

Am island, am sea, am father, farm, and friend,
Though I am here all things my coming attend;
I am, you have heard it, the Beginning and the End.

'Time', by Allen Curnow, from *Songs of Ourselves.*
Note: Lupins are a type of flower.

Worksheet for Text 1C: Time

1. Explain in your own words how Time is represented in the following lines of the poem:

   a. *I am the mileage recorded on the yellow signs.*

   b. *I am the sums the sole-charge teachers teach.*

   c. *I am the slap of the belting and the smell of the machine.*

   d. *I am recurrent music the children hear.*

2. What do the following devices contribute to the effect of the poem:

   a. alliteration

   b. repetition

   c. rhyme

3. Choose the line from the poem which you think best illustrates the role of Time, and give your reasons.

4. Write another three-lined rhymed verse for the poem, each line beginning 'I am.'

5 Write a paraphrase and summary of the final three verses of the poem.

_____

_____

_____

_____

_____

_____

_____

_____

6 Explain the use of capitals in the final line.

_____

_____

_____

_____

Cambridge IGCSE First Language English — **Comprehension and Summary**

Answers to Worksheet for Text 1C: Time

Note: This is a complex poem of ideas and the questions are designed to make students look at language and imagery, and to infer meanings, rather than to elicit 'correct' answers. Accept any reasonable attempts to convey understanding.

1   a   Time is shown by how long it takes to travel a distance.

    b   Time is the subject of maths problems asking how long it would take to perform a task.

    c   Time is measured in the passing of a day at work.

    d   Time makes music possible because notes have duration / form a beat.

2   a   Alliteration calls attention to phrases and connects their components memorably in logical collocations or surprising juxtapositions, e.g. *place in the park, father, farm and friend*.

    b   Repetition: the insistent use of *I am* at the start of lines has religious connotations and personifies Time as a domineering divine power which is everywhere and to which everything is subject; it stresses the concept of identity in its simplest and most inescapable form.

    c   The rhyming of each end-stopped line of the tercet (three-lined stanza) creates a regular and predictable pattern consistent with the fixed measure of Time.

5   Time is everything that has happened, however trivial and transitory; it is a constant and controlling force, both concretely and also in the form of memories, which are abstract products of the unconscious, tied to beloved people and places. Time is ever-present, yet always being waited for; it is the cause and symbol of beginnings and endings.

6   Time is capitalised and personified to signify its omnipotent and god-like status, and the capitals for *Beginning* and *End* emphasise the control Time has over the journey of a human life, from birth to death, and how nothing can exist outside of Time: past, present or future.

Answers – Unit 1

1. Example content for mindmap: dates, diaries, schedules and calendars, routine, seasons, ageing, change, decay, healing, regrets, hopes, prophecy, promises, horoscopes, memory, sport, examinations, travel

2. *procrastinate* – to delay or postpone deliberately the performance of an action

    optimise – to make the most effective use of something

    negotiate – to discuss in order to reach an agreement on something

    delegate – to entrust a task to another person

    prioritise – to rank items in order of importance

3. Argumentative language in Text 1A: rhetorical questions; triple structures; antithesis; use of inclusive 'we'; exclamations for lively tone; concessive language (*Of course, Which is not to say …*)

4. Fifteen 'Recommended strategies for improving time management':

    - Keep a to-do list and refer to it.
    - Don't aim to do too much each day.
    - Don't put things on the list you have no intention of doing.
    - Don't put jobs off, but at least make a start.
    - Allocate jobs according to the time of day you work best.
    - Turn work down that you don't really want or need to do.
    - Negotiate for an easier task or more time where possible.
    - Delegate when appropriate.
    - Retain good eating and sleep habits.
    - Be precise about the tasks.
    - Do the most urgent tasks first.
    - Don't spend too much time on the list.
    - Have long-terms goals and relate the tasks to them.
    - Resist distractions and avoid multi-tasking.
    - Take refreshment breaks every few hours.

5. a   What he observed on the journey in the machine:

    - high speed
    - hands moving fast towards the future
    - alternation of dark and light became slower
    - a continuous half-light
    - passing comets visible
    - Sun became redder and ceased to set
    - Sun finally became stationery
    - no Moon

- stars circled slowly
- when levers reversed, the hand indicating thousands (of years) stopped moving

b What he observed after the machine landed:

- black sky with bright stars in N.E.
- starless red sky overhead
- Sun on the S.E. horizon
- bright red rocks
- green vegetation
- sloping beach
- sea to S.W. with bright horizon
- no waves, but slight swell
- thick layer of pink-hued salt
- huge crabs

6 a Effective language in paragraph 5:

antennae – they are receiving signals and very aware; makes them seem more machine than animal

like carters' whips – pain-association of whips, and makes crabs seem in control, as carters control horses

waving and feeling – their antennae seem inescapable

stalked eyes gleaming – unpleasant image associated with sci-fi aliens

metallic front – reinforces idea of machines, and invulnerability

corrugated and ornamented – shell of its back impenetrably hard, like armour

greenish incrustation blotched it – all words associated with ugliness

its complicated mouth flickering and feeling – like the antennae, the mouth has a life of its own

b Their alertness and constant movement make the crabs threatening and dominating, and their ugly and alien aspect is alarming. The combined effect of the descriptive language is to convey a 'sinister apparition'.

Unit 2: The gentle touch

Topic outline

- **Main skills:** comprehension; summary; genres of response writing
- **Secondary skills:** selecting material; organising material
- **Outcome:** summary; interview; magazine article; *letter
- **Materials:** news article; Worksheet and answers for Text 2; Magazine article structure handout
- **Text:** Text 2: Monty's method

Lesson plan

1. Give out Text 2 and read it to the class. (5)

2. What sort of text is Text 2? Ask students to identify the characteristics of the genre, news reports, and collect a list on board, explaining how a news article differs from a news report in style, structure, voice and content. (10)

4. Give out the worksheet for Text 2 and ask students to complete it. (20)

5. Ask students to swap worksheets and give out answers while students mark each other's work. Collect marks (out of 25). (10)

6. Ask students to:
   a. find and list the points in paragraphs 4 and 5 for a summary of the process Monty uses for taming a wild horse
   b. turn them into a paragraph of about 75 words.

   Collect summaries for assessment. (15)

7. Ask students to plan and write a response to the following task: You are Monty Roberts being interviewed on a TV chat show. Write the replies you give to the following questions:
   a. How would you describe the 'magic' that you perform at public events?
   b. What are your beliefs about horses and children?
   c. Why do you think your method is so effective in your work with horses and children?

   Students should write half a page of average-sized writing in answer to each question. After students have checked their work, collect for assessment. (20)

8. Ask students to plan an article for their school magazine describing Monty's methods and how they can be applied in schools. They should scan the passage, select the relevant material, and organise a structure in their plans. (See the magazine article structure handout.) Write the acronym VARP – voice, audience, register, purpose – on the board as a reminder to students of what always needs to be considered before they write a response. (10)

Homework task

Write your magazine article, planned in Task 8, beginning *The school trip to see Monty Roberts was not only highly entertaining, but has caused us to reflect on the way students are treated in schools.* Remember to modify the voice, focus and style for the genre and audience of a school magazine article, and to change the order of the material to provide a new structure for a different purpose.

Additional task

Ask students to write a letter to their head teacher asking for the school to review its disciplinary procedures in the light of Monty's philosophy, and to adopt a system of contracts with students.

Text 2

Monty's method

Monty is the real-life Californian Horse Whisperer who can train a mustang to accept a saddle and rider in ten minutes.

On a cold Tuesday night in September, 1000 people are gathering in a barn the size of an aircraft hangar. In the queue, there's a man covered in blue denim from Stetson to cowboy boots whose spurs rattle as he walks. He looks the part. They are all here to see Monty Roberts. Outside, one of the volunteers who is putting up signs says 'In the horse world, he's a bit of a god.'

Monty Roberts is also gaining something of a reputation in the world of education as schools start to apply his **techniques** in the classroom. His theories on non-confrontational human relationships have been **credited with** turning round failing schools.

Back in the barn, the warm-up music of classic western themes fades and the night's star attraction appears. A big bear of a man with a gentle smile, he **acknowledges** the applause and walks into the fenced pen at the centre of the arena. 'Practically everybody here has read or heard something about me,' he begins. 'That's just the way it is today. But there won't be one horse who comes through that gate tonight that has read or heard anything about me.'

The first horse to enter the arena is a handsome animal called Socks. Like a magician about to perform a trick, Monty asks Socks's owner if they have ever met. He needs to rule out any **collusion** because what follows is so magical as to beggar belief. But it is not a trick. Socks is a 'starter', meaning he has never been ridden. In fact, he has never had anything on his back. He is wild – in the top five per cent of untrained horses. Socks starts to run round the pen, first one way then the other, as Monty throws a line softly on to his back and kicks up sawdust and dirt, **imitating** a predator. After a couple of minutes, Socks realises he is not in danger and starts to chew and lick his lips, just as Monty said he would. Then he stops, and drops his head to the ground.

And then the magic begins. Monty stands sideways on and walks slowly towards Socks, avoiding eye contact. Then Socks turns towards him, and Monty **scurries** away. This is not the action of a predator, the horse thinks. The third time he does this, something incredible happens. Socks begins to follow Monty across the ring, his head almost resting on his shoulder. In eight minutes, wild horse and civilised man have made friends, achieving what Monty calls 'join-up'. He signals for his rider to bring a saddle, and within ten minutes Socks is carrying a man on his back around the ring. 'Horses are stupid – that's what they said for 2000 years. Look at this young horse. Look at him learn. Horses are 50 million years old, and humans have been around for a much shorter period of time. Horses have been my teachers as much as I have been theirs.'

Monty Roberts has done this routine thousands of times. It's second nature to him. It's the reason he's famous. But it's not his *raison d'être*. During the evening he will 'join up' with five horses, gently curing them of habits of biting and bucking and refusing to go into boxes or through gates, without laying a finger on them except to pat their noses. But incredible though this is, it is only a sideshow.

Monty's main concern these days is to apply his non-violent methods to human relationships, to **revolutionise** the way we communicate. 'These are the most precious relationships,' he says. 'Every human being is more precious than all the horses I have worked with.' Like horses, children are flight animals, meaning that when threatened they flee, except that our predatory ancestry means we put up with a lot more ill-treatment before we run. 'Each of the animals that comes in that pen is just like a child,' says Monty. 'They have the same needs. They want trust, they want to be able to trust, they want safety and some love. They don't want to be hurt.'

His philosophy is simple: positive actions reap positive consequences; negative actions incur negative consequences. He encourages parents and children to draw up a series of contracts, verbal or written, and this gives even children as young as two a sense of responsibility. Children should never be rewarded for good behaviour with food or money, but allowed to go on an outing or do a favourite pastime instead. Breaking the contract means a task, but this should be something useful. It is important that the child decides on both the reward and the task and that both parties stick to the deal. 'There's not a bad kid born,' says Monty. 'There's not a bad horse born. Circumstances and life's environment are what make us either bad or good. And teachers have been the most important part of our sociological order since the beginning of time, because they represent what our future will be.'

Monty is a **charismatic**, articulate but modest man. He describes his work as a mission to leave the world a better place than he found it. In some places, in prisons and schools, thanks to him, it already is.

Adapted from article 'Monty's method', by Harvey McGavin, *Times Educational Supplement*, 21st September 2001.

Worksheet for Text 2: Monty's method

1. Explain in your own words *He looks the part*. (1)

2. Explain the meaning of *In the horse world, he's a bit of a god*. (1)

3. Why does Monty say that no horses have read or heard about him? (2)

4. Explain, using your own words, what the writer means by: (1 mark each: 3)

   a *so magical as to beggar belief*

   b *It's second nature to him.*

   c *it is only a sideshow*

5. Give another word for the words in bold in the text. (1 mark each: 8)

   a *techniques*

   b *credited with*

   c *acknowledges*

   d *collusion*

   e *imitating*

   f *scurries*

g *revolutionise*

h *charismatic*

6 Explain in your own words: (2 marks each: 4)

   a *our predatory ancestry means we put up with a lot more ill-treatment before we run.*

   b *positive actions reap positive consequences; negative actions incur negative consequences.*

7 What does Monty mean when he says *There's not a bad kid born. … There's not a bad horse born?* (2)

8 Quote two words or phrases which show that the writer is impressed by Monty's personality. (2)

9 Quote two words or phrases which show that the writer is impressed by Monty's achievement. (2)

[Total: 25 marks]

Answers to Worksheet for Text 2: Monty's method

1 His appearance is as one would expect it to be / he is wearing the clothes of a cowboy.

2 People who work with horses think he has divine powers.

3 He says this to make clear that the effect he has on horses can have nothing to do with his reputation.

4   a The animal's inexplicable behaviour is incredible / it seems to be under a spell.
    b He can do it without having to even think about it / it comes naturally.
    c It is not the main reason for his being there / it is not his main interest.

5   a skills / methods
    b given the recognition for / named as the person responsible for
    c notices / appreciates
    d partnership / working together
    e copying actions of / mimicking
    f moves quickly
    g completely change
    h charming / fascinating

6   a Because we are descended from hunters, we tolerate more maltreatment before escaping.
    b If you react to a situation with constructive measures, the outcome will be equally constructive, and the opposite is also true, so that destructive approaches lead to destructive outcomes.

7 He means that when they first come into the world, both children and horses are potentially good, and it is only what happens to them later which makes their behaviour difficult to handle.

8 *charismatic; modest*

9 *incredible; just as Monty said he would* (allow *magic*)

Answers – Unit 2

2 Text 2 has the news report features of: direct speech from interviewee, use of present tense, eye-witness account, short sentences, short paragraphs. These give the effects of immediacy, the personality of the subject, the authenticity of the event, and a sense of drama.

The text has the news article features of: lack of sense of immediacy, the personal attitude of the reporter, the use of the first person, long paragraphs. These give the effects of reflection, engagement and conviction, and the implication is that this is a significant and ongoing topic rather than just one ephemeral event.

Text 2 moves between the two styles and perspectives, even within the same paragraph.

6 a Points to be included:

- Monty throws line over horse's back.
- Monty kicks up earth in the arena.
- Monty walks sideways towards horse several times.
- Monty runs away each time horse turns towards him.
- Horse submits and follows Monty.
- A saddle is put on horse.
- Finally, horse is ridden around the arena.

b Having thrown a line over the horse's back, Monty kicks up earth in the arena. He then walks sideways towards the horse several times, and runs away each time that the horse turns towards him. Eventually, the horse submits and starts to follow Monty. At this point a saddle is put on the horse, so that finally it can be ridden around the arena. (64 words)

7 A good response will include the following points:

a Wild and unridden horses willingly allow a saddle to be put on their backs and a rider to mount them; horses lose their fears and bad habits within a few minutes; I can achieve this just by speaking to them and touching them gently.

b Horses are much wiser than humans; they have been around for much longer; they learn quickly; they are flight animals.

Children are more important than horses; they put up with a lot of abuse before running away.

Animals and children have similar needs: trust, safety and love. They are afraid of pain. Both horses and children are born potentially good, but get damaged by circumstances and the way they are treated. Both need enlightened teachers.

c Success is due to many years' experience of allowing horses to teach me; a positive approach is always more effective than a negative approach, i.e. rewards not punishments; instead of conflict, deals should be made which involve both sides; these encourage responsibility; rewards should consist of pleasurable and memorable experiences.

A good answer will have structure, sequence, clarity, and a variety of appropriate language used in the response.

Unit 3: To board or not to board

Topic outline

- **Main skills:** comprehension; summary; responses to reading
- **Secondary skills:** paraphrasing; selecting material; developing ideas; evaluating ideas; writers' effects; argument style
- **Outcome:** dialogue; speech; letter; *leaflet
- **Materials:** magazine articles; Worksheet and answers for Text 3A
- **Texts:** Text 3A: A boarding school student's view; Text 3B: A boarding school head's view

Lesson plan

1. Ask students to read Text 3A. (5)
2. Give out the worksheet for Text 3A and ask students to complete it. (15)
3. Ask students to check their answers. Collect the completed worksheets to assess. (5)
4. Ask students to underline or highlight the words or phrases in the first three paragraphs of Text 3A which best convey the feelings of the writer in a new country. (5)
5. Invite responses and collect on the board. Discuss why these words are effective. (5)
6. Ask students to prepare the answer (of about half a side) the writer might give if one of his children asked to be allowed to go abroad to boarding school. They will need to develop the ideas in Text 3A. (10)
7. Invite students to read out their answers. Judge whether they contain inference, development, persuasiveness, voice, sense of audience, and how well they cover the range of possible points. (10)
8. Ask students to read Text 3B. (5)
9. Ask students to identify features of argumentative style in Text 3B and give examples (e.g. short sentences, parallel structures, antithesis, repetition for effect, emphatic verbs, use of first person, use of absolutes). (5)
10. Ask students, in pairs, to underline or highlight in Text 3B the points in favour of boarding education. (5)
11. Ask students, in pairs, to collect ideas for questions and answers from both texts and to script an argumentative dialogue between the writers of Texts 3A and 3B, who should each speak at least five times. Students should include the stylistic features identified in Task 9. (10)
12. Invite pairs to perform their dialogues. Vote on the best dialogue, based on the range of material used and the persuasiveness of the speakers. (10)

Homework task

Your friend has been offered by his/her parents the chance of going to a boarding school in another country. Plan and write a letter to your friend of about 300 words, pointing out the things to be said for and against accepting the offer, based on the evidence in the two texts, and giving your own opinion. In the next lesson, you will swap letters with a partner and mark each other's letters according to the relevant assessment criteria.

Additional tasks

a. Ask students to write a dialogue between parents who are arguing about whether to send their child to boarding school.

b. Ask students to write a promotional leaflet for their own school, using some of the ideas from Text 3B and relevant ideas of their own. They should write about 300 words.

Text 3A

A boarding school student's view

I remember vividly that cold, dark Sunday evening 50 years ago when my parents first drove me to my new school, where the head received us in his study. Having only a few weeks earlier travelled by ship from East Africa, East Yorkshire in January was a shock. After pleasantries over a cup of tea, my parents left to make the long journey back to Dar es Salaam. I shall never forget that feeling of being left utterly alone. I remember tears welling up and the head telling me that I would have to grow up. He and I were never to get on. The following term, for no reason I could ever discern, he confiscated my favourite miniature car, which I kept in my locker. I never got it back.

For a child who had spent all his previous life in tropical open spaces, the north of England was an awful place. Where I came from, the Sun shone, there were palm trees, white sandy beaches, mangoes, houses with big gardens. I never saw a mango in Yorkshire; houses were joined to each other in terraces, and it was eternally dark and cold. Short trousers were a trial for an 11-year-old with hypothermia. I worked my way along corridors pressing my knees to radiators to restore circulation.

Life improved in some ways, but the long separation from the land that was home to me was something I never came to terms with. Like many others of my generation sent away to school in England, there was to be only one trip home a year, which was for the summer holiday. At Christmas and Easter I was parked with various relatives in unfamiliar towns. They took good care of me but they were strangers, albeit of a different kind. The school, with its long-established traditions imbued with an ethos fresh from the 19th century, was a place I never came to terms with. If you were academically able or good at cricket – or better still, both – it served you well. If not, that was your problem, not the school's.

Boarding school certainly makes one self-reliant, which comes in handy later in life. After that experience I had no problem surviving military academy. It was noticeable how much better the ex-boarders tended to fare in training than those who had been at day schools. But it can impair the parental connection – I never forgave mine for sending me away. For some reason I held my father to blame, which created a rift which was never properly mended, despite his very best efforts. I understand now, of course, that from my parents' perspective it would have seemed the most sensible course of action at the time.

My own experience and that of my wife Geraldine (who was sent to a convent boarding school) turned us against boarding for our own three children (even assuming we could have afforded it). But the world has changed markedly for the better. I have no doubt that these days boarding schools are far kinder places than once they were. And by the way, if anyone finds a coin under the floor of the dormitory on the top floor, it's mine; it rolled across the floor and dropped between the floorboards in February 1958.

Adapted from 'A boarder's view', in *The Alternative Old Pocklington Bulletin*, by Donald McGregor.

Text 3B

A boarding school head's view

Sending children away to boarding school has often been a controversial idea. Many cultures view this as at best incomprehensible and at worst tantamount to child abuse – the latter image encouraged by a number of notorious fictional representations. It is true that, in the past, boarding-school education was often rather spartan in nature, and even cruel at times. In several countries such schools were associated with preparing military officers and civil servants for the hardships they would endure in their careers of public service.

All this has changed. Anybody who visits a modern boarding school today comes away with an overwhelming impression of a happy, busy, motivated community of well-adjusted young people who are cared for and who live in comfortable, personalised living spaces. The era of huge, impersonal dormitories is long gone, as are inhuman matrons and housemasters. Boarding education today reflects the wider revolution which has taken place in education in recent years: student-centred, skills-based learning has replaced 'chalk-and-talk' and 'rote learning'. There is a profound emphasis on developing the individual, on helping and encouraging every student to achieve their best in whichever fields they have talent.

Many parents find it an agonising decision to send their beloved children away from home for three quarters of the year. They do it not because they are indifferent to their children; on the contrary, they do it because they care deeply about them and wish to give them the best opportunities and foundations for adulthood that they can. Boarding schools understand the sacrifice which parents are making, and communicate regularly with them. Most boarding schools operate an 'open-door' policy under which parents are welcome to visit the school at any time and to attend all school events.

Although there are of course good schools in every country, even the best cannot provide the range and quality of education which boarding schools can offer. In a boarding school, classes are smaller; staff are more highly qualified; there is an overriding commitment to a broad vision of education which does not end at 3 o'clock or at the classroom door. All boarding schools offer exceptional programmes of sporting, artistic, intellectual, cultural and physical activities. Any student with any special talent, interest or pursuit will find that it is nurtured by caring and patient staff at a boarding school. Because students are in the school seven days a week, so are the staff, and the students' time is employed fruitfully throughout the week.

The same is true for those who have special educational needs. The supportive atmosphere and the 24-hour-a-day availability of specialist staff mean that children who need help receive far more than can be offered in a day school.

Pastoral care is at the heart of boarding school life. Every adult in the school makes it their business to get to know each student, both in the classroom and beyond, and to offer them the opportunity to share their concerns and problems and to receive appropriate advice and guidance.

A key feature of the boarding-school experience which is not always appreciated is the educational value of learning to live together in a community: to get on with other people from a range of backgrounds and cultures, to share challenges and adventures together, to learn how to overcome adversity and cope with occasional failure, and to learn how to be a member of a team. Young people also, of course, learn to be independent, confident, self-reliant: in a word, they grow up faster and more successfully than those who have been sheltered at home. They are manifestly better-equipped for the transition to university and the workplace. They understand the importance of being a member of a community, and they make friendships for life.

Worksheet for Text 3A: A boarding school student's view

1 Why did the writer find East Yorkshire *a shock*? (1)

2 Explain in your own words the meaning of *pleasantries over a cup of tea*. (1)

3 Give the phrase which best describes how distressed the writer felt after his parents left him. (1)

4 Explain, using your own words, *He and I were never to get on*. (2)

5 State three ways in which the English landscape differed from that of Africa. (3)

6 What effect does the writer achieve by saying that he was *parked with various relatives*? (2)

7 Explain in your own words the two things he never came to terms with. (2)

8 Explain in your own words what, in the writer's view, ex-boarders have which day-school pupils lack. (2)

9 Put into your own words the phrase *impair the parental connection*. (2)

10 What two things is the writer implying by saying *even assuming we could have afforded it*? (2)

11 Give two reasons why the writer tells us that he lost a coin under the floorboards of his dormitory. (2)

[Total: 20 marks]

Answers to Worksheet for Text 3A: A boarding school student's view

1. It was cold and dark compared to East Africa.

2. trivial, polite conversation at tea-time

3. *the feeling of being utterly alone*

4. We continued to dislike each other / we did not manage to become friendly.

5. There was less sun, the vegetation was not tropical, and there was much less space.

6. He conveys the impression that he was being left with people he didn't know well and who didn't really want him.

7. He was never reconciled to being away from home, or to the school's atmosphere being so old-fashioned.

8. The ability to be depend on themselves and the ability to cope with disciplined training.

9. damage the relationship with one's mother and father

10. He is implying that boarding schools are very expensive, and that he and his wife were not well-off.

11. He is pointing out that he slept in a room with bare floorboards and no carpet when he was at school, and that he has not forgotten any of the distressing experiences he had when he was there.

[Total: 20 marks]

Answers – Unit 3

4 Text 3A – words conveying the writer's feelings:

Paragraph 1 – *shock, alone*

Paragraph 2 – *awful, dark and cold, trial*

Paragraph 3 – *separation from … home, unfamiliar, strangers*

6 Text 3A: sample answer:
Certainly not. My boarding school was a cold, unkind place and I was not happy there. You would feel very lonely, and there would probably be at least one teacher you didn't get on with and who was even cruel to you. The environment and climate would be very different from here and you would be homesick. It might not always be possible for you to come home for every school holiday, and you would hate being dumped on distant relatives. There are no luxuries and home comforts, you know; they don't even have carpet on the floor and you have to sleep in a dormitory with lots of other pupils and no privacy. Only students who are very academic or very sporty really enjoy boarding school. You might grow away from the family and would never forgive me for letting you go, just as I never forgave my own father. Although boarding schools are character-building – and they might have improved somewhat nowadays – I wouldn't want to take the risk of your being as unhappy as your mother and I were.

10 Text 3B: points in favour of boarding education:

- *happy, busy, motivated community*
- *well-adjusted young people*
- *students are cared for*
- *comfortable, personalised living spaces*
- *range and quality of education*
- *classes are smaller*
- *staff are more highly qualified*
- *commitment to a broad vision of education*
- *exceptional programmes of sporting, artistic, intellectual, cultural and physical activities*
- *any special talent, interest or pursuit is nurtured by caring and patient staff*
- *students' time is employed fruitfully throughout the week*
- *supportive atmosphere and the 24-hour-a-day availability of specialist staff*
- *every adult makes it their business to get to know each student*
- *receive appropriate advice and guidance*
- *get on with other people from a range of backgrounds*
- *share challenges and adventures*
- *learn how to overcome adversity and cope with occasional failure*
- *learn how to be a member of a team*
- *grow up faster and more successfully*
- *better-equipped for the transition to university and the workplace*
- *understand the importance of being a member of a community*
- *make friendships for life*

Unit 4: Virtual existence

Topic outline

- **Main skills:** comprehension; summary; responses to reading
- **Secondary skills:** identifying ideas; comparing texts; directed writing; collating material; developing ideas
- **Outcome:** blog post; summaries; evaluative letter; *speech
- **Materials:** blogs
- **Texts:** Text 4A: Empty promises; Text 4B: Teenage gaming addicts

Lesson plan

1. Ask students about their online activities: how many hours a day; what kind of platforms; what they feel they gain and lose by such activities. (5)

2. Give out Text 4A for students to read. (5)

3. Ask students to work in pairs to:
   a. give synonyms for the five verbs in bold in paragraph 1
   b. comment on the combined effect of the embolded words.

   Give answers. (10)

4. Ask students, in pairs, to re-read Text 4A and to collect a list of arguments, in their own words, for the claim that living online is diminishing humanity. (5)

5. Collect feedback and record on the board. (5)

6. Ask students to skim Text 4B for gist and say in one sentence what the debate is. (5)

7. Ask students, in pairs, to reduce Text 4B to two lists of summary bullet points (i.e. remove examples, direct speech, repetition, imagery, minor details) to represent both points of view. (10)

8. Elicit answers and put the agreed points on the board, to be copied by students. (5)

9. Put students into groups of four and ask them to discuss the arguments in Texts 4A and 4B (see lists on board) as to whether communication technology is damaging or enabling, using examples of their own and referring to their responses to Task 1. One student in each group should take notes and another should report to the class on the discussion. (15)

10. Ask students, in pairs, to compare Texts 4A and 4B and make notes on their differences, including examples. They should look at content and style. Elicit feedback. (10)

11. Ask students to plan and write a blog post of about 300 words in response to Text 4A. Their plan should show in note form the ideas they will use and the order in which they will use them. Collect for assessment. (15)

Homework tasks

a. Write in about 150 words, the summary of Text 4B from the notes prepared in Task 7. Points will need to be combined and sequenced for each side of the argument, and expressed in complex sentences.

b. Write a letter, of about 300 words, to the writer of Text 4B, in which you develop and evaluate some of the ideas (about five) used in the text, and give your own opinions. Pay attention to the clarity and coherence of your response, and the appropriateness of your style for a formal letter.

Additional task

Ask students to use the outcome of their group discussion and the content of both texts to write a speech, of about 350 words, to deliver in a school assembly, on the dangers of spending too much time online, entitled 'Are you virtually non-existent?' Remind them to briefly put the positive case for online platforms before presenting and developing their counter-argument.

Text 4A

Empty promises

I read a book today claiming that humans are **enslaved** by technology, **enthralled** and diminished by their laptops and smart phones, **infantilised** by cyber-surfing. Apparently the Digital Age has **stupefied** us and has **jeopardised** our future. It was shocking, I must admit, to learn that a South Korean couple had let their three-month-old daughter die of starvation because they had been too busy nurturing a virtual child online. That is scary, however you look at it. There's also mounting evidence that the ever-more-frequent school shootings are 'inspired' by computer games like *Doom* and *Grand Theft Auto*.

But it's apparently not just gaming addiction we need to worry about; it's all aspects of living online. Reality can't compete with the falsity of perfect Instagram pictures purveying apparent permanent success and happiness, especially staged to make you look good and your 'friends' to look like losers. Yes it's easier to shop from a screen, but you can't interact with the product or the seller in the way you can in a physical store, and you are likely to be disappointed with your order when it arrives at your house, because it doesn't look the same; it's the wrong colour, the wrong texture, the wrong size.

So many school-age kids (especially girls) are falling prey to mental health issues because of bullying and trolling. They check their inboxes every few seconds, unable to break the habit but hating how it makes them feel: inadequate, unpopular, left out of the party. They increasingly have only two states: asleep or online. They don't talk to people in the room, friends they are sitting next to, their loved ones; they are glued to their phones and their feeds; life is happening elsewhere – except it isn't. It's all an illusion, a bubble, a cocoon – an empty promise. They aren't collecting useful knowledge but destructive gossip. In the meantime, they are falling out with their peers, failing their exams, becoming obese. It used to be television that was blamed for removing the quality and quantity of interaction between parents and children; now it's the smaller screen.

Fantasy football means you don't have to leave the house and support a real team; virtual pets mean you don't have to bother with the mess and physical exercise of a real animal; online dating means you can treat a potential, and usually temporary, partner as just a commodity to be picked off the shelf. You don't even have to hail a visible taxi any more; everything is removed, non-physical, non-mental, non-existent.

Doom-mongers are claiming that it's inevitable, and soon, that a moment will come, when a computer will develop consciousness and upgrade its intelligence and performance. Hard to see how humanity could defeat AI, with its superior logic and freedom from doubt or empathy, or even survive. Call me old-fashioned, but I found all this pretty grim reading!

Text 4B

Teenage gaming addicts

Are teenage boys addicted to computer games? Well, this is hardly a new question, but it needs to be revisited periodically, so here goes...

I thought I'd start with some field research, so I asked my teenage son and stood back to await the blast of his wrath... but he was actually quite philosophical.

'The trouble with *old* people is that they just don't understand what's going on. They ask questions like, do you spend all your time watching television and playing on the computer? Are you always talking on your mobile phone? Well, the answer is a simple 'no'. I don't have a computer, or a television, and I never talk on the phone. But I do have a gaming console, a tablet and a smartphone, and I use them most hours of most days, usually with all three on the desk in front of me simultaneously. Am I addicted? No. Am I a highly accomplished multi-tasker employing multiple communication tools at once? Yes. I'm also top of my class at school, in three sports teams, play a musical instrument and love cycling and snow-boarding. Go figure.'

A robust response, and, as long as you understand the distinctions he is drawing – they never talk on their phones, but they do text all the time, take, send and receive photos, share and listen to music, run their social lives on multiple platforms and access more computing power than an Apollo mission, all on their 'phones'. They don't own a television because they stream visual content on their tablets and, of course, play games (not 'computer' games, how dated can you get...?) on their consoles – what he says is entirely true.

My son is a typical, well-adjusted, well-balanced, tech-savvy teenager who runs his busy, varied and very social life through high-tech platforms. But are all teenage boys like him?

Sadly not. News has come through this week that in China, the government claims that up to 24 million teenage boys are addicted to computer gaming, spending up to 20 hours at a time in front of a screen, engrossed in a game. The most severe cases are sent to residential centres such as the one run by Dr Tao Ran, a psychiatrist who is also an officer in the Chinese Army, one of 300 such centres in China. He explains:

'Internet addiction leads to problems in the brain similar to those derived from heroin consumption, but it can be even more damaging. It destroys relationships and damages the body without the person knowing. All my patients have eyesight and back problems and suffer from eating disorders. In addition, we have discovered that their brain capacity is reduced by eight per cent, and the psychological afflictions are serious. If someone is spending six hours or more on the internet, we consider that to be an addiction. 90 per cent of my patients suffer from severe depression and 58 per cent have attacked their parents. Many have committed serious crimes.'

Teenagers are sent to these centres for months at a time and are subject to a regime of military discipline to help them to break their habit. Dr Tao claims a 75 per cent success rate, but it is hard to know whether his patients are truly cured. If the government's figures are to be believed, he will busy for years to come.

So, in the light of that, I'm pleased that my son is only looking at his devices 'most hours of most days.'

Answers – Unit 4

3 a enslaved – without volition; enthralled – captivated; infantilised – reduced to state of early childhood; stupefied – numbed, befuddled, dumbfounded; jeopardised – endangered, threatened

b The combined effect of these passive verbs is that humans are not in control of their lives, any more than a young child is, and that we are at the mercy of a habit and concept which is leading us into danger.

4 making us addicted; making us childish; making us stupid; endangering our future; encouraging violence; making us dissatisfied; giving us unsatisfactory purchases; making us feel inadequate; making us neglect others; giving false impression of life; educationally, socially and physically damaging; breaking down family relationships; removing us from first-hand and tangible interactions; making us see partners as a replaceable commodity

6 The debate is whether there is a problem with the amount of time teenage boys spend on their digital communication devices.

7 Positive:

- just a new way of communicating and working
- multi-tasking is a valuable skill
- high-tech is fast and empowering
- doesn't necessarily affect educational, sporting or cultural attainment

Negative:

- huge numbers of teenage boys addicted to gaming in China
- addiction causes more brain damage than illegal drugs
- addiction causes physical and health problems
- family relations deteriorate
- addiction causes depression and violence
- addiction can lead to crime

10 Content and style text comparison:

Text 4A: content: impersonal; one-sided / entirely negative viewpoint;
style: argumentative; sophisticated vocabulary; triple structures; double structures; ironic use of single inverted commas; single dashes for assertive add-ons

Text 4B: content: personal; balanced viewpoint; direct speech / three voices;
style: discursive; questions; colloquial non-sentences; ellipses; long parentheses (and one inside another); lists; facts and statistics

…
Part 2: Comprehension and Writers' Effects

Unit 5: Colourful characters

Topic outline

- **Main skills:** comprehension; identifying and analysing writers' effects
- **Secondary skills:** narrative devices; punctuation revision
- **Outcome:** analysis of writers' effects; *descriptive writing
- **Materials:** autobiographical passages; Writers' effects questions handout
- **Texts:** Text 5A: My first drive; Text 5B: The Rose-beetle Man

Lesson plan

1. Assign roles from Text 5A (narrator, five children, older sister and mother) and read as drama. (5)

2. When do we use commas? Elicit the rules for comma usage and list on board. Ask students to find examples of each usage in Text 5A. (5)

3. When do we use hyphens? Ask students to circle all the hyphens in Text 5A and formulate a rule for their usage. Elicit the rule. (5)

4. How do we punctuate dialogue? Ask students, in pairs, to study the punctuation of the dialogue in Text 5A and formulate rules. Elicit the rules. (5)

5. Ask students to re-read Text 5A and, in pairs, identify and list the content and style features of narrative writing. (10)

6. Collect features on board and explain reason for and effect of each. (5)

7. Ask students, in pairs, to identify how:
   a. a sense of drama (i.e. conflict, tension and suspense) has been created in Text 5A, giving examples
   b. a sense of comedy has been created in Text 5A, giving examples.
   Discuss responses. (15)

8. Ask students to discuss, in pairs, and then as a class, the individual and overall effect of the phrases in bold in Text 5A. (10)

9. Ask students to work in pairs to decide on adjectives of their own to describe the character of the 'ancient sister', supported by evidence from Text 5A and referring to the character's speech and actions. Discuss suggestions. (5)

10. Ask students to a) underline words and phrases in Text 5B (at least ten) which convey the appearance of the Rose-beetle Man and b) draw a sketch of the Rose-beetle Man based on the description. Ask students to swap sketches and discuss differences, referring to the text. (5)

11. Ask students to transfer their underlined quotations to a list and to write an explanation of its meaning and effect against each one. (5)

12. Ask students to select from their list the three quotations they consider the most memorable in describing the Rose-beetle man, and to find three words or phrases in the passage which make them feel sorry for him. (5)

13. Ask students to use their selections to plan a response to the question: How has the writer given the impression that the Rose-beetle Man is a) weird and fascinating, and b) deserving of the reader's sympathy? They should refer to the Writers' effects process handout. (10)

Homework task

Write up your planned writer's effect analysis of The Rose-beetle Man, in about 250 words, making sure that you have shown an understanding of both meanings and effects for each of your choices, and linked them to convey an overall impression.

Additional task

Ask students to write a piece of description entitled 'A memorable character', using Text 5B as a model. They should give the character a context/surroundings, and describe in close detail their appearance and their manner, using imagery for effect.

Text 5A

My first drive

The weather was exceptionally mild that Christmas holiday and one amazing morning our whole family got ready to go for our first drive in the first motor-car we had ever owned. The driver was to be that 12-years-older-than-me-half-sister, who was now aged 21. She had received two full half-hour lessons in driving from the man who delivered the car, and this was considered quite sufficient. As we all climbed into the car, our excitement was so intense we could hardly bear it.

'How fast will it go?' we cried out. 'Will it do 80 kilometres an hour?'

'It'll do 90!' the ancient sister answered. Her tone was so confident it should have scared us to death, but it didn't. 'We shall probably go faster than that,' the sister announced, pulling on her driving-gloves and tying her scarf.

The canvas hood had been folded back because of the mild weather. My mother, half-brother, three sisters and I were all quivering with fear and joy as the driver let out the clutch and the **great, long, black automobile leapt into motion**.

'Are you sure you know what to do?' we shouted. 'Do you know where the brakes are?'

'Be quiet!' snapped the ancient sister. 'I've got to concentrate!'

Down the drive we went, and out into the village, with the driver pressing the rubber bulb of the horn every time we passed a human being. Soon we were entering a countryside of green fields and high hedges with not a soul in sight.

'You didn't think I could do it, did you?' cried the ancient sister, turning round and grinning at us all.

'Now you keep your eyes on the road,' my mother said nervously.

'Go faster!' we shouted. 'Put your foot down!'

Spurred on by our shouts, the ancient sister began to increase the speed. **The engine roared** and **the body vibrated**. The driver was clutching the steering-wheel **as though it were the hair of a drowning man**, and we all watched the speedometer needle creeping up. We were probably doing about 50 kilometres an hour when we came suddenly to a sharpish bend in the road. The ancient sister, never having been faced with a situation like this before, shouted 'Help!' and slammed on the brakes and swung the wheel wildly. The rear wheels locked and went into a fierce sideways skid, and then, **with a marvellous crunch of mudguards and metal**, we went crashing into the hedge. The front passengers all shot through the front windscreen and the back passengers all shot through the back windscreen. Glass flew in all directions, and so did we. But miraculously nobody was hurt very much, except me. My nose had been cut almost clean off my face and now it was hanging on by a single small thread of skin. My mother disentangled herself from the wreckage and grabbed a handkerchief from her purse. She clapped the dangling nose back into place and held it there.

Not a cottage or a person was in sight, let alone a telephone. Some kind of bird started twittering in a tree farther down the road, otherwise all was silent.

Adapted from *Boy*, by Roald Dahl.

Text 5B

The Rose-beetle Man

The extract describes the meeting on the Greek island of Corfu between a young boy and an itinerant seller of flying beetles tied to ribbons.

Perhaps one of the most weird and fascinating characters I met during my travels was the Rose-beetle Man. He had a fairy-tale air about him that was impossible to resist, and I used to look forward eagerly to my infrequent meetings with him. I first saw him on a high, lonely road leading to one of the remote mountain villages. I could hear him long before I could see him, for he was playing a rippling tune on a shepherd's pipe, breaking off now and then to sing a few words in a curious, nasal voice. As he rounded the corner both my dog and I stopped and stared at him in amazement.

He had a sharp, fox-like face with large slanting eyes of such a dark brown that they appeared black. They had a weird, vacant look about them, and a sort of bloom such as one finds on a plum, a pearly covering almost like a cataract. He was short and slight, with a thinness about his wrists that argued a lack of food. His dress was fantastic, and on his head was a shapeless hat with a very wide, floppy brim. It had once been bottle-green, but was now speckled and smeared with dust. In the band were stuck a fluttering forest of feathers. His shirt was worn and frayed, grey with sweat, and round the neck dangled an enormous cravat of the most startling blue satin. His coat was dark and shapeless, with patches of different hues here and there; on the sleeve a bit of white cloth with a design of rosebuds; on the shoulder a triangular patch of red and white spots. The pockets of this garment bulged, the contents spilling out, including a riot of handkerchiefs. His trousers, patched like his coat, drooped over a pair of scarlet leather shoes with upturned toes decorated with large black-and-white pompons.

Adapted from *My Family and Other Animals,* by Gerald Durrell.

Answers – Unit 5

2 Comma rules: to separate clauses; in pairs to create a parenthesis, including appositional phrases; to separate single items in a list (including multiple adjectives); after initial adverbials in a sentence. The general rule is that if words can be removed from a sentence whilst leaving it grammatically intact, then this is indicated by putting a comma before and after them..

3 Hyphen rules: to connect two or more words acting as one and which cannot exist meaningfully alone in the context; to differentiate the prefix from the rest of the word where confusion might occur; to show a word has been split because of lack of room on a line. The general rule is that hyphens work within words as a joining device and leave no space either side of them.

4 Rules for the punctuation of dialogue:

- Start a new line for a change of speaker.

- Include some form of punctuation before closing inverted commas.

- Use a small letter for the beginning of the word which continues the sentence after the speech closes, even if the final speech punctuation is a question or exclamation mark (and it cannot be a full stop).

- Use a comma to introduce speech within a sentence before opening inverted commas.

Note: Although printed text uses single inverted commas for speech, in handwriting double for speech, and single for titles, jargon and ironic usage.

5 Text 5A: features of narrative writing:
Although Text 5A is autobiographical, it has the same features as fictional narrative: two or three main characters (more becomes confusing); dialogue (for dramatic effect, variety, and to allow voices to reveal character); changes of pace (to build up tension or convey panic); figurative language (similes and metaphors create images to clarify meaning); multiple adjectival usage (to give maximum detail of setting or character); time references (to create apprehension and expectation); references to season and weather and time of day (to enable reader to picture the scene).

7 a How Text 5A has been made dramatic:

Because the weather was **exceptionally mild** and the morning was amazing we are expecting something extraordinary to happen, and the phrase it **should have scared us to death** foreshadows that it will not be a good thing. The children are quivering with fear and joy which are strong emotions and create a heightened mood. Calling his 21-year-old half-sister ancient prepares us for her being unsatisfactory or a figure of fun. Emphasis is placed on the car by describing it as **the great, long, black automobile**, and the fact that it is personified as having **leapt into motion** signifies that something will happen because of the car, which makes us expect there to be an accident. Because the sister **snapped** when they asked if she knew how to drive, we know that she is stressed and this means that she may make a mistake. The mother is behaving nervously which reveals she is afraid. The simile **as if it were the hair of a drowning man** is an unpleasant image to introduce the idea of life-threatening danger. When the sister shouts **Help!** we realise that the car is out of control at high speed and so a collision is inevitable, since she is unable to do anything to stop it, as is shown by the word **wildly**. The verb **slammed** is violent and calls attention to the emergency situation. The alliterative phrase **marvellous crunch of mudguards and metal** strongly emphasises the severity of the crash, as in this case **marvellous** means amazing, like something that might happen in a film. Glass **flew in all directions** is an exaggeration for dramatic effect, but we associate even a small amount of broken glass with injury. That his nose is now only attached by a **single small thread of skin** emphasises how nearly it has come off completely, and how it may still do so.

The syntax in the passage is exaggerated or extreme, and the number of short questions and exclamations give an overall effect of tension and drama to the events. There is a lot of noise to lead up to the climax and provide a contrast to the sudden silence, which shows that something awful has now happened and they don't know what to do about it.

b How Text 5A has been made comic:

- The multiple hyphenation of his sister's age makes it sound ridiculous.
- His sister doesn't have a name, as though being his sister is her only function.
- The children are fixated on speed, without any regard for safety, which is foolish and will have inevitable consequences.
- The sister is presented as over-confident, which indicates she is heading for a deserved fall.
- The children have an unrealistic unanimous voice: *we shouted* and no names are mentioned.
- *Do you know where the brakes are*? foreshadows the crash.
- The description of people they pass as *a human being* is amusing as it makes it sound as though they consider themselves above human status.
- *Help!* is a futile and cartoon-like cry.
- The detail and duration of the description of the crash is another cartoon effect; the verbs *skid*, *crunch* and *crash* are associated with comic books.
- The family flying in both directions, along with the glass, creates an exaggerated and therefore comic image.
- The painless description of the severed nose is another extreme cartoon effect, and the idea of a *dangling nose* is inherently funny.
- The comment of the bird *twittering* in a tree is incongruous and therefore amusing.

Generally, comedy can only be created where pain and distress is absent and there is no empathy between the reader and the characters suffering the disaster. All of the above put the reader at a distance from the actual experience being described.

8 Phrases in bold in Text 5A:

Note that longer phrases should be split and the parts examined separately in order for explanations and effects to be more focused and specific.

great, long, black automobile – triple adjectival qualification gives the car powerful and threatening qualities of size and colour; there is an association with a funeral vehicle

leapt into motion – the speed of an animal of prey, such as a cheetah, is connoted.

The engine roared – this continues the big cat image, with the addition of a threatening sound

the body vibrated – again the car is being described as if it were alive and therefore an adversary

as though it were the hair of a drowning man – life-threatening simile to evoke the difficulty the sister is having with the steering

marvellous crunch of mudguards and metal – incongruous but alliterative use of 'marvellous' suggesting the boy is rather enjoying the drama and noise of the crash, but the onomatopoeic and assonantal word 'crunch' conveys that there was significant damage to the car.

The overall effect is that the car is a powerful and uncontrollable monster until it reverts back to being a machine when it crashes.

9 Adjectives to describe the character of the 'ancient sister' should indicate that she is:

over-confident (*considered quite sufficient, We shall probably go faster than that*); showing off (*It'll do 90!; pressing the rubber bulb of the horn*); bad-tempered (*Be quiet!*); self-satisfied (*grinning*); flustered (*Help!*).

Cambridge IGCSE First Language English — Comprehension and Writers' Effects

10 and 11

a He is made to seem weird and fascinating, and *impossible to resist*, because the reference to *fairy-tale* suggests that he has magic powers. His *curious, nasal voice* when he sings makes him sound different from other people, and his eyes are *such a dark brown* that they seem black and his *sharp* face was more *fox-like* than human. Describing his clothing as *fantastic* again connects him to fairy tales. He does not just have one feather in his hat, but a *fluttering forest* of them, which stresses how many of them there were, and that they were in constant movement. Likewise, *a riot of handkerchiefs* suggests not only quantity but also noise and violent movement. He is wearing *a mixture of different hues* which are so many and so bright and the effect so startling that even the dog *stopped in amazement*, as he had never seem any human like this before. The exact detail of *a triangular patch of red and white spots* creates a bizarre visual effect of contrasting colours and shapes. The main colour is bright red, which reminds us of the costume of a clown. The overall effect is that everything about the figure is unusual and forms a bizarre spectacle, which the onlooker's gaze becomes fixed on because of the surprise combinations of colour and the constant movement.

b The reader feels sympathy for him because the *pearly covering* on his eyes suggests he cannot see properly, and the *thinness about the wrists* shows he does not get enough to eat. Because his hat is *speckled and smeared with dust* and his clothing is *worn and frayed*, we assume that he only has one set of clothes, which he has to patch, and that he has no one to look after him or care about him. Because his cravat is of *blue satin*, which is a material associated with luxury, we get the impression that previously he was better off and better dressed than he is now. The fact that his hat is *floppy*, his trousers *drooped*, and his shoes have *upturned toes* and *pompons* contribute to a total picture of a clown whose clothes are all too big for him. This means that we think of him as someone who is brightly and comically dressed, yet who may be sad.

Unit 6: Hide-and-seek

Topic outline

- **Main skills:** comprehension; analysing writers' effects; inference
- **Secondary skills:** description; voice, setting and atmosphere in narrative
- **Outcome:** writers' effects response; narrative continuation; story plan; *story or opening
- **Materials:** writers' effects grid; short story extracts; poem
- **Texts:** Text 6A: Games at Twilight (opening); Text 6B Hide-and-seek; Text 6C: Games at Twilight (ending)

Lesson plan

1. Give out Text 6A for students to read. Ask them to discuss in pairs and make notes of the answers to the following questions (on the board):

   a. What is the setting? What does it make you expect?

   b. What is the atmosphere? What does it make you expect?

   c. What kind of narrative opening is used? What is the effect?

   d. What kind of sentences are used? What is their effect?

   e. What do you predict will happen next? Why?

   Go through the elicited answers. (15)

2. Give out the grid following Text 6A and ask students to put the embolded phrases into it with an explanation of their meaning, the name of the literary device, and their effect. Go through the answers. (The first one has been completed as an example.) (20)

3. Ask students to choose six of the writer's effects from the grid and write a response in continuous writing, of about 250 words, to be collected for assessment. (They may need to be referred to the Writers' effects process handout.) (15)

4. Read Text 6B to students. Ask them to say in one sentence what happens in the poem. (5)

5. Ask students to consider the effects of the words in bold in Text 6B and offer answers to be evaluated. (10)

6. Ask students to work in pairs to comment on the use of the following (list on the board) in Text 6B:

   i. second person

   ii. imperative voice

   iii. direct speech

   iv. occasional rhyme

   v. question at the end (10)

7. Collect feedback for discussion. (10)

8. Read Text 6C to the class, the ending to the short story begun in Text 6A. A similar thing happens in both the short story and the poem. Ask the class to discuss the similarity and interpret what they think the texts are saying about the boys playing hide-and-seek, or about any children playing any game. (5)

Homework tasks

a. The next paragraph of Text 6A begins: *Ravi heard the whistling and ....* Write a continuation of the story, of about a page, in the same style, focusing on Ravi and his choice of hiding place. Describe the place, and how Ravi is feeling, using imagery.

b. Plan your own short story called 'Hide-and-seek'. Decide on the characters, voice, setting and atmosphere, how the story will end, where direct speech will be used, and what kind of imagery you will use. The title can be taken metaphorically rather than literally.

Additional task

Ask students to write the opening to their story, of about a page, or their whole story.

Text 6A

Games at Twilight (opening)

It was still too hot to play outdoors. They had had their tea. They had been washed and had their hair brushed, and after the long day of confinement in the house that was not cool but at least a protection from the sun, the children strained to get out. Their faces were red and bloated with the effort, but their mother would not open the door, everything was still curtained and, shuttered in a way that stifled the children, made them feel that **their lungs were stuffed with cotton wool** and their noses with dust and if they didn't burst out into the light and see the sun and feel the air, they would choke.

'Please, ma, please,' they begged. 'We'll play in the veranda and porch — we won't go a step out of the porch.'

'You will, I know you will, and then—'

'No — we won't, we won't,' they wailed so horrendously that she actually let down the bolt of the front door so that they burst out **like seeds from a crackling, over-ripe pod** into the veranda, with such wild, maniacal yells that she retreated to her bath and the shower of talcum powder and the fresh sari that were to help her face the summer evening.

They faced the afternoon. It was too hot. Too bright. The white walls of the veranda **glared stridently** in the sun. The bougainvillea hung about it, purple and magenta, in **livid balloons**. The garden outside was **like a tray made of beaten brass**, flattened out on the red gravel and the stony soil in all shades of metal - aluminium, tin, copper and brass. No life stirred at this arid time of day - the birds still drooped, **like dead fruit**, in the papery tents of the trees; some squirrels lay limp on the wet earth under the garden tap. The outdoor dog lay stretched as if dead on the veranda mat, his paws and ears and tail all reaching out **like dying travellers in search of water**. He rolled his eyes at the children - **two white marbles rolling in the purple sockets**, begging for sympathy - and attempted to lift his tail in a wag but could not. It only twitched and lay still.

Then, perhaps roused by the shrieks of the children, a band of parrots suddenly fell out of the eucalyptus tree, tumbled frantically in the **still, sizzling air**, then sorted themselves out into battle formation and streaked away across the white sky.

The children, too, felt released. They too began tumbling, shoving, pushing against each other, frantic to start. Start what? Start their business. The business of the children's day which is — play.

'Let's play hide-and-seek.'
'Who'll be It?' 'You be It.'
'Why should I?

You be—' 'You're the eldest—'
'That doesn't mean—'

The shoves became harder. Some kicked out. The motherly Mira intervened. She pulled the boys roughly apart. There was a tearing sound of cloth but it was lost in the heavy panting and angry grumbling and no one paid attention to the small sleeve hanging loosely off a shoulder.

'Make a circle, make a circle!' she shouted, firmly pulling and pushing till a kind of vague circle was formed. 'Now clap!' she roared and, clapping, they all chanted in melancholy unison: 'Dip, dip, dip - my blue ship-' and every now and then one or the other saw he was safe by the way his hands fell at the crucial moment - palm on palm, or back of hand on palm - and dropped out of the circle with a yell and a jump of relief and jubilation.

Raghu was It. He started to protest, to cry 'You cheated - Mira cheated - Anu cheated—' but it was too late, the others had all already streaked away. There was no one to hear when he called out, 'Only-in the veranda - the porch - Ma said - Ma said to stay in the porch!' No one had stopped to listen, all he saw were their brown legs flashing through the dusty shrubs, scrambling up brick walls, leaping over compost heaps and hedges, and then the porch stood empty in the purple shade of the bougainvillea and the garden was as empty as before; even the limp squirrels had whisked away, leaving everything gleaming, brassy and bare.

Only small Manu suddenly reappeared, **as if he had dropped out of an invisible cloud or from a bird's claws**, and stood for a moment in the centre of the yellow lawn chewing his finger and near to tears as he heard Raghu shouting, with his head pressed against the veranda wall, 'Eighty-three, eighty-five, eighty-nine, ninety...' and then made off in a panic, half of him wanting to fly north, the other half counselling south. Raghu turned just in time to see the flash of his white shorts and the uncertain skittering of his red sandals, and charged after him with such a bloodcurdling yell that Manu stumbled over the hosepipe, fell into its rubber coils and lay there weeping, 'I won't be It - you have to find them all - all - All!'

"I know I have to, idiot,' Raghu said, superciliously kicking him with his toe. 'You're dead,' he said with satisfaction, licking the beads of perspiration off his upper lip, and then **stalked off in search of worthier prey**, whistling spiritedly so that the hiders should hear and tremble.

From *Games at Twilight and Other Stories*, by Anita Desai, Heinemann.

Phrase	Meaning	Device	Effect
their lungs were stuffed with cotton wool	they could barely breathe	metaphor	sustains the meaning of the previous metaphorical verb 'stifled' to stress how desperate they were to get outdoors

Text 6B

Hide-and-seek

Call out. Call loud: 'I'm ready! Come and find me!'
The sacks in the toolshed smell like the seaside.
They'll never find you in this **salty dark**,
But be careful that your feet aren't sticking out.
Wiser not to risk another shout.
The floor is cold. They'll probably be searching
The bushes near the swing. Whatever happens
You mustn't sneeze when they come prowling in.
And here they are, whispering at the door;
You've never heard them sound so hushed before.
Don't breathe. Don't move. Stay dumb. Hide in your blindness.

They're moving closer, someone stumbles, mutters;
Their **words and laughter scuffle**, and they're gone.
But don't come out just yet; they'll try the lane
And then the greenhouse and back here again.
They must be thinking that you're very clever,
Getting more puzzled as they search all over.
It seems a long time since they went away.
Your legs are stiff, **the cold bites** through your coat;
The **dark damp smell of sand** moves in your throat.
It's time to let them know that you're the winner.
Push off the sacks. Uncurl and stretch. That's better!
Out of the shed and call to them: 'I've won!
Here I am! Come and own up I've caught you!'
The **darkening garden watches**. Nothing stirs.
The **bushes hold their breath**; the sun is gone.
Yes, here you are. But where are they who sought you?

'Hide-and-seek', by Vernon Scannell.

Text 6C

Games at Twilight (ending)

The game proceeded. Two pairs of arms reached up and met in an arc. The children trooped under it again and again in a lugubrious circle, ducking their heads and intoning

'The grass is green,
The rose is red;
Remember me
When I am dead, dead, dead, dead ...'

And the arc of thin arms trembled in the twilight, and the heads were bowed so sadly, and their feet tramped to that melancholy refrain so mournfully, so helplessly, that Ravi could not bear it. He would not follow them, he would not be included in this funereal game. He had wanted victory and triumph – not a funeral. But he had been forgotten, left out and he would not join them now. The ignominy of being forgotten – how could he face it? He felt his heart go heavy and ache inside him unbearably. He lay down full length on the damp grass, crushing his face into it, no longer crying, silenced by a terrible sense of his insignificance.

From *Games at Twilight and Other Stories*, by Anita Desai, Heinemann.

Answers – Unit 6

1. **a** setting: indoors and unbearably stifling and burning hot; the imagery is of aridness and metal; we expect a strong reaction when the children are finally set free to roam outdoors, and one which may reflect harshness rather than gentleness.

   b atmosphere: things are referred to as dying; we expect something to end on this day; the title of the story includes the word 'twilight', which has associations with death because it means the end of day / the loss of light.

   c narrative opening: *in medias res* (middle of the action) indicated by the word 'still'; the effect is to convey that there have been many previous hours of incarceration in the house that have built up to this bursting point.

   d sentences: the sentences are glaringly short and simple, which reflects the children's voice but also suggests constraint and impatience. They are in the mood for brisk action and not for leisurely communication.

   e Someone will be made to pay for the pent-up frustration of the children. At worst they will turn on a weaker member of the group with physical or verbal violence; at best they will ignore or neglect him/her in pursuit of their own pleasure in finally being outside and free.

2.

Phrase	Meaning	Device	Effect
their lungs were stuffed with cotton wool	they could barely breathe	metaphor	sustains the meaning of the previous metaphorical verb 'stifled' to stress how desperate they were to get outdoors
like seeds from a crackling, over-ripe pod	they burst out through the door	simile	conveys the large number of children, their noisiness, and their need for more space
glared stridently	the walls were very bright	mixed metaphor and personification	the whiteness was so strong it was hard to look at and seemed to be shouting
livid balloons	has large circular purple flowers	metaphor and pun	the flowers are purple, but the adjective 'livid' also connotes anger, which adds to the idea of the children's frustration and hostility
like a tray made of beaten brass	the earth is flat, brown and metallic-looking	simile	the heat seems to have flattened the garden violently and dried up the vegetation
like dead fruit	the birds are unmoving and inanimate	simile	continues the recurring image of dryness (*cotton wool*, *crackling pods*) and introduces the death of nature to emphasise the assault on living things being made by the Sun
like dying travellers in search of water	walkers in the desert are desperately thirsty	simile	recurring image of drought and death
two white marbles rolling in the purple sockets	the dog's eyes are unfocused	metaphor	an image of exhaustion as it's the only part of its body it can move
still, sizzling air	sweltering and breezeless air	alliteration and assonance, metaphor	connotes frying and reinforces the extremely high temperature
as if he had dropped out of an invisible cloud or from a bird's claws	his arrival wasn't observed	double simile	conveys how small and delicate the boy is, and suggests he is vulnerable in this situation, aligned with nature which has been subdued by the heat
stalked off in search of worthier prey	went to find someone more challenging to beat	metaphor	Raghu does not consider Manu to be worth bullying as he is so weak and timid; reveals Raghu's aggressive character and desire for dominance; equates him with the sun which is destroying the life in the garden

4 A boy hiding in a shed realises, after a long time has passed, that the other children have given up looking for him and gone somewhere else, so that he cannot enjoy having outwitted them.

5 Effects of the words in bold in Text 6B:

- **salty dark** – darkness cannot be literally salty, but this taste image suggests sweat caused by fear, or that the shed smells like seaweed because of its coldness and dampness

- **words and laughter scuffle** – this is another transference; it is the children who are shifting their feet, but as he cannot see them it is the noise they are making which seems to be scuffling; this image makes him seem excluded as well as invisible

- **the cold bites** – the personification of the cold makes it seem painful, as if he is being attacked by an animal

- **dark damp smell of sand** – the double alliterative, monosyllabic phrase evokes the clamminess and earthiness of the shed, synthesising sight, smell and touch images; smells cannot be dark, so this is another transferred epithet

- **darkening garden watches** – the light is fading so the garden seems to have become darker; another unfriendly personification shows how much time has passed, as well as conveying the idea of being watched expectantly

- **bushes hold their breath** – another personification, and alliteration, continues the suggestion that something dramatic and shocking is about to happen

Overall, the images create an atmosphere of his being in an alien place surrounded by personified, antipathetic natural elements, making the boy seem isolated and uncomfortable when he is in the shed and exposed to humiliation and judgement when he comes out.

6
   i   second person – the narrator seems to be on the side of the boy victim and wanting to warn him; it could be that the narrator is addressing his younger self pityingly, or that the boy is talking to himself. The use of 'you' contrasts with the anonymous use of 'they' throughout, making it a two-sided contest.

   ii imperative voice – the commands add to the preponderance of monosyllabic diction, which gives an urgency to the poem, conveying how seriously the boy is playing the game and what is at stake for him. The narrator seems to want to warn the boy and to prevent the inevitable ending.

   iii direct speech – this is the script, the time-honoured script of the game of Hide-and-seek, being given by the narrator to the boy, but also the instructions the boy is giving to himself, stressing that, unlike the others, who are exchanging words and laughter, he has no one but himself to talk to. The game goes wrong (the outcome isn't as it should be) and the ironic words add pathos to the poem.

   iv occasional rhyme – the occasional rhymes and half rhymes create echoes, which could be the seekers' voices in the garden, or a pattern to suggest the inevitability of what is going to happen.

   v question at the end – this is the question the poem is asking the reader, the philosophical realisation that people move on, forget each other and appear uncaring, and that this is a painful fact of life: that what we think is important may not seem so to others, who are governed by impatience and intent on their own gratification, and that our timing does not coincide with the decisions and actions taken by others.

8 Texts 6A and 6C are saying that games are not games but are taken seriously and can be distressing: children bully and cheat to dominate the group. The hiders both feel very nervous and fearful of being seen and caught, as if everything depends on being successful, in their own self-esteem and in the eyes of the others. In both cases, one of the children is forgotten about as the others move on without them, and they suffer a huge sense of loneliness and injustice. Games are a metaphor for life.

Unit 7: Same difference

Topic outline

- **Main skills:** comprehension; inference; identifying and analysing writers' effects; text comparison
- **Secondary skills:** summary; stylistic analysis; narrative style
- **Outcome:** encyclopedia entry; text comparison; narrative continuation; *short story

- **Materials:** informative text; short story opening; Worksheet and answers for Text 7B
- **Texts:** Text 7A: Two of a kind; Text 7B: The day of the party

Lesson plan

1 Ask students to give their reactions to the idea of identical twins, describe those they have known, and say whether they would like to be one. (5)

2 Ask students to skim-read Text 7A. (5)

3 Ask students to identify and underline the facts (ignoring the opinions, details, examples, repetitions, images) in Text 7A, and list them in their own words. (10)

4 Ask students to write a 150-word summary for an encyclopaedia entry of Text 7A on the topic of twins, using and re-ordering their key points from Task 3 and writing in the style of Text 7A. (They may need to be referred to the summary process handout.) Collect pieces to assess for a) content and b) style and structure. (10)

5 Ask students to analyse the language and style of Text 7A in a column of points, with examples next to each point. (5)

6 Choose four students to read the three speaking parts and the narration, which is the opening of a short story, in Text 7B. (5)

7 Students work in pairs to complete the Worksheet for Text 7B. (25)

8 Go through the worksheet questions and discuss validity of answers offered or solicited. (15)

9 Ask students to make a column of language and style points plus examples for Text 7B, next to the previous one made in Task 5. (5)

Homework tasks

a Write a comparison of the writers' vocabulary, sentence structures and other stylistic devices in Texts 7A and 7B, selecting from your lists of points from tasks 5 and 9. Express your points as pairs of opposites, and include examples to support each point. Explain how the purpose of each text is reflected in its style. Write about 250 words.

b Write a continuation and ending to the story to explain what happens at the party. Use the same style as Text 7B.

Additional task

Ask students to plan, draft and write their own story with twins as the main character. It should include dialogue, and descriptive and figurative language to create setting and atmosphere.

Text 7A

Two of a kind

Everyone is fascinated by identical twins: they look the same – even advanced digital imaging systems sometimes fail to tell them apart – and yet they have different personalities and abilities. Literature and detective stories depend upon them for providing a plot twist or a mystery. In reality, too, there have been numerous cases of one twin impersonating the other for a joke, to escape punishment or to advance a romantic interest.

They may have the same eyes, the same hair colour, the same smile, but one will be shy and the other more outgoing, or one cleverer or funnier or kinder than the other. And this despite their having the same DNA. They do not, however, have the same fingerprints, which are believed to be determined by environmental factors.

Twins like spending time with each other – often to the exclusion of others. In 50 percent of cases, they even develop their own secret language. Furthermore, it is commonly believed that they have the ability to communicate telepathically so that, for instance, one is able to draw a picture of what the other is thinking. There have been innumerable claims that a twin has shared the physical or mental pain of the other – known as 'crisis telepathy' – even when they could not have known it was happening.

Monozygotic twins – who share everything before birth – usually share everything after birth, too: the same tastes in food, music, sport or politics … One might think that this could be explained by the fact that parents often give their newborn twins confusingly similar names, continue to dress them exactly alike until they are well into their teens, and generally treat them in the same way throughout their upbringing.

However, there are well-documented cases of identical twins brought up separately from birth who, nonetheless, made the same decisions and life choices. In the 1980s, there was the much-publicised case of the identical twin 'Jim' brothers. Born in Ohio USA in 1939, Jim Springer and Jim Lewis were put up for adoption as babies and raised by different couples, who happened to give them the same first name. When Jim Springer reconnected with his brother at age 39, in 1979, a string of other similarities and coincidences was discovered. Both men were six feet tall and weighed 180 pounds. Growing up, they'd both had dogs named Toy and taken family vacations on the same beach in Florida. As young men, they'd both married women named Linda, and then divorced them. Their second wives were both named Betty. They named their sons James Alan and James Allan. They'd both served as part-time sheriffs, enjoyed home carpentry projects, and suffered from severe headaches.

Scientists study twins in order to collect evidence for the age-old nature versus nurture debate: how much of their behaviour is hereditary and how much conditioned by their environment; what are people actually born with and what is caused by experience? Because identical twins come from a single fertilised egg that splits in two and share virtually the same genetic code, any differences between them must be due to environmental factors. Studying the differences between identical twins to pinpoint the influence of environment, and comparing identical twins with fraternal ones to measure the role of inheritance has been crucial to understanding the interplay of nature and nurture in determining our personalities, behaviour, and vulnerability to disease.

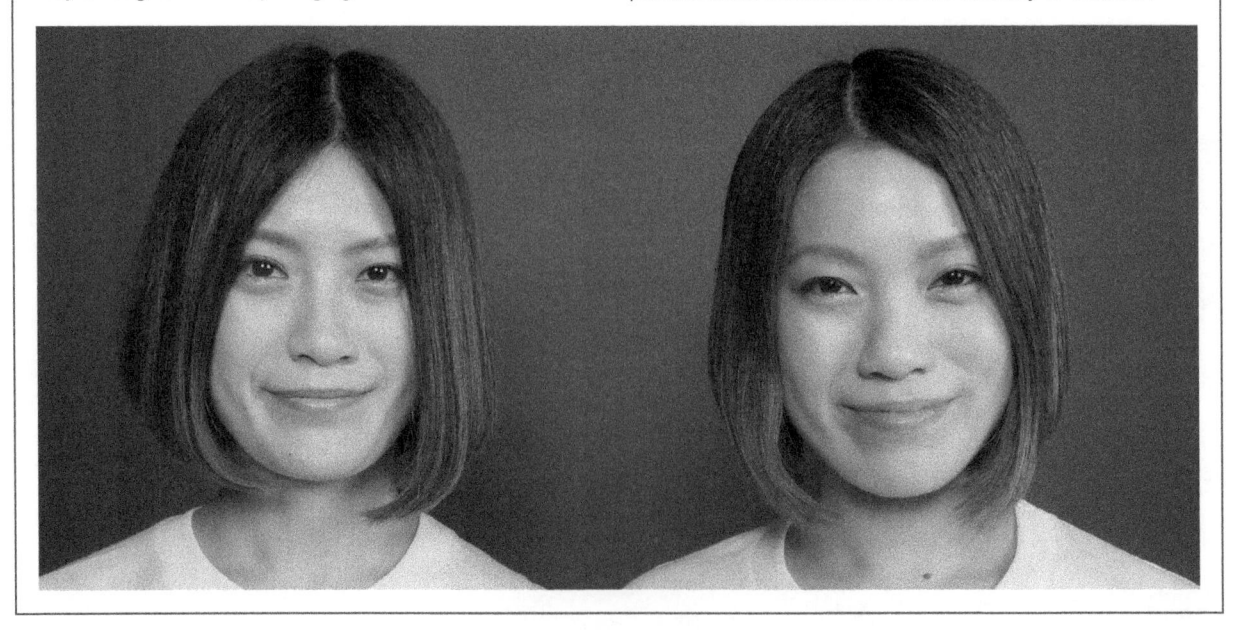

Text 7B

The day of the party

Peter Morton woke with a start to face the first light. Rain tapped against the glass. It was January the fifth.

He looked across a table on which a night-light had guttered into a pool of water, at the other bed. Francis Morton was still asleep, and Peter lay down again with his eyes on his brother. It amused him to imagine it was himself whom he watched, the same hair, the same eyes, the same lips and line of cheek. But the thought **palled**, and the mind went back to the fact which lent the day importance. It was the fifth of January. He could hardly believe a year had passed since Mrs Henne-Falcon had given her last children's party.

Francis turned suddenly upon his back and threw an arm across his face, blocking his mouth. Peter's heart began to beat fast, not with pleasure now but with uneasiness. He sat up and called across the table, 'Wake up.' Francis's shoulders shook and he waved a clenched fist in the air, but his eyes remained closed. To Peter Morton the whole room seemed to darken and he had the impression of a great bird swooping. He cried again, 'Wake up,' and once more there was silver light and the touch of rain on the windows.

Francis rubbed his eyes. 'Did you call out?' he asked.

'You are having a bad dream,' Peter said. Already experience had taught him how far their minds reflected each other. But he was the elder, by a matter of minutes, and that brief extra interval of light, while his brother still struggled in pain and darkness, had given him self-reliance and an instinct of protection towards the other who was afraid of so many things.

'I dreamed that I was dead,' Francis said.

'What was it like?' Peter asked.

'I can't remember,' Francis said.

'You dreamed of a big bird.'

'Did I?'

The two lay silent in bed facing each other, the same green eyes, the same nose tilting at the tip, the same firm lips, and the same premature modelling of the chin. The fifth of January, Peter thought again, his mind drifting idly from the image of cakes to the prizes which might be won. Egg-and-spoon races, spearing apples in basins of water, blind man's buff.

'I don't want to go,' Francis said suddenly. 'I suppose Joyce will be there … Mabel Warren.' Hateful to him, the thought of a party shared with those two. They were older than he. Joyce was eleven and Mabel Warren thirteen. The long pigtails swung **superciliously** to a masculine stride. Their sex humiliated him, as they watched him **fumble** with his egg, from under lowered scornful lids. And last year … he turned his face away from Peter, his cheeks scarlet.

'What's the matter?' Peter asked.

'Oh, nothing. I don't think I'm well. I've got a cold. I oughtn't to go to the party.'

Peter was puzzled. 'But Francis, is it a bad cold?'

'It will be a bad cold if I go to the party. Perhaps I shall die.'

'Then you mustn't go,' Peter said, prepared to solve all difficulties with one plain sentence, and Francis let his nerves relax, ready to leave everything to Peter. But though he was grateful he did not turn his face towards his brother. His cheeks still bore the badge of a shameful memory, of the game of hide-and-seek last year in the darkened house, and of how he had screamed when Mabel Warren put her hand suddenly upon his arm. He had not heard her coming. Girls were like that. Their shoes never squeaked. No boards whined under the tread. They slunk like cats on padded claws.

When the nurse came in with hot water Francis lay tranquil leaving everything to Peter. Peter said, 'Nurse, Francis has got a cold.'

The tall starched woman laid the towels across the cans and said, without turning, 'The washing won't be back till tomorrow. You must lend him some of your handkerchiefs.'

'But, Nurse,' Peter asked, 'hadn't he better stay in bed?'

'We'll take him for a good walk this morning,' the nurse said. 'Wind'll blow away the germs. Get up now, both of you,' and she closed the door behind her.

'I'm sorry,' Peter said. 'Why don't you just stay in bed? I'll tell mother you felt too ill to get up.' But rebellion against destiny was not in Francis's power. If he stayed in bed they would come up and tap his chest and put a thermometer in his mouth and look at his tongue, and they would discover he was **malingering**. It was true he felt ill, a sick empty sensation in his stomach and a rapidly beating heart, but he knew the cause was only fear, fear of the party, fear of being made to hide by himself in the dark, uncompanioned by Peter and with no night-light to make a blessed **breach**.

From *The End of the Party*, by Graham Greene.

Cambridge IGCSE First Language English
Comprehension and Writers' Effects

Worksheet for Text 7B: The day of the party

1. Give synonyms to replace the five embolded words in the text.

   _____
   _____

2. Select words and phrases from the text which convey the difference in character between the twins.

   _____
   _____
   _____
   _____

3. What can you infer about the character of the nurse, and what is your evidence?

   _____
   _____
   _____
   _____

4. Explain the effect of each of the following images from the text:

   Rain tapped against the glass.

   _____
   _____

   a night-light had guttered into a pool of water

   _____
   _____

   a great bird swooping

   _____
   _____

   the touch of rain

   _____
   _____

They slunk like cats on padded claws.

5 a What are the recurring images in the text?

  b What is their combined effect?

6 Write a complex sentence to explain the situation so far in the short story.

7 a Say what you think is likely to happen in the story.

  b Give your reasons by referring to evidence in the text.

Answers to Worksheet for Text 7B: The day of the party

1. **palled** – became uninteresting; **superciliously** – disdainfully; **fumble** – catch clumsily; **malingering** – feigning illness, pretending to be ill; **breach** – gap, break, rupture

2. Peter: *It amused him; self-reliance and an instinct of protection; his mind drifting idly; prepared to solve all difficulties*

    Francis: *afraid of so many things; I dreamed that I was dead; humiliated; Perhaps I shall die; nerves; leaving everything to Peter; rebellion against destiny was not in Francis's power; fear*

3. The nurse is unyielding, unsympathetic and practical; she likes to follow a strict routine. We know this because she is 'starched', she believes in the power of fresh air and her response to being told that Francis is ill is to tell Peter to lend him handkerchiefs.

4. *Rain tapped against the glass.*

    Rain is a device of pathetic fallacy to give a miserable atmosphere to the story from the start. It is personified as a person trying to get into the room. This begins a recurring image of Francis' fear of being touched by someone malignant, and of the power of water to snuff out life.

    a night-light had guttered into a pool of water

    This is one of the images of light being drowned; 'guttered' is an unpleasant-sounding word with connotations of being brought low. Although it is dawn, and it is party day, the imagery is dark and forebodes extinction.

    a great bird swooping

    Large dark birds are associated in literature with predation, death and evil. Many people are afraid of birds and associate their wings with the idea of smothering and blocking out the light.

    the touch of rain

    A repeat of the image in the opening paragraph that rain has fingers and is capable of touching. This symbolises the sudden terror of the feel of Mabel Warren's hand upon Francis' arm last year.

    They slunk like cats on padded claws.

    This is another predatory image, implying creeping up on a victim and causing injury with just a touch of the claws.

5. a. The recurring images are of darkness, birds, and water, all working against the light and symbol of life.

    b. These are all things which can touch and extinguish, an idea further reinforced by the words 'palled' and 'blocking'. Francis stayed in the dark longer at birth, and again on the morning of this story, being embroiled in a nightmare and waking up later than his brother. The effect of the imagery is to suggest that the weak and passive Francis will be vanquished by the 'masculine' girls, just as cats prey upon smaller creatures and as the hen is preyed upon by the falcon (in the name of the hostess of the party Francis fears so much). Hide-and-seek is a game played in the dark, closed-in and trapped like being back in the womb.

6. When he wakes after a nightmare, Francis is frightened of having to go to the party that evening, because of the girls who will be there and the games he will have to play, so he claims to be ill and desperately hopes that his more confident twin will be able to get him out of going.

7. a. **(Example answer)** It is likely that Francis will be forced to go to the party and that the same thing may happen again, this time with more serious consequences because Francis has such a morbid fear.

    b. A sombre mood is created by the weather, the nightmare and the recurring imagery. The date may be ironic, as it is the eve of Epiphany, which means the coming of the light. The refusal of the nurse to be accommodating suggests that Francis will not find escape or rescue, since even his sympathetic brother seems unable to help him. The references to death and increased heart beats are an indication of impending tragedy.

Answers – Unit 7

3 Text 7A key facts:
- have close physical similarities
- show different behaviour traits
- have same genetic code
- have different fingerprints
- enjoy each other's company
- often communicate in their own language
- believed by some to be telepathic
- sometimes claim to share emotions and physical sensations
- tend to like the same things
- have been known to make the same decisions although brought up independently
- are the subject of scientific study to establish relative power of genes versus environment
- develop from one egg.

4 **(Example answer)** encyclopedia entry

Identical twins are the product of a single fertilised egg, which means that they share DNA molecules and a genetic code – though not fingerprints – and therefore have close physical similarities. However, they often have different personalities and are the object of scientific study to determine the extent to which this is caused by external factors. It is known that they usually have the same tastes, enjoy being together, and often devise an exclusive secret language. This has led to a widespread belief that they have telepathic abilities which allow them to communicate powerful feelings and sensations to each other when apart. Studies of twins raised separately have shown an extraordinary similarity of life choices.

5 Text 7A: characteristics of informative writing style and their effect:
- rule of three (knowledgeable and authoritative, gives a range of examples)
- discourse markers (e.g. *however*, *furthermore* (to show change of direction of argument)
- use of 'one' (impersonal and universal)
- use of passive voice (more scientific and official)
- precise, concise and varied vocabulary (effective and economical means of communicating and retaining reader interest)
- variety of sentence structures and punctuation devices (to alleviate the factual nature of the content)

9 Text 7B: characteristics of narrative writing style and their effect:

prolixity of expression (to create mood); metaphors and similes (for atmosphere); use of dialogue (for characterisation and suspense); repetition (to emphasise an idea); non-sentences (to reflect thought); ellipses (to reflect speech and emotion); short simple sentences (to convey childish expression); questions (to convey anxiety)

Homework task a comparison of vocabulary, sentence structures and other stylistic devises in Texts 7A and 7B:

Both texts deal with the topic of identical twins and how they can understand each other and even share thoughts telepathically. Text 7A, being an informative text, uses initial adverbials and discourse markers to link ideas logically, whereas the linkage in Text 7B is by question and answer and a chronological progression of events. The rule of three gives information economically in Text 7A, whereas the triple repetitions in Text 7B are to give emphasis and build up emotion and expectation. The use of the impersonal 'one' and the passive verbs in Text 7A is in marked contrast to the active verbs and full range of personal pronouns used in Text 7B, where characters and their differences, and who is performing the actions, are essential features of the story. The prolix wording of Text 7B, dwelling on an idea and illustrating it with a lot of detail, contrasts in style with the concise wording of Text 7A, but the narrative passage is more limited in sentence types and lengths as the interest lies in the tension and suspense being built up, and one type of sentence is needed for consistency of character creation.

Unit 8: Dislocation

Topic outline

- **Main skills:** identifying and explaining writers' effects
- **Secondary skills:** vocabulary building; descriptive writing
- **Outcome:** analysis of effects; *descriptive composition
- **Materials:** novel and short story extracts; Worksheet for Text 8A; Worksheet for Text 8B
- **Texts:** Text 8A: The island; Text 8B: The causeway; Text 8C: The river

Lesson plan

1 Tell students they are going to study three passages about people who feel out of place in their new and alien surroundings. Have they ever experienced this feeling themselves? Ask for examples. Elicit ideas on how this effect may be achieved by writers, with examples. (10)

2 Ask students to brainstorm ideas associated with being stranded on an island. Collect them on the board and discuss why islands have these particular associations. (5)

3 Ask students, in pairs, to complete the gap-fill task on the Worksheet for Text 8A, taking careful note of parts of speech. (10)

4 Invite and evaluate suggestions for each of the ten gaps. Then ask students to read the original, complete version of Text 8A and to underline and comment on the original words. (10)

5 Ask students, in pairs, to select words to complete the gap-fill task on the Worksheet for Text 8B after discussing each of the three possible choices. (10)

6 Read out the original ten words used in Text 8B (underlined in the text). Give students the chance to argue that their choices are more in keeping with the overall effect. (5)

7 Ask students what they would notice and feel if they were travelling up the Amazon River, deeper and deeper into tropical jungle. (5)

8 Read Text 8C while students listen. Which words or phrases can they remember? Write these on the board. (5)

9 Invite reasons why those particular words and phrases stood out from the passage and what effect they convey. (5)

10 Ask students to read Text 8C, comparing the underlined words and phrases with the ones on the board to see how many are the same. (5)

11 Ask students, in pairs, to write explanations of the meanings and effects of the underlined words or phrases. (10)

12 Ask students to read out their responses and discuss them as a class. (10)

Homework tasks

a Choose either Text 8A or Text 8B and write a response to the question: How does the passage create the effects of isolation and threat caused by natural elements?

b Set a piece of descriptive writing, of about 250 words, with the title of either 'The island' or 'The river'.

Additional task

Ask students to choose a passage in a book, which describes a place with a powerful atmosphere, and to read it next lesson to the class. They should comment on why they find it effective as descriptive writing.

Text 8A

The island

Here, on the other side of the island, the view was utterly different. The filmy enchantments of mirage could not endure the cold ocean water, and the horizon was hard, clipped blue. Ralph wandered down to the rocks. Down here, almost on a level with the sea, you could follow with your eye the ceaseless, bulging passage of the deep sea waves. They were miles wide, apparently not breakers or the banked ridges of shallow water. They travelled the length of the island with an air of disregarding it and being set on other business; they were less a progress than a momentous rise and fall of the whole ocean. Now the sea would suck down, making cascades and waterfalls of retreating water, would sink past the rocks and plaster down the seaweed like shining hair: then pausing, gather and rise with a roar, irresistibly swelling over point and outcrop, climbing the little cliff, sending at last an arm of surf up a gully to end a yard or so from him in fingers of spray.

Wave after wave, Ralph followed the rise and fall until something of the remoteness of the sea numbed his brain. Then gradually the almost infinite size of this water forced itself on his attention. This was the divider, the barrier. On the other side of the island, swathed at midday with mirage, defended by the shield of the quiet lagoon, one might dream of rescue; but here, faced by the brute obtuseness of the ocean, the miles of division, one was clamped down, one was helpless, one was condemned, one was …

From **Lord of the Flies,** **by William Golding.**

Text 8B

The causeway

On the causeway path it was still quite dry underfoot but to my left I saw that the water had begun to seep nearer, quite silent now, quite slow. I wondered how deeply the path went under water when the tide was at its height. But on a still night such as this, there was plenty of time to cross in safety, though the distance was greater, now I was traversing it on foot, than it had seemed when we trotted over in Keckwick's pony cart, and the end of the causeway path seemed to be receding into the greyness ahead. I had never been quite so alone, nor felt quite so small and insignificant in a vast landscape before, and I fell into a brooding, philosophical frame of mind, struck by the absolute indifference of water and sky to my presence.

Some minutes later, I could not tell how many, I came out of my reverie, to realize that I could no longer see very far in front of me, and when I turned around I was startled to find that Eel Marsh House, too, was invisible, not because the darkness of evening had fallen, but because of a thick, damp sea-mist that had come rolling over the marshes and enveloped everything, myself, the house behind me, the end of the causeway path and the countryside ahead. It was a mist like a damp, clinging cobwebby thing, fine and yet impenetrable … I felt confused, teased by it, as though it were made up of millions of live fingers that crept over me, hung onto me and then shifted away again. Above all, it was the suddenness of it that had so unnerved and disorientated me.

From *The Woman in Black,* by Susan Hill.

Text 8C

The river

Towards the evening of the second day we judged ourselves about eight miles from Kurtz's station. I wanted to push on; but the manager looked grave, and told me the navigation up there was so dangerous that it would be advisable, the <u>Sun being very low</u> already, to wait where we were till next morning. Moreover, he pointed out that if the warning to approach cautiously were to be followed, we must approach in daylight – not at dusk, or in the dark. This was sensible enough. Eight miles meant nearly three hours' steaming for us, and I could also see <u>suspicious ripples</u> at the upper end of the reach. Nevertheless, I was annoyed beyond expression at the delay, and most unreasonably too, since one night more could not matter much after so many months. As we had plenty of wood, and <u>caution was the word</u>, I brought up in the middle of the stream. The reach was narrow, straight, with <u>high sides like a railway cutting</u>. The dusk came gliding into it long before the sun had set. The current ran smooth and swift, but a dumb immobility sat on the banks. The living trees, lashed together by the creepers and every living bush of the undergrowth, might have been <u>changed into stone</u>, even to the slenderest twig, to the lightest leaf. It was not sleep – <u>it seemed unnatural, like a state of trance</u>. Not the faintest sound of any kind could be heard. You looked on amazed, and began to suspect yourself of being deaf – then the night came suddenly, and <u>struck you blind</u> as well. About three in the morning some large fish leaped, and the loud splash made me jump <u>as though a gun had been fired</u>. When the sun rose there was <u>a white fog</u>, very warm and clammy, and more blinding than the night. It did not shift or drive; it was just there, standing all round you like something solid. At eight or nine, perhaps, it lifted as a shutter lifts. We had a glimpse of the <u>towering multitude of trees, of the immense matted jungle</u>, with the blazing little ball of the sun hanging over it – all perfectly still – and then the white shutter came down again, smoothly, as if sliding in <u>greased grooves</u>. I ordered the chain, which we had begun to heave in, to be paid out again. Before it stopped running with a muffled rattle, a cry, a very loud cry, <u>as of infinite desolation</u>, soared slowly in the opaque air.

From *Heart of Darkness*, by Joseph Conrad.

Worksheet for Text 8A: The island

Fill each blank with one word.

Here, on the other side of the island, the view was utterly different. The (1)_____ enchantments of mirage could not endure the cold ocean water, and the horizon was hard, (2)_____ blue. Ralph wandered down to the rocks. Down here, almost on a level with the sea, you could follow with your eye the ceaseless, (3)_____ passage of the deep sea waves. They were miles wide, apparently not breakers or the banked ridges of shallow water. They travelled the length of the island with an air of disregarding it and being set on other business; they were less a progress than a (4)_____ rise and fall of the whole ocean. Now the sea would (5)_____ down, making cascades and waterfalls of retreating water, would sink past the rocks and plaster down the seaweed like (6)_____ hair: then pausing, gather and rise with a roar, irresistibly swelling over point and outcrop, climbing the little cliff, sending at last an arm of surf up a gully to end a yard or so from him in (7)_____ of spray.

Wave after wave, Ralph followed the rise and fall until something of the (8)_____ of the sea numbed his brain. Then gradually the almost infinite size of this water forced itself on his attention. This was the divider, the barrier. On the other side of the island, (9)_____ at midday with mirage, defended by the (10)_____ of the quiet lagoon, one might dream of rescue; but here, faced by the brute obtuseness of the ocean, the miles of division, one was clamped down, one was helpless, one was condemned, one was …

Worksheet for Text 8B: The causeway

Choose the best word from the three choices to fill each blank.

On the causeway path it was still quite dry underfoot but to my left I saw that the water had begun to (1)_____ nearer, quite silent now, quite slow. I wondered how deeply the path went under water when the tide was at its (2)_____. But on a still night such as this, there was plenty of time to cross in safety, though the distance was greater, now I was (3)_____ it on foot, than it had seemed when we trotted over in Keckwick's pony cart, and the end of the causeway path seemed to be receding into the (4)_____ ahead. I had never been quite so alone, nor felt quite so small and (5)_____ in a vast landscape before, and I fell into a brooding, philosophical frame of mind, struck by the absolute indifference of water and sky to my presence.

Some minutes later, I could not tell how many, I came out of my reverie, to realize that I could no longer see very far in front of me, and when I turned around I was (6)_____ to find that Eel Marsh House, too, was invisible, not because the darkness of evening had fallen, but because of a thick, damp sea-mist that had come (7)_____ over the marshes and (8)_____ everything, myself, the house behind me, the end of the causeway path and the countryside ahead. It was a mist like a damp, (9)_____ cobwebby thing, fine and yet impenetrable … I felt confused, teased by it, as though it were made up of millions of live fingers that crept over me, hung onto me and then (10)_____ away again. Above all, it was the suddenness of it that had so unnerved and disorientated me.

1	drift	seep	creep
2	height	maximum	highest
3	crossing	covering	traversing
4	blackness	whiteness	greyness
5	insignificant	unimportant	lost
6	surprised	puzzled	startled
7	flooding	rolling	flowing
8	enveloped	shrouded	hid
9	sticky	transparent	clinging
10	shifted	moved	ran

Answers – Unit 8

1 How writers create the effect of alienation:

The persona is alone; climate, vegetation or wildlife is different from what they are used to and extreme; the place is not at all what they were expecting; aspects of the place are personified; the weather or environment is threatening; the atmosphere is tense with expectation of an impending event; the arrival has been long-awaited after an arduous journey; the persona is dreading what they will find there; the persona feels unwell, physically or psychologically; the persona will not be able to leave the place because of its isolation or lack of transport.

2 Islands:

Probable responses – because these are traditional in literature and films – are isolation: lack of food; lack of comforts; lack of means of escape; lack of communication; fear of possible natives; dangerous animals; poisonous vegetation; division and fighting among the group; disappearances; supernatural events.

7 The Amazon:

Tropical rivers and jungle conjure up images of watchers among the foliage: piranhas, crocodiles and other predators in the water; alarming screeching noises of parrots and exotic animals; humid and dark atmosphere; lurid green vegetation; powerful creepers and tall/thick trees full of dangerous creatures, including snakes; the idea of the unknown and unknowable in the heart of the jungle.

11 Text 8C: effects of underlined words:

sun being very low – light is going / darkness is coming; this is a bad time to arrive in a strange place

suspicious ripples – suggestions of something dangerous moving under the water; not naming it makes it more frightening

caution was the word – this implies that there are a lot of things one must be careful of

high sides like a railway cutting – it would be impossible to escape by climbing

changed into stone and like a state of trance – remind the reader of bewitchment and spells

it seemed unnatural – this implies that the stillness is supernatural and that something will happen because of it, and because of the silence

struck you blind – this is a violent image, showing the power of darkness to remove the ability to see

as though a gun had been fired – this simile introduces the idea of danger and death

a white fog – another image of blindness, which always makes someone feel vulnerable to attack by something unseen

towering multitude of trees, of the immense matted jungle – these make the vegetation seem gigantic and easily able to defeat or swallow humans

greased grooves – this alliterative phrase shows how swiftly the fog returned, like the action of a gun

as of infinite desolation – the cry sounds inhuman and unbearably tragic; it creates an impression of belonging to something unearthly and desperate

Part 3: Response to Reading

Unit 9: Missing persons

Topic outline

- **Main skills:** genre transformation; inferring; selecting material; sequencing
- **Secondary skills:** paraphrasing; news reporting; formal register
- **Outcome:** news report; formal report; *plot synopsis
- **Materials:** informative account; memoir; news report structure handout; formal report structure handout
- **Texts:** Text 9A: The disappearance of Jim Thompson; Text 9B: The lighthouse keepers

Lesson plan

1. Ask students to read Text 9A. (5)
2. Ask students to discuss, in pairs, their theories about what might have happened to Jim Thompson, using the clues in the text. (5)
3. Elicit feedback with supporting evidence. (5)
4. Give out the News report structure handout. Ask students to plan a news report for the disappearance of Jim Thompson. (The theories can be included as speculation if attributed to agencies or interviewees. Direct speech can be used.) (10)
6. Ask students to write their news reports, including a suitable headline. (15)
7. Ask students to swap their reports with a partner to check for accuracy. Then collect for assessment. (5)
8. Read Text 9B while students follow text and underline unknown words. (5)
9. Ask students to guess the meanings of unknown words using the recommended methods (i.e. breaking down words into constituent parts including prefixes, family word connections, other language similarities, logical guess from context). (10)
10. Ask students to infer what they think happened to the three lighthouse keepers. (5)
11. Ask students to re-read Text 9B, in pairs, and underline only factual material. (5)
12. Class agrees on material selected. (5)
13. Ask students to work individually to copy the points, in their own words, into a plan for a formal report to the authorities made at the time of the disappearances.

    First give out the formal report structure handout and remind students that no inference or speculation can be included. (10)
14. Ask students to number the points in their plan logically and chronologically to show their sequence and how they will be grouped into complex sentences. The first order of the points in their plan is not necessarily the sequence required for the type of response. (5)

Homework task

Write the formal report, of about 300 words, selecting a suitable voice and register. Check it for accuracy when completed.

Additional tasks

a. Ask students to imagine they are a Hollywood screenwriter and to write their version of the story, entitled 'Lost in Malaysia', of what happened to Jim Thompson, as the basis for a future film script. They should use the facts about his disappearance and their own inferences. They should write about 400 words.

b. Ask students in groups of three to plan a drama sketch, lasting about five minutes, to illustrate their theory of what happened to the three lighthouse keepers. They can perform it to the class.

Text 9A

The disappearance of Jim Thompson

James Thompson arrived in Thailand as an American military intelligence officer at the end of the Second World War. He decided to stay in the country but was divorced by his wife who did not wish to live in Southeast Asia. The former architect from Delaware began by renovating the celebrated Oriental Hotel in Bangkok, which had been damaged during the Japanese occupation. While he was doing this, Thompson became fascinated by Thailand's rich, exotic, hand-woven silks and he set about reviving the declining cottage industry. His skill as a designer and textile colourist was noted by fashion editors and film producers, which led to the creation of his empire founded on silk.

But Thompson was not to enjoy his dream for long. On 26th March 1967, while he was visiting some friends in the Cameron Highlands, Malaysia, they went for a picnic on Mount Brinchang. His friends returned home, but Thompson vanished. The area contains wild, untamed jungle, but Thompson was familiar with such terrain from his survival training when he was a commando. It drops steeply down into a valley shrouded in oaks, laurels, cinnamon trees and rhododendrons. There is an overgrown trail which leads to the Lutheran Mission where Thompson was last seen. The person who last saw Thompson remembers that he had a camera around his neck. He turned to wave goodbye and was never seen again.

Search parties, including police, soldiers and helicopters, were mobilised, scouring a 100-kilometre area of jungle and mountains. A 25,000-dollar reward was offered, but after ten days the operation was called off. Locals suggested a tiger attack; a tiger had been recently witnessed making off with a dog from the same spot. But tiger attacks usually leave something behind, perhaps a belt buckle or shoes. Others believe he was accidentally shot by a tribal blow-dart. But less than six months later, his elderly sister was murdered in America, which added to the mystery. Two or three people go missing each year in this area of misty highlands, but they are generally found within a few days once the tribal trackers are sent out. No one else has ever vanished without trace in the area, which gives a chilling poignancy to Thompson's case.

During the following months the case was characterised by false alarms, mystical visions and bizarre theories. Some investigators favoured the idea of a communist kidnapping plot, as there were terrorists active throughout the 450 square kilometres of the Cameron Highlands until they finally surrendered in 1989. Thompson disappeared at the height of the Vietnam War, when the USA was battling communism, and there were rumours that he was still working for the American CIA. It also emerged after his death that he had fallen out with the Thailand Society and had removed them from his will. There were reported sightings of Thompson in places as far apart as Canton, Laos and Tahiti, but finally in 1974 Thompson was declared dead in the USA and Thailand. His file, however, is still open in the nearby police station, labelled 'Missing in action'. His famous house in Bangkok now resembles the *Marie Celeste*, untouched exactly as he left it. Forty years have offered no further clues to this mystery, which is worthy of treatment by Hollywood's most imaginative scriptwriters.

Adapted from: 'Jim Thompson's House', The James H.W. Thompson Foundation.

Text 9B

The lighthouse keepers

We were a hardened lot, the lighthouse keepers of the Flannan Isles. The Outer Hebrides do not breed soft men; if it does, they do not live long. The storms come screaming down from the Arctic, and we are often cut off from the world outside for weeks on end. It is impossible to feel more alone – or so I thought until that day in December 1900 – a propitious day, it should have been, looking to the new year and the new century.

I was sailing with Captain James Harvey, an experienced sailor for the Northern Lighthouse Board, on a routine trip to replace one of the three keepers of the Eilean Mor lighthouse. Our sailing had been delayed by a fierce storm, but the seas were calm as we approached the landing stage. It was immediately clear that all was not well, because there was no keeper waiting to greet me. The captain sounded his fog-horn and launched a flare as I rowed over, somewhat concerned.

As I climbed the steep rock-cut stairs, I felt an overwhelming sense of foreboding. It has always been said that the island was an evil place, and none but the keepers would spend a night there. When I reached the lighthouse the door was open, two oilskin coats were missing – and keeper was there none. I searched, in increasing agitation, but there was no denying it; and the kitchen clock had stopped.

I hastened back to the landing and the ship; the good Captain was nonplussed, and sent two stout sailors to pass the night with me while he sought assistance. I can say that we did not sleep easy that night.

We searched every inch of that cursed island over the next three days, but to no avail, except to note that all was not as it should be at the landing stage – the storm had damaged the crane and loading installations, and loose ropes were strewn around. But of the three men with whom I had worked for years, no sign or hint.

Mr Robert Muirhead, the Board Superintendant, came to the island in person, and he it was who came upon the journal which told an incomprehensible story. Starting on the 12th December, the diary told of storms fierce beyond living memory, and of keepers – hardened men, all – in fear for their lives and weeping. The storm continued unabated, from the diary entries, until 15th December, when the final entry stated: 'Storm over. Sea calm. God is over all.'

Well, indeed He is, but what in the name of the heavens did that mean? There was no further entry to dispel the mystery. Shortly after, all three men vanished from the island and from this life as if they had been swept up.

But what is passing strange is that there was no storm on the 12th, or 13th, or 14th, or 15th December. The tempest which wrought such destruction upon the landing stage started only on the 17th December. The island is clearly visible from the mainland and nothing had been reported.

Muirhead investigated the damage to the landing stage and pronounced that the destruction of the storm had been exceptional. Had the keepers ventured forth to attempt the rescue of their equipment? But why, contrary to all regulation, would all three go? And if so, why had one left his oilskin behind, in a raging winter tempest? And if the third had not been swept away with the other two, where then was he?

No body was ever washed ashore. No trace was ever found. No explanation was ever offered which I could put my hand to. It is my profound belief that the ancient curse of the Island brewed up a false storm to terrify the keepers and lure them to their death. The temerity of Man in building the new lighthouse just the year before would surely have been an affront which needed to be avenged. And avenged it was.

Answers – Unit 9

2 Theories about the disappearance of Jim Thompson:

- Business rivals in the silk industry got rid of him.
- He fell down a gorge and his body remained hidden by undergrowth.
- Wild animals devoured him in the jungle.
- Tribespeople poisoned him.
- He was killed by someone with a grudge against his family.
- He was kidnapped by communists because he worked for the CIA.
- The Thailand society wanted revenge for being cut out of his will.
- He was abducted by aliens.

11 Facts from Text 9B:

- The Outer Hebrides have stormy Arctic weather.
- There were three keepers of the lighthouse at Eilean Mor.
- Captain James Harvey took a replacement keeper there in December 1900.
- The sailing had been delayed but the seas were then calm.
- No keeper was present to greet the replacement.
- A fog-horn was sounded and a flare launched by the captain.
- There were no keepers in the lighthouse.
- The clock had stopped.
- Two sailors stayed with the replacement keeper while the captain returned to the mainland.
- The island was searched for three days.
- There was damage and disarray at the landing stage.
- The Board Superintendant arrived and found a journal.
- It was claimed there had been exceptionally bad storms for three days in mid-December.
- In fact, there were no storms at that time but there was two days later.
- No trace of the three missing men was ever found.
- The lighthouse had been built the year before.

Cambridge IGCSE First Language English — Response to Reading

Unit 10: Home and away

Topic outline

- **Main skills:** genre transformation; adopting a voice
- **Secondary skills:** summarising; selecting material; style analysis
- **Outcome:** dialogue; news report; journal; *speech
- **Materials:** monologues; novel extract; journal content handout
- **Texts:** Text 10A: Brothers at war; Text 10B: When the locusts came

Lesson plan

1. Choose two students to read out Text 10A in role. (5)
2. Ask students to highlight the key information about the experience of Luis and of Amaral during the time they were apart (i.e. after the abduction by Unita and the MPLA, and before the reunion). (5)
3. Ask students to transfer the highlighted material, in their own words, to two columns, one for each brother. (5)
4. Ask students, in pairs, to write the dialogue between the brothers at their meeting after 29 years. They should explain:
   a. what happened to them
   b. how they felt then about the war and their separation
   c. how they feel now about the war and their reunion. (15)
5. Ask pairs to perform their dialogues. The class votes on the best script in terms of content and voice. (15)
6. Ask students to skim-read Text 10B. (5)
7. Ask students to say, in one sentence, how the villagers felt about the coming of the locusts. (5)
8. Discuss in class the effect of the following features of Text 10B:
   a. the short and simple / compound sentences
   b. starting sentences with 'And' and 'But'
   c. the simple and monosyllabic diction (10)
9. Ask students to scan Text 10B to identify and highlight relevant information for a news report about the coming of the locusts, and to transfer it, in their own words, to a plan in an appropriate order for the response genre. First they should revise news report structure (see handout). (10)
10. Ask students to write their news report, with a suitable headline, and submit it for assessment. (15)

Homework task

Write Okonkwo's journal entry, of about 300 words, for the day the locusts came. (Refer to the journal content handout.)

Additional task

Ask students to write a speech on the topic of 'Child soldiers', referring to the experiences described in Text 10A.

Text 10A

Brothers at war

LUIS: I was with my mum in the fields in November 1975 when my dad ran to tell her that the Portuguese were leaving Angola. Although our country was free of the Portuguese, there was then civil war between two factions – the MPLA and Unita. Like many people, my parents were caught in the middle. Now, from being people who worked hard and had good times, we became people who had little and were often on the run. Our lives were a nightmare.

In December 1976 tragedy struck. It was a Sunday in the Christmas holidays, when my brother was home. We were in church praying, and the choir was singing, when suddenly faces appeared at every window. It was MPLA soldiers who marched in and announced to the congregation: 'Everyone outside – but we only want the teenage boys.' Shocked and scared, everyone left the church and the soldiers seized six boys, including Amaral, who was 14. My father rushed to stop them, but the soldiers immediately set on him and beat him.

That night my brother managed to escape the soldiers and fled back to our village. Amaral and his friends hid for the next few days, but some nights later, as they sat in our kitchen planning what to do, we heard the terrible sound of soldiers' boots marching towards our house. This time it was the Unita soldiers, who didn't wear uniform. As they marched in, I was like a mouse, trying to hide in the corner. 'Don't beat me – just take me,' pleaded my brother. It was all over very quickly. I had to wake my parents and tell them my brother had been abducted a second time. I didn't see my brother again for 29 years.

As the days went on, I could see in my parents' faces an increasing sense of hopelessness. My father was frequently beaten by MPLA soldiers because my brother was serving in the Unita forces. I understood all too well that I could be taken too, and I was afraid all the time – especially at night. To be safe I'd often sleep with the cattle in the field. At night my mum used to make a fire with green leaves underneath. As it burnt she'd call 'Amaral, come back!' But he didn't. At school the teachers would say: 'You, boy, does your brother come to see your parents at night?' One teacher made me kneel on a pile of small stones, trying to get information out of me about Unita.

I knew nothing, but I still have the scars from the stones.

In 1981 I moved to a small town to continue my studies. But when I was 15, the inevitable happened – I was abducted by the MPLA, on my way to school. I was a soldier until 1992, and it was a very hard life. As a soldier you have to be bad and kill people. I soon became a tank-company commander on the front line. But in 1990 our brigade was completely destroyed by Unita. What I didn't know was that my brother was also on the front line – on the other side. We may even have fought each other.

In early 1992 I was demobilised. When my brother didn't reappear we had to accept he was dead, so we held a funeral for him. We didn't know that he was in a refugee camp in Zambia. One day my father received a letter from him through the International Red Cross. I'll never forget the day we were reunited. I walked into my sister's house in Huambo. There were my sisters, my father, and a man with a mutilated leg. I couldn't speak. We embraced each other. Over a big lunch we tried to tell each other our stories.

AMARAL: I left Luis when he was only four years old, when I was abducted. Because of the civil war the two opposing political parties wanted young people who were able to read and write to serve in their armies. The first time I was abducted I managed to escape and went back to the village, but a few nights later I was abducted again with three friends by Unita soldiers. I didn't cry, but I was frightened because I didn't know where they were taking me. On the way to the camp we had to climb mountains and cross rivers and I was afraid I'd be killed.

At the camp there were six other boys the same age as me, but Unita did not have enough weapons for us, so we were given sticks and taught to ambush MPLA soldiers. If we had not done what we were told, the commander would have shot us. I was always thinking about running away but I was too scared. And then I stepped on a land mine and lost my leg. As things got worse and our fellow soldiers were dying around us in battles, we developed anger and wanted revenge against the MPLA soldiers. But all of us were black, and we could not understand why we were killing each other.

During our 29-year separation I prayed that I would see my brother again. I missed him a lot. I left him as a child and I could only try to imagine how he was growing up. I never thought that I would find him so well educated. When we met at my sister's house we were surprised and nobody spoke. I had not expected that my brother and I would ever meet again, and soon I was crying. I had been worried how it would be, because I had been Unita and Luis had been MPLA. But when we talked about it we didn't have any anger, because we were forced to do what we did.

Adapted from article, 'Relative Values: Amaral Samacumbi and his brother, Luis', *The Sunday Times.*

Text 10B

When the locusts came

This novel extract is set in the fictional village of Umuofia, Nigeria, around 1900.

In this way the moons and the seasons passed. And then the locusts came. It had not happened for many a long year. The elders said locusts came once in a generation, reappeared every year for seven years and then disappeared for another lifetime. They went back to their caves in a distant land, where they were guarded by a race of stunted men. And then after another lifetime these men opened the caves again and the locusts came to Umuofia. They came in the cold *harmattan* season after the harvests had been gathered, and ate up all the wild grass in the fields.

Okonkwo and the two boys were working on the red outer walls of the compound. This was one of the lighter tasks of the after-harvest season. A new cover of thick palm branches and palm leaves was set on the walls to protect them from the next rainy season. Okonkwo worked on the outside of the wall and the boys worked from within. There were little holes from one side to the other in the upper levels of the wall, and through these Okonkwo passed the rope, or tie-tie, to the boys and they passed it round the wooden stays and then back to him – and in this way the cover was strengthened on the wall.

The women had gone to the bush to collect firewood, and the little children to visit their playmates in the neighbouring compounds. The harmattan was in the air and seemed to distil a hazy feeling of sleep on the world. Okonkwo and the boys worked in complete silence, which was only broken when a new palm frond was lifted on to the wall or when a busy hen moved dry leaves about in her ceaseless search for food.

And then quite suddenly a shadow fell on the world, and the sun seemed hidden behind a thick cloud. Okonkwo looked up from his work and wondered if it was going to rain at such an unlikely time of the year. But almost immediately a shout of joy broke out in all directions, and Umuofia, which had dozed in the noon-day haze, broke into life and activity.

'Locusts are descending,' was joyfully chanted everywhere, and men, women and children left their work or their play and ran into the open to see the unfamiliar sight. The locusts had not come for many, many years, and only the old people had seen them before.

At first, a fairly small swarm came. They were the harbingers sent to survey the land. And then appeared on the horizon a slowly-moving mass like a boundless sheet of black cloud drifting towards Umuofia. Soon it covered half the sky, and the solid mass was now broken by tiny eyes of light like shining star dust. It was a tremendous sight, full of power and beauty.

Everyone was now about, talking excitedly and praying that the locusts should camp in Umuofia for the night. For although locusts had not visited Umuofia for many years, everybody knew by instinct that they were very good to eat. And at last the locusts did descend. They settled on every tree and on every blade of grass, they settled on the roofs and covered the bare ground. Mighty tree branches broke away under them, and the whole country became the brown-earth colour of the vast, hungry swarm.

Many people went out with baskets trying to catch them, but the elders counselled patience till nightfall. And they were right. The locusts settled in the bushes for the night and their wings became wet with dew. Then all Umuofia turned out in spite of the cold harmattan, and everyone filled his bags and pots with locusts. The next morning they were roasted in clay pots and then spread in the sun until they became dry and brittle. And for many days this rare food was eaten with solid palm-oil.

From *Things Fall Apart*, by Chinua Achebe.

VOCABULARY

harmattan: dry, dusty wind on the West African coast, occurring from December to February.

Answers – Unit 10

2 Text 10A: main points:

Luis' experiences:

- watched parents lose hope
- father beaten by MPLA soldiers
- so afraid of being abducted he slept (with the cattle) in the field
- mother lit fires to call for Amaral to return
- tormented by MPLA supporters to give information about Unita
- transferred to another school in town
- abducted by MPLA on way to school aged 15
- became a tank-company commander and sent to front line
- brigade destroyed by Unita in 1990 and many killed
- demobilised in 1992
- assumed Amaral was dead so funeral was held
- received letter from Amaral through the International Red Cross

Amaral's experiences:

- frightened by the journey to the camp with three friends
- with six other boys in camp, the same age of 14
- they were given sticks instead of weapons
- too scared to disobey or run away
- had a leg blown off by a mine
- developed a hatred for the MPLA
- couldn't understand why people were killing each other
- missed his baby brother and didn't expect to see him again
- worried by the meeting after 29 years because they'd been on opposing sides

7 The villagers were delighted by the coming of the locusts as they had not been for a very long time and they provided food.

8 The effect of the following features of Text 10B:

a the short and simple / compound sentences – simple, uneducated people living an unpretentious existence reliant on basic necessities for survival

b starting sentences with 'And' and 'But' – the people people make simple connections between thoughts and events, and the practicalities of life are what matter to them

c the simple and monosyllabic diction – their vocabulary and knowledge is restricted by their life and surroundings; they express themselves in clear but basic language in order to be understood

9 News report content and sequence:
- locusts arrived unexpectedly in Umuofia the day before yesterday
- they appeared as a thick cloud hiding the Sun at noon
- a small swarm came ahead of the huge mass covering half the sky
- 'It was a tremendous sight, full of power and beauty' said one young villager
- the inhabitants of the village were glad to see the locusts, as they knew they could eat them
- it was the first time in living memory for most of the inhabitants
- local belief is that they come only once in a generation, for seven years in a row
- when they come it is always during the harmattan season and after the harvest, to clear the fields
- in the evening they settled on and covered every surface
- the village elders advised the villagers to wait until dusk to collect them
- villagers filled many receptacles with the creatures
- yesterday there was great feasting after the locusts were roasted and dried, then eaten with solid palm-oil
- the village has enough locusts to provide meals for many days

Unit 11: Of sharks and whales

Topic outline

- **Main skills:** response to reading; genre transformation; selecting; collating
- **Secondary skills:** concision; formal expression
- **Outcome:** summary; dialogue; news report; letter; *journal entry; *interview
- **Materials:** news article; fact sheet; novel extract; formal letter structure handout
- **Texts:** Text 11A: The Trojan shark project; Text 11B: Shark myths and facts; Text 11C: The Great White Whale

Lesson plan

1. Ask students to skim-read Text 11A and say, in one sentence, what the article is about. (5)

2. Ask students to scan, in pairs, Text 11A for points about a) the Trojan shark and b) real Great White sharks, highlighting them in different colours. Write points on board in two columns. (10)

3. Ask students, to show, in pairs, with brackets how the short paragraphs could be combined into longer paragraphs in Text 11A, and to say why internet news articles (as well as news reports) contain unusually short paragraphs. (5)

4. Ask students to work in pairs to rewrite the three passages in bold in Text 11A, (each containing three sentences), in one complex sentence each. (10)

5. Ask students to read Text 11B, to order and combine the points, and to write a summary of approximately 120 words, in complex sentences, of a) the facts and b) the myths about sharks. Collect for assessment. (10)

6. Ask students to work in pairs to write a dialogue for a news programme between Fabien Cousteau and a shark expert who believes that the Trojan shark project is pointless and dangerous. They should use material from both Text 11A and Text 11B. They should begin the dialogue with the expert saying: 'Unsettling Great Whites is always inadvisable'. (15)

7. Ask pairs to perform their dialogues and the class can judge the best, giving reasons. (10)

8. Ask students to read Text 11C, noting unknown words. Go through the unknown words, using the recommended methods of working out their meaning. (10)

9. Ask students to underline the material in Text 11C which could be adapted for use in a news report of the attack of Moby Dick on Captain Ahab. (10)

Homework tasks

a. Plan and write your news report, of about 300 words, under a suitable headline. You may make up the necessary additional information about places and ages, etc.

b. Plan and write Ishmael's letter home, of about 300 words, explaining his thoughts and feelings about Moby Dick and why he has taken an oath of revenge on the whale. the whale. Use your own words.

Additional tasks

a. Ask students to plan and then write Fabien's journal for the final day of the Trojan shark project, including the relevant material in Text 11A and developing his thoughts and feelings.

b. Ask students to write an interview transcript between a reporter for the Nantucket News and Captain Ahab, after his return to land. The three questions to ask are:

1. Can you tell us what the whale looked like and why it was so special?
2. Why were you so intent on pursuing the whale?
3. How do you feel now about the whale that took off your leg?

Text 11A

The Trojan shark project

Deep beneath the waves a weird fish has swallowed the grandson of the late Captain Jacques Cousteau, the ocean explorer. Fabien Cousteau, 36, is these days to be found inside the belly of a submersible built in the shape of a Great White shark.

It might seem a foolhardy enterprise, but Cousteau is using the robotic fish to get as close as possible to real Great Whites, the most ferocious killers of the sea, in the hope of filming them without disturbing their natural behaviour.

The 'Trojan shark', built from steel and plastic, is 4 metres long and was created by a Hollywood prop expert at a cost of $115,000.

'The whole point,' says Cousteau, 'is to fool them into thinking I am a shark.'

It is hardly the most comforting of environments in which to get cosy with the predatory fish. Cousteau's diving contraption is covered with Skinflex, a malleable material mixed with glass beads and sand to simulate the texture of shark skin, right down to the ugly scars that commonly disfigure the biggest Great Whites.

The head swings open on hinges to allow Cousteau to enter the body. There he lies flat, holding a joystick in each hand to control speed, left and right movement, and pitch – 'just like a fighter plane,' he says.

The shark's eyes are camera lenses and a third camera is positioned in a rubber 'pilot fish' clamped, in another lifelike touch, to the underbelly of the submarine.

A 'pneumatic propulsion system' invented by the American Navy powers the shark's tail. It enables it to move quietly and without creating bubbles.

'Bubbles make noise the sharks would feel and hear,' explains Cousteau. 'It's an artificial stimulus that could spook them or alter their behaviour in some way.'

Unsettling Great Whites is inadvisable. They have been blamed for three deaths this year and numerous attacks on swimmers and surfers. Some have been known to attack the metal cages used by divers. In the image popularised by the Steven Spielberg film *Jaws*, a Great White is even thought capable of biting a small boat in half.

With the Trojan shark, Cousteau is protected by a stainless steel skeleton made from 5 cm thick ribs beneath the shark's skin.

Perhaps because of their fearsome reputation, the Great White remains little understood. Scientists have yet to establish where they breed, how long they live and how big they can grow. The largest on record is 6.4 metres.

Cousteau's device has enabled him to study the fish with unprecedented insight. Over the past few months he has been filming Great Whites from Mexico to Australia for American television. His findings contradict popular conceptions.

In fact, he says, 'Great White sharks do not go around chomping up boats'. Instead he claims they are 'very timid creatures'.

The new mechanical shark – called Troy but nicknamed Sushi by some of Cousteau's crew – has proved successful. Real sharks tend to accept the intruder as a dominant female, says Cousteau, even though they may be baffled by some of its features. The mouth can open and close but does not eat. And Troy, unlike real sharks, is odourless and incapable of great bursts of speed.

With the help of Troy, Fabien, born in Paris but now living in New York, may become the most effective torchbearer of his grandfather's mission.

He could not have better credentials: he began diving at the age of four when his grandfather designed a junior scuba outfit for him.

He was only six when he sneaked into a cinema to watch *Jaws*, which his parents had forbidden him to see.

He says he was horrified by the film because 'it went against everything I'd ever been taught'.

That experience still underlies his desire to show audiences that sharks are not evil creatures but natural predators. He may yet change the popular perception of Great Whites, assuming Troy continues to perform as planned – and Cousteau does not end up inside the wrong shark.

Adapted from article 'Cousteau and his incredible Trojan shark', by Matthew Campbell, The *Sunday Times*.

Text 11B

Shark myths and facts

Myths

- sharks attack swimmers if they have come to expect to be fed by people
- all sharks are predators
- they see humans as no more than shark bait
- sharks are unpredictable and attack without warning
- divers are only safe if wearing chain-mail or in cages

Facts

- divers are merely regarded as other predators by sharks
- of the hundreds of shark species, few pose a threat
- those that are threatening are rarely seen and account for few deaths
- attacks are usually the result of mistaken identity, as a surfer looks like an injured seal
- if sharks are moving slowly and gracefully, they are not likely to attack
- cages only need to be used when a shark has been deliberately enticed to feed by 'chumming' (pouring fish blood into the water)

Text 11C

The Great White Whale

In this extract from a 19th-century American novel, Ishmael is recounting why he has dedicated himself to catching the Great White Whale, Moby Dick, and what happened to his ship's captain, Ahab.

I, Ishmael, was one of that crew; my shouts had gone up with the rest; my oath had been welded with theirs; and stronger I shouted, and more did I hammer and clinch my oath, because of the dread in my soul. A wild, mystical, sympathetical feeling was in me; Ahab's quenchless feud seemed mine. With greedy ears I learnt the history of that murderous monster against whom I and all the others had taken our oaths of violence and revenge.

For some time past, though at intervals only, the unaccompanied, secluded White Whale had haunted those uncivilized seas mostly frequented by the Sperm Whale fishermen. But not all of them knew of his existence; only a few of them, comparatively, had knowingly seen him; while the number who as yet had actually and knowingly given battle to him, was small indeed. It was hardly to be doubted, that several vessels reported to have encountered, a Sperm Whale of uncommon magnitude and malignity, which whale, after doing great mischief to his assailants, had completely escaped them; to some minds it was not an unfair presumption, I say, that the whale in question must have been no other than Moby Dick.

Nor did wild rumors of all sorts fail to exaggerate, and still the more horrify the true histories of these deadly encounters. So that in many cases such a panic did he finally strike, that few who by those rumors, at least, had heard of the White Whale, few of those hunters were willing to encounter the perils of his jaw.

Nevertheless, some there were, who even in the face of these things were ready to give chase to Moby Dick; and a still greater number who, chancing only to hear of him distantly and vaguely, without the specific details of any certain calamity, and without superstitious accompaniments, were sufficiently hardy not to flee from the battle if offered.

One of the wild suggestions referred to, as at last coming to be linked with the White Whale in the minds of the superstitiously inclined, was the unearthly conceit that Moby Dick was ubiquitous; that he had actually been encountered in opposite latitudes at one and the same instant of time.

But even stripped of these supernatural surmisings, there was enough in the earthly make and incontestable character of the monster to strike the imagination with unwonted power. For, it was not so much his uncommon bulk that so much distinguished him from other sperm whales, but, as was elsewhere thrown out—a peculiar snow-white wrinkled forehead, and a high, pyramidical white hump. These were his prominent features; the tokens whereby, even in the limitless, uncharted seas, he revealed his identity, at a long distance, to those who knew him.

The rest of his body was so streaked, and spotted, and marbled with the same shrouded hue, that, in the end, he had gained his distinctive appellation of the White Whale; a name, indeed, literally justified by his vivid aspect, when seen gliding at high noon through a dark blue sea, leaving a milky-way wake of creamy foam, all spangled with golden gleamings.

Nor was it his unwonted magnitude, nor his remarkable hue, nor yet his deformed lower jaw, that so much invested the whale with natural terror, as that unexampled, intelligent malignity which, according to specific accounts, he had over and over again evinced in his assaults. More than all, his treacherous retreats struck more of dismay than perhaps aught else. For, when swimming before his exulting pursuers, with every apparent symptom of alarm, he had several times been known to turn round suddenly, and, bearing down upon them, either stave their boats to splinters, or drive them back in consternation to their ship.

His three boats stove around him, and oars and men both whirling in the eddies; one captain, seizing the line-knife from his broken prow, had dashed at the whale, blindly seeking with a six inch blade to reach the fathom-deep life of the whale. That captain was Ahab. And then it was, that suddenly sweeping his sickle-shaped lower jaw beneath him, Moby Dick had reaped away Ahab's leg, as a mower a blade of grass in the field. Small reason was there to doubt, then, that ever since that almost fatal encounter, Ahab had cherished a wild vindictiveness against the whale, all the more fell for that in his frantic morbidness he at last came to identify with him, not only all his bodily woes, but all his intellectual and spiritual exasperations.

It is not probable that this monomania in him took its instant rise at the precise time of his bodily dismemberment. Then, in darting at the monster, knife in hand, he had but given loose to a sudden, passionate, corporal animosity; and when he received the stroke that tore him, he probably but felt the agonizing bodily laceration, but nothing more. Yet, when by this collision forced to turn towards home, and for long months of days and weeks, Ahab and anguish lay stretched together in one hammock, rounding in mid winter that dreary, howling Patagonian Cape; then it was, that his torn body and gashed soul bled into one another; and so interfusing, made him mad. At intervals during the homeward passage, he was a raving lunatic; and, though unlimbed of a leg, yet such vital strength yet lurked in his Egyptian chest, and was moreover intensified by his delirium, that his mates were forced to lace him fast, even there, as he sailed, raving in his hammock. In a strait-jacket, he swung to the mad rockings of the gales.

Abridged extract from *Moby Dick*, by Herman Melville.

Answers – Unit 11

1 Text 11A is about the use of a manned mechanical shark which enables researchers to get closer to real sharks in order to film them, allowing them to discover new information which overturns some of the myths associated with Great White sharks.

2 Text 11A: summary points:

a Trojan shark [18 points]
- submersible in the shape of a Great White
- built from steel and plastic
- 4 metres long
- created by a Hollywood prop expert
- cost of £115 000
- skin made of malleable material which simulates texture of shark skin
- hinged head allows entrance to body
- joysticks control speed and angle
- shark's eyes are camera lenses and a third camera is positioned beneath
- American Navy invention propels shark's tail
- moves quietly and without creating bubbles
- has a five-centimetre-thick, stainless steel skeleton
- named Troy but nicknamed Sushi
- mouth opens and closes but Trojan does not eat
- it is odourless
- it is unable to move fast
- device has enabled unprecedented opportunity to study sharks
- accepted by real sharks as a dominant female

b Real Great White sharks [15 points]
- the most ferocious marine predators
- large ones disfigured by ugly scars
- attended by pilot fish
- blamed for several deaths and attacks on swimmers and surfers every year
- have been known to attack metal cages containing divers
- considered capable of biting a small boat in half (because of film *Jaws*)
- the Great White remains little understood
- scientists don't know where they breed, how long they live and how big they can grow
- the largest on record is 6.4 metres
- Great Whites can be found from Mexico to Australia
- many false perceptions about sharks

- sharks actually very timid
- Great White sharks do not attack and eat boats
- they have a smell
- they are capable of great speed

3 Text 11A: paragraph joining (there is an alternative for paragraph 15):

1 + 2 + 4 + 15
3 + 5 + 6 + 7
8 + 9 + 10 + 11 (+ 15)
12 + 13 + 14
16 + 17 + 18 + 19 + 20

Logically, the 20 paragraphs in Text 11A should be only five paragraphs. These paragraphs can be joined because there is no change of time, place or topic between them. News reports and articles tend to use simple or compound sentences for dramatic effect and simplicity of expression, as befits informative writing for a mass readership. They also use shorter paragraphs than other genres of writing because they are purely informative and information is more easily assimilated if it is broken up for the reader. Newspapers rely on sales achieved through the accessibility of their layout for people who have a limited attention span, or who do not have the time or ability to wade through dense text, so their pages must have 'white space'. Because sub-editors cut news reports from the bottom upwards if they are too long for the space available, the information is given in descending order of importance. Internet articles do not use columns, which makes it even more necessary for them to use short paragraphs, usually one per sentence, in order to create white space and make text seem accessible.

4 (Example answers)

Unsettling Great Whites is inadvisable, as they have been blamed for three deaths this year and have made numerous attacks on swimmers and surfers, some of them even attacking the metal cages used by divers.

Perhaps because of their fearsome reputation, the Great White remains so little understood that scientists have yet to establish where they breed, how long they live and how big they can grow, although the largest on record is 6.4 metres.

Cousteau's device has enabled him to study the fish with unprecedented insight, while over the last few months he has been filming Great Whites from Mexico to Australia for American television, since his findings contradict popular conceptions.

5 Divers are viewed as other predators by sharks, not as prey or providers of food. Very few of the many hundreds of shark species are dangerous, and even those which are a threat are rarely seen and cause few deaths. Sharks do not attack without warning or reason, the most common attack being mistaken identity for an injured seal. When moving slowly and gracefully, sharks are not likely to be planning an attack, so divers are safe even without additional protection, provided that they are not trying to entice the sharks with fish blood, in which case they should be in a cage. [102 words]

Cambridge IGCSE First Language English — Response to Reading

Unit 12: Marital Misery

Topic outline

- **Main skills:** genre transformation; inferring; selecting, supporting
- **Secondary skills:** developing ideas; explaining; empathy; adopting a voice; narrative structure
- **Outcome:** subtext dialogue; journal; letter; *narrative continuation
- **Materials:** novel extracts
- **Texts:** Text 12A: Misapprehension; Text 12B: Apprehension

Lesson plan

1. Ask students to follow Text 12A while listening to a reading of it. (5)

2. Ask students to a) explain the ironies of the extract and b) say which character they empathise with and why. (10)

3. Ask students, in pairs, to scan Text 12A for material which implies the character of Mrs Weldon, and to make a list of their own words which would describe her character. Discuss in class which words are the best fit and why. (10)

4. Ask students in groups of four to imagine and write a double script for a) the conversation Mr and Mrs Weldon have when he gets home and b) what they would say if they were being honest with each other. Give each character five speeches of a few lines each. (15)

5. Perform the dialogues with two students playing each character, one saying the actual words and the other following them with the sub-text of the character's real thoughts. Judge the best dialogue according to how much detail from Text 12A has been used, how well the sub-text has been inferred and developed, and how well the characters' voices have been captured. (15)

6. Ask students to read Text 12B and say in one sentence what happens in the extract. (5)

7. Ask for their view on whether they empathise with Mr or Mrs Foster, and why. (5)

8. Ask students, in pairs, to scan Text 12B to identify and explain the implied evidence that Mr Foster is deliberately torturing his wife. (10)

9. Divide students into two groups, Text 12A and Text 12B, and ask them to discuss and decide on a plausible climax and an ending for the story, to be fed back to the rest of the class. They must give evidence of foreshadowing from the texts to support their predictions. (Both stories end with the death of one or both of the characters.) (15)

Homework tasks

a. Write a journal entry, of about 300 words, for Mr Weldon, in which he records his thoughts and feelings about his home and his wife, referring to details in Text 12A and things that happened in the past or might happen in the future.

b. Write a letter from Mrs Foster to her daughter in Paris, a few days before she sets off to visit her, hinting at how her husband is behaving and how distressing she finds it.

Additional task

Write a continuation, of about 250 words of either Text 12A or Text 12B, relating what happened when Mr Weldon got home, or what happened when the Fosters set off for the airport. Use a style consistent with that of the original passage.

Text 12A

Misapprehension

Mrs. Ernest Weldon wandered about the orderly-living room, giving it some of those feminine touches. She was not especially good as a touch-giver. The idea was pretty, and appealing to her. Before she was married, she had dreamed of herself as moving softly about her new dwelling, deftly moving a vase here or straightening a flower there, and thus transforming it from a house to a home. Even now, after seven years of marriage, she liked to picture herself in the gracious act.

But, though she conscientiously made a try at it every night as soon as the rose-shaded lamps were lit, she was always a bit bewildered as to how one went about performing those tiny miracles that make all the difference in the world to a room The living-room, it seemed to her, looked good enough as it was – as good as it would ever look, with that mantelpiece and the same old furniture. Delia, one of the most thoroughly feminine of creatures, had subjected it to a long series of emphatic touches earlier in the day, and none of her handiwork had since been disturbed. But the feat of making all the difference in the world, so Mrs Weldon had always heard, was not a thing to be left to servants. Touch-giving was a wife's job. And Mrs Weldon was not one to shirk the business she had entered.

With an almost pitiable air of uncertainty, she strayed over to the mantel, lifted a small Japanese vase, and stood with it in her hand, gazing helplessly around the room. The white-enameled bookcase caught her eye, and gratefully she crossed to it and set the vase upon it, carefully rearranging various ornaments to make room. To relieve the congestion she took up a framed photograph of Mr Weldon's sister in evening gown and eye-glasses, again looked all about, and then set it timidly on the piano. She smoothed the piano-cover ingratiatingly, straightened the copies of 'A Day in Venice,' 'To a Wild Rose,' and Kreisler's 'Caprice Viennois,' which stood ever upon the rack, walked over to the tea-table and effected a change of places between the cream-jug and the sugar-bowl.

Then she stepped back, and surveyed her innovations. It was amazing how little difference they made to the room.

Mrs Weldon gave the elderly daffodils a final pat, now, and once more surveyed the room, to see if any other repairs suggested themselves. Her lips tightened as the little Japanese vase met her gaze; distinctly, it had been better off in the first place. She set it back, the irritation that the sight of the mantel always gave her welling within her.

She had hated the mantelpiece from the moment they had first come to look at the apartment. There were other things that she had always hated about the place, too – the long, narrow hall, the dark dining-room, the inadequate closets. But Ernest had seemed to like the apartment well enough, so she had said nothing, then or since. After all, what was the use of fussing? Probably there would always be drawbacks, wherever they lived. There were enough in the last place they had had.

So they had taken the apartment on a five-year lease – there were four years and three months to go. Mrs Weldon felt suddenly weary. She lay down on the davenport, and pressed her thin hand against her dull brown hair.

Mr Weldon came down the street, bent almost double in his battle with the wind from the river. His mind went over its nightly dark thoughts on living near Riverside Drive, five blocks from a subway station – two of those blocks loud with savage gales. He did not much like their apartment, even when he reached it. As soon as he had seen that dining-room, he had realized that they must always breakfast by artificial light – a thing he hated. But Grace had never appeared to notice it, so he had held his peace. It didn't matter much, anyway, he explained to himself. There was pretty sure to be something wrong, everywhere. The dining-room wasn't much worse than that bedroom on the court, in the last place. Grace had never seemed to mind that, either.

Abridged extract from the short story 'Too Bad', by Dorothy Parker.

Text 12B

Apprehension

It was really extraordinary how in certain people a simple apprehension about a thing like catching a train can grow into a serious obsession. At least half an hour before it was time to leave the house for the station, Mrs Foster would step out of the elevator all ready to go, with hat and coat and gloves, and then, being quite unable to sit down, she would flutter and fidget about from room to room until her husband, who must have been well aware of her state, finally emerged from his privacy and suggested in a cool dry voice that perhaps they had better be going now, had they not? Mr Foster may possibly have had a right to be irritated by this foolishness of his wife's, but he could have had no excuse for increasing her misery by keeping her waiting unnecessarily.

Mind you, it is by no means certain that this is what he did, yet whenever they were to go somewhere, his timing was so accurate – just a minute or two late, you understand – and his manner so bland that it was hard to believe he wasn't purposely inflicting a nasty private little torture of his own on the unhappy lady. And one thing he must have known – that she would never dare to call out and tell him to hurry. He had disciplined her too well for that. He must also have known that if he was prepared to wait even beyond the last moment of safety, he could drive her nearly into hysterics. On one or two special occasions in the later years of their married life, it seemed almost as though he had wanted to miss the train simply in order to intensify the poor woman's suffering.

Assuming (though one cannot be sure) that the husband was guilty, what made his attitude doubly unreasonable was the fact that, with the exception of this one small irrepressible foible, Mrs Foster was and always had been a good and loving wife. For over thirty years, she had served him loyally and well. There was no doubt about this. Even she, a very modest woman, was aware of it, and although she had for years refused to let herself believe that Mr Foster would ever consciously torment her, there had been times recently when she had caught herself beginning to wonder.

Mr Eugene Foster, who was nearly seventy years old, lived with his wife in a large six-storey house in New York City, on East Sixty-second Street, and they had four servants. It was a gloomy place, and few people carne to visit them. But on this particular morning in January, the house had come alive and there was a great deal of bustling about. One maid was distributing bundles of dust sheets to every room, while another was draping them over the furniture. The butler was bringing down suitcases and putting them in the hall. The cook kept popping up from the kitchen to have a word with the butler, and Mrs Foster herself, in an old-fashioned fur coat and with a black hat on the top of her head, was flying from room to room and pretending to supervise these operations. Actually, she was thinking of nothing at all except that she was going to miss her plane if her husband didn't come out of his study soon and get ready.

'What time is it, Walker?' she said to the butler as she passed him.

'It's ten minutes past nine, Madam.' 'And has the car come?' 'Yes, Madam, it's waiting. I'm just going to put the luggage in now.' 'It takes an hour to get to Idlewild,' she said.

'My plane leaves at eleven. I have to be there half an hour beforehand for the formalities.* I shall be late. I just know I'm going to be late.'

'I think you have plenty of time, Madam,' the butler said kindly. 'I warned Mr Foster that you must leave at nine-fifteen. There's still another five minutes.'

'Yes, Walker, I know, I know. But get the luggage in quickly, will you Please?'

She began walking up and down the hall, and whenever the butler carne by, she asked him the time. This, she kept telling herself, was the one plane she must not miss. It had taken months to persuade her husband to allow her to go. If she missed it, he might easily decide that she should cancel the whole thing. And the trouble was that he insisted on coming to the airport to see her off.

'Dear God,' she said aloud, 'I'm going to miss it. I know, I know, I know I'm going to miss it.' The little muscle beside the left eye was twitching madly now. The eyes themselves were very close to tears.

'What time is it, Walker?'

'It's eighteen minutes past, Madam.'

'Now I really will miss it!' she cried. 'Oh, I wish he would come!'

This was an important journey for Mrs Foster. She was going all alone to Paris to visit her daughter, her only child, who was married to a Frenchman. Mrs Foster didn't care much for the Frenchman, but she was fond of her daughter, and, more than that, she had developed a great yearning* to set eyes on her three grandchildren. She knew them only from the many photographs that she had received and that she kept putting up all over the house.

They were beautiful, these children. She doted on them, and each time a new picture arrived she would carry it away and sit with it for a long time, staring at it lovingly and searching the small faces for signs of that old satisfying blood likeness that meant so much. And now, lately, she had come more and more to feel that she did not really wish to live out her days in a place where she could not be near these children, and have them visit her, and take them out for walks, and buy them presents, and watch them grow.

She knew, of course, that it was wrong and in a way disloyal to have thoughts like these while her husband was still alive. She knew also that although he was no longer active in his many enterprises, he would never consent to leave New York and live in Paris. It was a miracle that he had ever agreed to let her fly over there alone for six weeks to visit them. But, oh, how she wished she could live there always, and be close to them!

'Walker, what time is it?'

'Twenty-two minutes past, Madam.'

As he spoke, a door opened and Mr Foster came into the hall. He stood for a moment, looking intently at his wife, and she looked back at him – at this diminutive but still quite dapper old man with the huge bearded face that bore such an astonishing resemblance to those old photographs of Andrew Carnegie.

'Well,' he said, 'I suppose perhaps we'd better get going fairly soon if you want to catch that plane.'

'Yes, dear – yes! Everything's ready. The car's waiting.'

'That's good,' he said.

With his head over to one side, he was watching her closely. He had a peculiar way of cocking the head and then moving it in a series of small, rapid jerks. Because of this and because he was clasping his hands up high in front of him, near the chest, he was somehow like a squirrel standing there – a quick clever old squirrel from the Park.

'Here's Walker with your coat, dear. Put it on.'

'I'll be with you in a moment,' he said. 'I'm just going to wash my hands.'

Extract from the short story 'The Way Up to Heaven', by Roald Dahl, in *Kiss Kiss*.

Answers – Unit 12

2 a) ironies:

Mrs Weldon spends her life doing something she's not good at; she has a servant to look after the house so doesn't need to do anything to it; she pointlessly swaps ornaments around, and then returns them to their original position; she hates the mantelpiece and many other features of the house, some of them the same ones that her husband hates, but he believes that she likes the apartment, and she believes he likes it; neither of them say anything about it because they don't want to make a fuss; it was the same situation with the previous apartment, but they have learnt nothing and made the same mistakes again

b) empathy:

the reader probably feels more able to sympathise Mr Weldon because he has the additional discomfort of the apartment being too far from the subway and having to put up with inclement weather; because he dreads coming back from a day at work to an unsatisfactory home; we learn more about Mrs Weldon and we do not find her sympathetic. It would be possible to argue that we feel more sorry for Mrs Weldon, as she is bored, leads a pointless and trivial existence trapped in a home she doesn't enjoy, and is 'almost pitiable'.

3 Mrs Weldon is shallow; impressionable; stubborn; delusional; time-wasting; insensitive; inadequate; incompetent; fearful; indecisive; dissatisfied; unattractive.

6 Text 12B summary:

A wealthy elderly couple in New York are due to go to the airport so that the wife can fly to Paris to visit her daughter and grandchildren for six weeks, but the husband is delaying their departure and making her more and more worried about missing her plane.

7 The sympathy is clearly with Mrs Foster, who is the victim of her husband's unkind and distressing behaviour. In return, she does not complain nor show any disloyalty to him – because he has 'disciplined her too well for that' – although she is unhappy and would rather be living with her daughter's family in Paris. Although her obsession is irritating, it does not justify his causing her so much anxiety and even physical symptoms; he is a sadistic, sarcastic bully and his wife is governed by him; she had to persuade him to let her make the trip and he might cancel it yet. He would never leave New York, despite his wife's desperate desire to do so.

8 The writer does not ever say explicitly that Mr Foster is deliberately torturing his wife, but implies it by the number of times the writer alludes to the idea, using modifying adverbs, modal verbs and negatives to avoid actually stating the fact but ironically planting it in the reader's mind:

- 'who must have been well aware of her state'
- 'he could have had no excuse for increasing her misery'
- 'it was hard to believe he wasn't purposely inflicting a nasty private little torture'
- 'he could drive her nearly into hysterics'
- 'it seemed almost as though he had wanted to miss the train'
- 'though one cannot be sure'
- 'refused to let herself believe'
- 'insisted on coming to the airport'

Part 4: Directed Writing and Coursework 1

Unit 13: Fur and against

Topic outline

- **Main skills:** evaluative writing; selecting points; supporting views
- **Secondary skills:** summary; persuasive devices; interviewing; text comparison
- **Outcome:** formal letters; *debate speech
- **Materials:** magazine article; website interview; Rhetorical devices handout; argument structure handout
- **Texts:** Text 13A: Embrace your heritage!; Text 13B: Fur FAQs (PETA)

Lesson plan

1. Ask students to give their opinion on the wearing of animal fur, with reasons. (5)
2. Ask students to read Text 13A. (5)
3. Ask students to re-read Text 13A and make a list in their own words of the arguments in favour of wearing fur. (10)
4. Read out or write points on board and ask students to amend their list if necessary. (5)
5. Ask students, in pairs, to identify in Text 13A a) the stages in the structure of the article and b) the devices employed to persuade the reader. (10)
6. Ask students, in pairs, to think of interview questions a journalist might ask representatives of the anti-fur campaign. (5)
7. Choose students to read out Text 13B. Comment on the number of questions correctly anticipated in Task 6. (5)
8. Invite students to say which fact in Text 13B they found the most persuasive, and why. (5)
9. Ask students to decide, giving reasons and examples, whether Text 13A or Text 13B is more strongly argued and has more persuasive devices. Ask whether any of them have changed their view since the opening discussion, and, if they have, why. (5)
10. Ask students to turn the answers in Text 13B into a letter from PETA to the editor of *The Sunday Times* in response to the article 'Embrace your heritage!'. They should address and refute several of the points in Text 13A, and pay particular attention to the structuring and sequencing of their letter. They should first look at formal letter structure handout and the rhetorical devices handout to help them with the structure and style of their letter. (20)
11. Ask students to swap letters, suggest improvements, and then correct their own responses. Collect them for assessment. (5)
12. Ask students to plan a letter, in their own person, to the author of Text 13A, engaging with and developing or refuting the ideas in the passage. (10)

Homework task

Turn your plan into a formal letter of about 350 words or a draft for a coursework assignment of about 600 words. You should check it using the success criteria handout and improve it before giving it in for assessment or comment, bearing in mind the relevant mark scheme band descriptors.

Additional task

Ask students to prepare for and debate the motion 'Fur or Against'. They need to gather points from the relevant passage for the side they are supporting and add others of their own. The class votes on the motion according to the persuasiveness of the speeches.

Text 13A

Embrace your heritage!

Our most distant ancestors came through the Ice Age without going black with frostbite because they wore second-hand skin: fur. We are, as I'm sure even the least perceptive of you will have noticed, nude underneath our pyjamas. Naked apes. We don't have enough hair, fur, fluff or feathers to deflect even the finest drizzle. We shiver in pathetically bald bodies for a reason – and the reason is that we look better in suede than cows do.

We shed our thick, short and curlies because it was our natural selection, our destiny, our personal ecology, and instead gained those uniquely human attributes: taste and vanity. We wore other species' skins when they had no further use for them, and we've been doing it for a long time. How fur went from being practical and chic, stylish and sensible for 100 000 years, and then all of a sudden became the coat of shame in the past decade, is one of the oddest about-faces in all civilisation.

There have always been people who are funny about their relationship with animals – vegetarians who got religion, a few people who swept the street in front of them so as not to hurt a flightless fly – but the majority of us, the vast, vast majority, have gone on eating anything dumb enough to taste good with chips, and squashing cockroaches wherever possible. But that odd prejudice, the ban on fur, has become automatic and universal in our select and ethically compromised bit of the First World. The virulence and viciousness of fur vigilantes mean that few of us now brave the spittle-flecked venom of self-righteous pressure groups and dim, new-age absolutists. The argument against fur has always been more about class and money than about dumb critters. Fur, restricted to the point of prohibitive expense, is now symbolic of wealth and power.

Enough. A number of furriers are now taking back the morality of skin. They are mostly from the north – Scandinavia, Greenland, Russia, Iceland and Denmark – where fur has always been a practical business in a most practical part of the world. Of all the animals that we kill for our personal use, mink have by far and away the easiest passing: well fed and unstressed, they're gently gassed.

One of my favourite shops is a remarkable furrier in Reykjavik. Eggert Johannsson makes beautiful, sensible clothes out of pelts. He is a missionary for what he calls 'ethical fur': well-sourced, responsibly farmed and humanely culled. Seals, for instance. The European Union is debating whether to ban sealskin on anyone except a seal. In Greenland, hunting them is the subsistence income of the east coast. It's what they do. It's what they've always done. There is nothing else to do. There is nothing else. They can't grow cut flowers instead. In Iceland, parts of the shore where the seals congregate were sold as agricultural assets. Farmers would facilitate the natural seal colonies, protecting them from predators, and once a year they'd cull them. But since the seal market has collapsed, so have the care and value of the shoreline, and so have the seals. All over the North Sea, their populations are fluctuating. They're caught in fishing nets, shot by fishermen. They hang around ports and fish farms like water foxes. The seals have gone from being valuable, protected and plentiful, to being waterborne vermin and endangered, because we have removed their value thanks to ignorant squeamishness and class politics.

The argument goes that once we may have needed fur, but now we don't; we have, instead, technology. Well, leaving aside the attraction of the real thing, I assume you all know how polymers such as nylon, polyester, Terylene and so on are made. That they use fossil fuels, and intensely polluting processes that involve some of the most toxic chemicals on the planet ... I've been there. I've seen the greatest environmental disaster on the globe, greater than an armful of runways or nuclear bombs, worse than deforestation or any city's urban sprawl: the murder of the Aral Sea in central Asia by the drying-up of the Oxus River, reducing an area the size of Denmark to a toxic, salted dust bowl – and all caused by cotton. Compared with a cotton shirt, a fur coat is morally blameless.

The most poignant argument for fur is not where it comes from, or who first wore it; it's what it looks like and how it feels. A polyamide coat connects you to an oil well and a factory; fur joins you to your heritage. It is 100 000 years of history and culture. We wear fur because it is our story. If you haven't put on a fur coat recently, or ever, try it. Cast aside your prejudice and feel it. You can sense it's not simply a statement of fashion, wealth or even warmth; the connection is ancient, truly visceral. Fur is the cover, the binding, of our long, long, story. And if you're still not convinced, then would you for a moment consider your own cushions, your pillow. The feathers inside, the bird fur, where do you imagine that came from? How do you imagine all that duck and goose skin was gleaned? I'd hate for you to be a hypocrite. Sleep well.

Adapted from article, 'Fur and against', by AA Gill, *The Sunday Times.*

Text 13B

Fur FAQs (PETA)*

Aren't there laws to protect animals on fur farms?
Currently, there are no federal laws providing protection for the millions of animals – including chinchillas, foxes, minks, and raccoons – who suffer and die on fur farms. The fur industry remains completely self-regulated, which means that animals are kept in crowded, filthy wire cages, where they often develop neurotic behaviors and become sick or wounded, and fur farmers kill them by breaking their necks while they are fully conscious or by electrocuting them. Click here to see pictures of caged animals on fur farms.

Isn't animal fur more environmentally friendly than synthetic fur?
Absolutely not! Fur has fallen so far from grace that furriers are now trying to convince consumers that pelts are 'eco-friendly', but furs are loaded with chemicals to keep them from decomposing in buyers' closets, and fur production pollutes the environment and wastes precious resources. It takes more than 15 times as much energy to produce a fur coat from ranch-raised animals than it does to produce a fake fur. Plus, the waste produced on fur farms poisons our waterways. And don't forget … unlike faux fur, the 'real thing' causes millions of animals to suffer every year. Click here for more information about fur and the environment.

Animals in cages on fur farms don't suffer that much because they've never known anything else, right?
Wrong! Animals on fur farms are prevented from acting on their most basic instinctual behaviors, which causes them tremendous suffering. Even animals who have been caged since birth feel the need to move around, groom themselves, stretch their limbs, and exercise. All confined animals suffer from intense boredom – some so severely that they begin displaying neurotic behaviors such as pacing, turning in endless circles, self-mutilation, and even cannibalism. Click here to learn more about cruelty on fur farms.

Aren't animals better off on fur farms, where they are fed and protected, than they are out in the wild, where they can die of starvation, disease, or predation?
A similar argument was used to support the claim that black people were better off being slaves on plantations than being free men and women! Animals on fur farms suffer so much that it is inconceivable that they could be worse off in the wild. The wild isn't 'wild' to the animals who live there – it's their home. The fact that they might suffer there is no reason to ensure that they suffer in captivity. Click here to learn more about what a lifetime in a cage is like.

Is the fur industry as cruel as people make it out to be?
It's even crueller. PETA's undercover investigations on fur farms have found that animals are killed by anal electrocution, during which an electrically charged steel rod is inserted into the animal's rectum, literally frying his or her insides. Exposed broken bones, upper respiratory infections, and cancerous tumors were among the wounds and diseases that animals endured without veterinary treatment on one fur farm that we investigated.

Animals caught in steel-jaw leghold traps are in so much pain that some actually chew off their limbs in order to escape. Since they are unable to eat, keep warm, or defend themselves against predators, many die in horrible ways before the trapper arrives to kill them. Others suffer in the traps for days until they are caught and killed. To avoid damaging the pelt, trappers often beat or stomp animals to death. Whether they are enduring the excruciating pain of a leghold trap or a lifetime of agony in a tiny cage, these animals suffer immensely. Click here to learn more about fur trapping.

Why should animals have rights?
Supporters of animal rights believe that animals have an inherent worth – a value completely separate from their usefulness to humans. We believe that every creature with a will to live has a right to live free from pain and suffering. For more information, click here.

Adapted from, www.furisdead.com.

*PETA – People for the Ethical Treatment of Animals

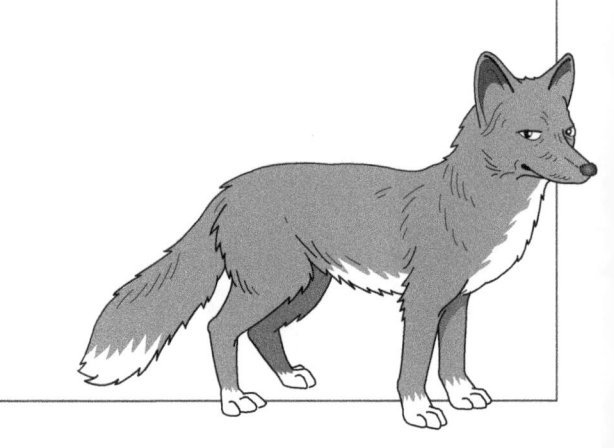

Answers – Unit 13

3 Text 13A: summary points pro-fur [14 points]:

- long tradition of wearing fur
- humans don't have enough natural hair / are meant to use animal skins
- it's only a recent and passing fad to feel ashamed of wearing fur
- the majority of humans are meat-eaters
- we kill insects
- pressure groups have made people afraid to wear it
- anti-fur campaigners don't care about animals, only about the politics of class/wealth
- modern fur farms kill animals humanely
- some countries' economies are dependent on the sale of animal skins
- animals have a more painful death if not culled by furriers
- some species have become endangered by the collapse of the fur market
- the production of fake fur and even natural materials involves the use of pollutants and toxic chemicals
- the look and feel of fur is wonderful, and part of our natural heritage
- we use feathers, a type of animal fur, in bedding so it's hypocritical to be against fur coats

5 a Text 13A: article structure:

1. gives historical and scientific facts
2. cites normal human behaviour
3. attacks motives of the extremists
4. informs us of humane approaches of furriers of northern 'practical' nations
5. points out inconsistency that animals killed for fur suffer less pain than those killed for meat, so if we allow one, why not the other?
6. introduces personal acquaintance as evidence
7. uses positive-sounding terminology of 'ethical fur'
8. pleads on behalf of countries which have no other industry
9. claims that seals are now suffering because of ignorant and politically motivated anti-fur activists
10. dismisses ecological argument against fur production by claiming other fabrics cause more pollution
11. returns to the beginning, the heritage argument, that it is natural and right for humans to wear fur and only the prejudiced won't admit how good it looks and feels
12. says anyone who owns a feather-stuffed cushion is a hypocrite if they are against fur coats

b Text 13A: persuasive devices:

humorous comparisons; irony (*flightless fly*); mockery; insult (*spittle-flecked*); ridicule; short and non sentences (*Seals, for instance.*); surprise information (*about cotton*); reversing common beliefs; derogatory description of animals (*dumb critters*); use of triple structures (*well sourced, responsibly farmed and humanely culled*); use of abrupt command (*Enough, try it*); accusing the reader of prejudice and hypocrisy; analogy and antithesis; rhetorical questions; alliteration (*virulence and viciousness of fur vigilantes*); personal testimony (*I've been there*); switch from inclusive *we* to accusatory *you* in final paragraph; conclusive, dismissive and sarcastic final sentence.

9 Which text is more persuasive and why:

Text 13A is more personal in its attack on the hypocrisy of the reader. It uses wit to woo the reader, and mockery to make the reader not want to be associated with 'self-righteous' pressure groups, which are blamed for making it possible for only the rich to be able to afford the fur, which should be available for everyone, and so raises anger against them. It has a large number of points to make to support its case.

Text 13B uses shocking factual material and attacks what it sees as the myths which the pro-fur lobby uses to defend its position. The 'click here' commands imply that a wealth of evidence, including photographic proof, exists to support their case, which has been based on extensive research. The emphasis throughout is on the pain and suffering of animals trapped and killed for their coats, and this evokes pity in the reader.

Either text can be chosen as the answer to this question: both texts have widened the issue from fur coats to the environment and pollution in order to influence a wider group than just animal lovers. However, the most persuasive device of all is a linked and progressive structure to the stages of an argument, so Text 13A is perhaps more effective overall, although Text 13B has the greater emotional impact.

Unit 14: Caught in the web

Topic outline

- **Main skills:** evaluation; persuasive devices; selecting material
- **Secondary skills:** summary; comprehension; supporting opinions; discursive writing
- **Outcome:** summary; blog post / coursework assignment; *letter; *magazine article
- **Materials:** blogs; magazine article
- **Texts:** Text 14A: Long live the internet!; Text 14B: Down with the internet!; Text 14C: What's with the fake news?

Lesson plan

1. Ask students for their opinion on the role of the internet in modern life. Elicit both positive and negative views. (5)

2. Ask students to skim-read Text 14A. (5)

3. Ask students to re-read Text 14A in pairs and underline the key points. (5)

4. Ask students to plan and write a summary, in their own words, of the benefits of the existence of the internet. They should mention no more than 12 relevant points and write no more than 120 words. The points should be resequenced in the plan so that similar ideas can be expressed in the same sentence. (15)

5. Ask students to check their summaries for accuracy and style. Collect them for assessment. (5)

6. Read out Text 14B while students listen and make notes of the points being presented. (5)

7. Give students a copy of Text 14B and ask them to read it to confirm that they selected all the relevant points, or to amend their list. (5)

8. Invite students to discuss and critically evaluate the claims made in Text 14B. They should consider which of the arguments can be refuted, and, if any can, how. (10)

9. Ask students, in pairs, to study the style and punctuation of Text 14B and identify the features of argumentative speech. (5)

10. Elicit features and examples of argumentative style. List them on the board and discuss their persuasive effect. (10)

11. Ask students to read Text 14C and write one sentence to summarise the argument being presented. Hear the sentences and comment on their content and expression. (10)

12. Ask students to plan their response to Text 14C in the form of a blog post or coursework assignment. It should engage with some of the writer's claims and opinions, and present their own views on the topic and how it relates to their country and situation. (10)

Homework tasks

a. Write your blog post or coursework piece in response to Text 14C. It should contain specific examples of your own to illustrate the concept of fake news.

b. Write a letter to the writer of Text 14B, evaluating the quality of the arguments, developing some of the ideas, and saying whether or not you share the same viewpoint. Use your notes from Task 8.

Additional task

Ask students to write a school magazine article discussing the role of the internet in their education and their social life.

Text 14A

Long live the internet!

It's hard to imagine that, just 30 years ago, the internet did not exist. For most people living today, the internet is where their lives are mostly lived. It has become taken for granted to such an extent that many people do not even realise that they are using the worldwide web in their day-to-day transactions. It is true that smartphones are an integral part of this development, but not because they are telephones; many people rarely use them to speak into. But they are part of the web of connectivity, using the internet as much as phone networks, which shapes our daily lives.

Because it is so familiar, we forget how difficult everything was before. So let's remind ourselves.

In the Old Days, you wanted to look up an old friend, but didn't know their current address. Simply, you couldn't do it. Now, you do a Google search, or a Facebook search; you find them, send them an email or use social media. You are re-united. Then there's the new friends you can meet in chat-rooms and maybe form a meaningful relationship with. You can also keep in touch with distant relatives without having to resort to pen and paper or make expensive phone calls, and you can send them photos or videos you've taken yourself to keep them happy.

You wanted to book a flight or a hotel? You had to travel into a town and find a travel agent, wait while they laboriously filled forms and made calls – and pay a hefty premium for doing so. Now you shop the world through comparison sites, find spectacularly cheap deals, book, pay and confirm instantly. All other kinds of goods and services are now also at your fingertips, and you can arrange for your weekly food shop to arrive at your doorstep so that you never have to waste time wandering around a supermarket again.

You wanted to meet up with friends for the evening? You sat by the phone; dialled each of them; they weren't in; you kept dialling. Now? Facebook or Twitter or text. You can reach them anywhere, any time, and not just individually. Groups organise all their discussions and meetings through messenger or group chat or website postings – even quicker than emailing and communications can happen in real time.

And that's just the beginning. You have at your fingertips more data than all the libraries in the world; you can access millions of experts. You can find people who share your interests, no matter how obscure. And, increasingly, you can find a partner, for a brief romance or for life.

Or to entertain yourself solitarily you have the facility to stream music and films, and the endless amusement of Youtube clips. These help get you painlessly through the hour at the gym, the several hours on the train or plane, the day in bed sick.

If you're setting up your own small business, or promoting your talents, or trying to sell something, how much easier and cheaper to do it through blogs and online ads, which enable you to compete against the big firms. Crowd-funding has changed for ever the way good or obscure causes are financed, and benefitted more people and charity projects than could be helped before, when the message couldn't be spread so wide or so fast. The internet is thoroughly egalitarian in its opportunities and democractic in its operations, providing a vital channel for free expression under repressive regimes, which therefore hate it.

And best of all? This cornucopia of wonders is, mostly, free.

So what's not to like? Okay, you need to be careful about maintaining some privacy; by venturing onto the web you are putting yourself out in the world. Not everybody may like you, but most people will; not everybody will help you, but many will. There are criminals and bad people, for sure, as there are everywhere, and the important thing is to stay alert, be sensible, think before you give too much away. That way, the internet and the connected web can infinitely broaden your horizons, offer you experiences you never dreamed of, and immeasurably enrich your life.

Text 14B

Down with the internet!

'The Internet should be banned': there's a headline to catch the reader's attention. Surely everybody believes that the web has redefined social life, that it IS the future? No, not everybody; and it is not only repressive governments which think that the unlimited and instant global communication nexus is a very mixed blessing indeed.

One area of rapid growth in recent years has been in so-called 'social sites', where anyone can easily (and without cost) publish their own web page with personal photos, and provide an opportunity for their 'friends' to leave messages – and for prospective employers to scrutinise these sites for evidence of what a job candidate really thinks, believes and does.

These networking sites have created an unprecedented opening for cruel bullying, especially among the teenagers (and pre-teens) who constitute a huge proportion of those with pages on sites such as Facebook. The bullying is anonymous – although the victim is not – and there is no censorship, so there are no limits to the viciousness of the attacks. Even if the site is deleted and replaced by a new one, the bullies can find it in seconds. School counsellors have been inundated with cases of profoundly depressed teenagers. This 'cyber-bullying' is a wholly new phenomenon which could never have existed before social websites.

An arguably more fundamental issue concerns information and opinion forming. In most countries, the broadcast media are reasonably responsible, have to adhere to a code of conduct, and are overseen by watchdogs. They have to maintain at least a degree of impartiality. Laws of libel and slander protect reputations and deter the media from publishing unsubstantiated rumours. None of these restrictions apply in practice, however, to the Internet. No-one does or can censor what appears on individual websites; many are hosted in countries where there is no policing of content. The craze for 'blogging' (web-logging), where individuals write their thoughts about anything and everything, might be thought to be harmless – and indeed no-one has to read them – but in practice some build up huge followings and their writings are politically influential. Some would describe this as democracy at work, but it may be that many people prefer to have their prejudices reinforced; it is now illegal in civilised countries to preach racism, for example, but plenty of blogs do so.

One of the greatest threats facing the world today is that of global terrorism. The Internet and email make it possible for conspirators to communicate instantly with one another, at any time, wherever they are in the world; and, possibly, without being detected. There is a real danger of mathematically competent terrorists with advanced digital encryption technology planning global atrocities with impunity if they can keep one step ahead of the intelligence agencies who attempt to monitor them. There are now online tutorials for bomb-making.

In the case of email, it has revolutionised communication, but it has also brought with it unwelcome side effects. 'Spam' mail is more than a minor irritant; the time wasted in deleting it costs billions every day, and much of its content is offensive. Even if the USA – the source of more than 90 per cent of 'spam' – were to ban it, the spammers would simply move their operations elsewhere.

And then there are more serious dangers too. Online fraud has increased exponentially in recent years. Believe it or not, there are still people – thousands of them – so gullible that they send their bank details to complete strangers when promised a million-dollar 'inheritance' from someone they have never heard of. More recently, the scam has taken the form of sending emails to all of a 'victim's' friends claiming they have lost their money on holiday and been arrested or in an accident, and need an urgent loan.

But there are other issues: the decline of literacy because it is considered acceptable to write even formal emails in a debased language with copious abbreviations and symbols; the fact that the tone of an email is misinterpreted by the recipient more than half the time. Instant communication is miscommunication.

There is also a significant threat to the academic world. Now that huge quantities of prepared essays are available on the Internet (at a price, for this is a very profitable business) students at every level, from GCSE coursework to university dissertations, are able to purchase work they could not have written. In the process they gain academic qualifications to which they are not entitled, and the social consequences are very worrying. There is no foolproof way of detecting plagiarism of this kind.

So much of the world now depends on computers and networked systems that we are much more vulnerable than previously to malicious attack from enemies who can damage our society without leaving their bedroom. Every country has a massive 'cyber warfare' department seeking ways of destroying an enemy's infrastructure. The Internet makes it possible for outsiders to gain access to the most critical of systems which run power stations and communications, and which manage air traffic control. 'Denial of Service' attacks have already crippled some of the most powerful corporations on the planet.

Furthermore, there are the morally corrosive effects of the unlimited availability to everyone (including children) of violence on the Internet; such images will inevitably desensitise their viewers and arguably lead to more extreme atrocities. It isn't called a world wide web for nothing: it is a snare which has trapped us all, depriving us of privacy, scholarship, security and morality. Until it can be properly policed, the net is a powerful weapon for criminals of all kinds, and it should be taken away from them to protect the rest of us.

Text 14C

What's with the fake news?

The internet was not planned; no one controls it, and like most unparented children, it grows in directions, and adopts habits, which no one anticipated. The most recent of these developments was the panic, starting in 2016, over what has come to be called 'fake news'.

In truth, nothing new happened on the internet in 2016, but what did happen was that a new political movement which had been stealthily gathering momentum over the preceding eight years burst into public view with two spectacular achievements.

Since the end of the Second World War, in 1945, and especially since the end of the Cold War (1989–92), the dominant political orthodoxy in much of the world has been international democratic liberalism. Democracy gave power to the people and prevented tyranny; liberalism removed barriers of prejudice which had blighted the lives of millions of people; and internationalism brought economic benefits and removed the possibility of wars of the kind which had killed millions in the twentieth century.

This orthodoxy was shaken by the financial crash of 2008, an economic event originating in the USA whose worldwide repercussions no one, or almost non one, foresaw. During the years that followed, the steady improvement in the lot of ordinary people since 1945 was reversed; most people in western countries were worse off in 2016 than in 2008. As time passed, and the political elites proved incapable of restoring economic growth or full employment, and as, in parallel, the super-rich became dramatically richer and flaunted their wealth through highly-publicised celebrity lifestyles, the whole international liberal democratic model came to be increasingly challenged. However, the counter-movement built up steam out of sight of conventional commentators: it spread like wildfire through social media, recruiting millions of supporters, until it burst into the open in the unexpected British referendum decision to leave the European Union (so-called 'Brexit') and the surprising election of Donald Trump as President of the USA.

The traditional political elites and media flailed around for an explanation of these unforeseen world-changing events, and they lighted upon 'fake news' as their scapegoat. What they discovered was that the 'new populism', with its anti-foreigner, anti-immigrant, anti-tolerant, anti-elite views, was a product of the social media generation. What had happened, without anyone noticing, was that a significant proportion of people in western countries – overwhelmingly, the least well-off, the least well-educated, the least well-informed, the ones who had suffered most from the economic downturn – had abandoned traditional news media and were instead 'listening' only to alternative sources of news and opinion, on social media and the internet. Traditional mass media, print and broadcast, are constrained by law and tradition from presenting blatantly biased or false material. The new media, by contrast, chose to deliver to their self-selecting audience a torrent of one-sided propaganda, spiced up with exaggeration, misrepresentation and downright lies. Exposed to a constant diet of such venom, pandering directly to the audience's prejudices, these brainwashed victims came to believe that liberals, democrats and foreigners were responsible for their economic woes, and were told what to do to put it right: vote for isolationism, vote for nationalism, vote for conservatism – and enough of them did so to swing referendum and election results (although they were still very close.)

Once the spotlight of media attention was turned on this phenomenon, it was immediately apparent what had happened, and the label 'fake news' was attached to it. Thousands of examples of pernicious untruths were exposed. What was most worrying, though, for the traditional elites, was the attitude of the consumers of this material: a majority said, when asked, that they didn't care whether news was true or not, as long as it fitted with their views – what is now called 'confirmation bias' – or was 'interesting.'

And that is the real problem. There has always been 'fake news' – every country has had tabloid newspapers filled with extreme views and outright lies – but until now nobody took them seriously. Most people were canny enough to see it for what it was, and it was balanced by the more rational coverage in other media. What is new is the 'bubble' mentality where people only listen to opinions they agree with and lose any grasp of reality. And that state-sponsored interference can use this method to de-stabilise and influence the outcome of national elections in other countries.

Answers – Unit 14

3 Text 14A: key points [14 points]:

- contact old friends
- meet new friends
- take and send videos and photos
- instant booking
- comparison sites find good deals
- shopping ordered and delivered
- groups organise themselves
- information discovered
- partnerships formed
- music and films accessible
- sales promoted and businesses advertised
- fund-raising channel
- symbol and means of free expression
- mostly doesn't cost anything

4 Summary of benefits of the internet:

Social contact and group communication through the internet is quick and efficient, also allowing pictures to be taken and sent. Purchases of all sorts and online bookings can be quickly made and at low prices. It is easy to find like-minded people through the internet for romance or hobby-sharing, and to retrieve required information. There is access to unlimited sources of music and films. Small businesses and personal skills can be promoted effectively, and money for causes can be raised easily. Because the internet is low-cost, it gives freedom to ordinary people world-wide and is a tool against political oppression. [100 words]

6 Text 14B: key points [16 points]:

- social sites encourage bullying
- rumours cannot be prevented
- no policing of content
- bloggers with prejudices have political influence
- false information quickly spreads around the world
- global terrorism made possible through communication of conspirators
- spam wastes billions of dollars of work time every day
- platform for online fraud
- emails debase the use of language and are often misinterpreted
- students can cheat and plagiarise to gain qualifications dishonestly
- hackers can get confidential information
- cyber warriors can destroy computer systems and damage society
- violent images are available to children

10   Text 14B: argumentative features and effects:

provocative title arouses interest and fury; rhetorical questions force reader to feel engaged; strong language, such as *bullying, viciousness*, evokes sympathy; triple structures are the most convincing form of persuasion; epigrammatic phrases, such as *instant communication is miscommunication*, are short, memorable sayings; paragraph openers give the impression of how many arguments there are to support the adopted view (*One of …, And then there are …, So much of …, In the case of …, There is also …, But there are other …*); examples derived from life-threatening scenarios and threats of terminal dangers to society concentrate the reader's mind and arouse fear (e.g. references to terrorism, enemies, criminals)

11   Fake news is the product of the overwhelming rise in the use of social media sites which, over recent years, and in reaction to mis-management by politicians and resentment at wealth inequalities in societies, has enabled the growth of a populist movement no longer tuned in to mainstream media sources but which is reliant upon news stories which tell them people they want to hear or always suspected, thus confirming their prejudices.

Unit 15: Praise or blame?

Topic outline

- **Main skills:** evaluative writing; argumentative writing; persuasive devices
- **Secondary skills:** identifying arguments; giving supporting evidence; style analysis; comparing texts
- **Outcome:** interview; text comparison; letter / coursework assignment; *magazine article
- **Materials:** argument texts (book extract and newspaper article)
- **Texts:** Text 15A: All about me; Text 15B: Punishment, not praise

Lesson plan

1. Ask students to define and give their views on the concept of self-esteem, giving examples of personal experiences and suggesting people they associate with having a high degree of it, and whether they think one can have too much of it. (5)
2. Ask students to skim-read Text 15A for gist. (5)
3. Ask students to scan-read Text 15A and highlight the points in the argument. (5)
4. Invite students to read out their selections and compare them with those of others', disputing the inclusion or omission of points if necessary. (5)
5. Ask students to read Text 15B for gist. (5)
6. Ask students to re-read Text 15B to identify and underline the persuasive devices used. (5)
7. Go through the devices, asking for explanations of how they position and manipulate the reader in each case. (5)
8. Ask students to decide which of the two texts is more persuasive and why. They need to give at least five detailed references to support their judgement. (10)
9. Ask students to make notes for a comparison of Text 15A and Text 15B. They should look at how the opinions have been conveyed through voice, content and style, (15)
10. Ask students to work in pairs to script a university entrance interview between an admissions tutor and a student educated according to the Self-esteem Programme. It should begin with the tutor asking: 'So, can you explain why you believe you deserve a place at this university?' and include four other questions. They need to use ideas from Text 15A. (20)
11. Ask students to perform their interviews. The class should judge the appropriateness and effectiveness of the content and give constructive criticism on each. (10)

Homework tasks

a. Write your textual comparison using about 300 words. Check your work carefully before submission for sequencing and linking of ideas, supporting detail, and accuracy of expression.

b. Write a letter to the author of Text 15B and explain why, as a teenager and student, you do not agree with his opinion, giving detailed support for your view. Use some of the devices identified in Task 7. This may be extended as a coursework assignment. (You may wish to remind yourself of the formal letter structure handout.)

Additional task

Ask students to write a school magazine article or coursework assignment discussing the points raised in Text 15A and Text 15B, relating them to the educational philosophy practised by their school.

Text 15A

All about me

From the 1970s onwards, a quiet revolution took place in American education. Whereas life in high schools in America used to centre upon Grade Point Averages and Honour Rolls, where every student knew his or her place in the academic hierarchy, the advocates of the so-called 'Self-Esteem' movement threw all this aside in order that all children should 'feel good about themselves'. They argued that failing or getting a low grade was an unpleasant experience – so it should be banned. Many high schools taught courses in Self-Esteem. Teachers were told not to mark or evaluate students' work; some went so far as to give every piece of work an A, and banned the use of red pens by teachers in case they offended the students. Honour rolls were abolished, and the fiction was maintained that all students were equally talented and were high achievers, no matter how little they did. An especially worrying feature of the more extreme versions of the Self-Esteem movement was the idea that correct spelling was an unreasonable tyranny, so children should be praised for spelling words in any way they fancied. Parents, too, were sucked in, and told that they should praise their children, all the time, whatever they did. The development of 'individuality' was considered more important than effective socialisation.

Since the turn of the century, a reaction has, not surprisingly, set in – occasioned not least by the mis-match between what the schools (and parents) were saying and the reality of life after school. Universities and employers refused to buy in to this nonsense; universities needed students with knowledge, skills and suitable attitudes – and so continued to select using real criteria – and employers needed employees who were capable of doing the job. Both of these key groups found that students who had never been taught the concept of standards, and thought that an A grade could be earned by writing their name (whether spelled correctly or not), were of no use to them at all.

The attack came from a number of fronts. Roy Baumeister, a leading psychologist who conducted an extensive review of the phenomenon, found that the self-esteem programmes did not actually result in any of the benefits claimed by their exponents: students did not achieve better grades (in any real sense, as opposed to inflated grades given for nothing); nor did the programmes reduce violence, cheating or anti-social behaviour. On the contrary, he found that those who had been exposed to the programmes were often more violent and more likely to cheat than those who had not; they were self-centred and cynical about the whole educational process, because they knew that the praise and grades they received were meaningless. Baumeister concluded, 'After all these years, I'm sorry to say, my recommendation is this: forget about self-esteem and concentrate more on self-control and self-discipline.'

American social commentator Jean M. Twenge coined the phrase 'Generation Me' in her 2006 book of the same name to describe a phenomenon which she observed developing in the society around her. Under the influence of the so-called 'Self-Esteem Movement', parents were coming under pressure not to set any standards of behaviour for their children; rather than punishing them if they did wrong, parents, it was argued, should boost their children's 'self-esteem' by praising them for anything they did. The consequence of this, she claimed, was a generation of self-obsessed children who had no standards against which to judge their behaviour or achievements and who were, ironically, deprived of the key learning experience of being valued for something they had worked for and truly accomplished.

Most crucially, Twenge argued, the 'Self-Esteem' movement was anti-educational because students could not understand the value of anything. They were not being prepared in any way for life. Protecting them from criticism in childhood meant that they were completely unprepared for it, and unable to deal with it, when it inevitably came in adult life.

Twenge also argued that the movement was fundamentally misguided and based upon false premises. Whilst it is true that many American (and British) schools in the 1950s and 1960s were obsessed with grades and hierarchies at the expense of individual development, what was really needed to counteract this was the educational philosophy increasingly adopted in Europe over the past 30 years: that every child matters, every child has ability in some field, and that the purpose of education is to help every child to achieve his or her potential, whether it be in academic work, sport, drama, community service or anything else. It was also important that children should learn from their mistakes (not have them reinforced), and should receive constructive feedback to help them to improve their performance. Children cannot evaluate either conduct or achievement unless they understand and accept the objective standards applied by trusted adults such as parents and teachers. An essential element of 'education for life' is to develop empathy with and respect for others. Psychologists have found that those whose self-esteem is artificially induced are often 'narcissistic' – obsessed with themselves, devoid of secure judgement and incapable of appreciating the viewpoint or needs of others.

It is also vital that children should be helped to establish realistic expectations, and Twenge is especially scornful of those who tell children to 'follow their dream' – that they can have anything if they want it enough – because it simply is not true in the real world. What children need to be told, if they are to develop into true and effective individuals, is that they are valued for themselves and for their talents, whatever they may be, but they need to work hard to achieve goals and career success. As Baumeister puts it, self-control and self-discipline deliver results: self-esteem delivers a cruel illusion.

Text 15B

Punishment, not praise

Well, all I can say is that I hope you are counting. How many times have you praised your out-of-control little monster today? If government advice on school discipline applies, as logically it should, in the home, then parents across the country will need to keep a constant check on their response to the undesirable behaviour of their offspring. Five to one is the ratio of praise to punishment, ladies and gentlemen. Criticise rarely; keep punishment to the barest possible minimum; praise and reward however monstrous the offence. Follow the latest ministerial guidance and your children will understand the difference between right and wrong and learn to act with adult responsibility in every circumstance. Just pat them on the head and tell them how wonderful they are.

Of course it is important to praise children, and, looking back as a parent and a teacher, I would be the first to admit that I probably did not praise enough. Few of us do. A little recognition goes a long way, and everyone who has responsibility for children needs to remind themselves of this commonsense truth. To that extent the government's advice is sensible. How, though, did it come up with this 5:1 statistic? This is a finger-in-the-wind generalisation that is meaningless in any specific circumstance.

Meaningless, and, what is worse, insidious. Yes, children should be praised when they do something good. To suggest it is somehow wrong to punish them when they do something bad, or, more ridiculous still, actually to reward unacceptable behaviour, is to send a message that is not so much stupid as dangerous. Children need boundaries. They need to know what they are allowed to do and what they are not allowed to do. And they need to understand that if they choose to break the rules, the consequences are unpleasant.

Talk to any head teacher who has turned round a failing school. The first thing they will tell you is that they had to deal with pupils who would not accept the conventions of normal schooling. Without order, nothing. It is not rocket science. Punctuality, attendance, uniform, behaviour; the heads would make their expectations clear, and they would ensure everyone knew what would happen to those who stepped out of line. Good behaviour would be praised and bad behaviour would be punished. Make the rules clear and apply them fairly. Children know where they are and teachers can start teaching again.

From article 'Well done class, you learnt zilch', by Chris Woodhead, *The Sunday Times*.

Answers – Unit 15

4 Text 15A: list of arguments:

- American teachers stopped correcting children's work as they believe criticism damages their self-esteem.
- Psychologists are warning that these trends have not only made no improvement to grades and behaviour but have increased the likelihood of cheating and violence in schools.
- Psychologists claim that what is needed is not more self-esteem but more self-discipline.
- Attempting a challenge is more character-building and rewarding than not trying at all, or being allowed to give up because of laziness or fear of failure.
- Failing can be a positive experience.
- All children are good at something.
- True self-worth comes from learning new skills and applying one's talents, not from being told you are wonderful simply because you exist.
- Self-control can achieve the ends which self-esteem has failed to bring about, and equips a child to cope with adversity and be protected from misery.
- Children sheltered from failure and shielded from challenges cannot deal with life's disappointments.
- Competition is necessary to stretch children to perform their best.
- Self-esteem is the easier option and therefore attractive to students and teachers.
- Rewards should only be for achievement, not for doing nothing, otherwise children become cynical.
- It is not fair to tell children they can do and be anything they want, because it isn't true.
- Hard work is necessary for getting somewhere in life.
- Self-esteem fosters unrealistic expectations.

7 Text 15B: persuasive devices and their effects:

colloquialisms – to create conversational effect and invite reader trust (e.g. *Well* and *Yes*)

addressing reader as 'you' – for intimacy and presupposition that the reader will agree

rhetorical questions – to engage and involve reader

triple structures – to make utterances memorable and effective

sarcasm – for mockery of opponents so that reader will not wish to identify with them

imperatives – to sound authoritative and superior (e.g. *Follow, Talk*)

repetition of words – for emphasis (e.g. *meaningless, need*)

short categorical sentences – to give the impression that there can be no counter argument

insults – to ridicule opponents (e.g. *little monster, stupid*)

non-sentences – to make the sentiment sound decisive (e.g. *Without order, nothing.*)

modern idiom – to show the writer is up to date (e.g. *It is not rocket science*)

lists – to give the impression that the writer is well-informed

antithesis – to make it seem a simple, two-sided issue

admission of fallibility – to make what follows seem honest and therefore true

Cambridge IGCSE First Language English — **Directed Writing and Coursework 1**

Unit 16: Community spirit

Topic outline

- **Main skills:** selecting and structuring material; voice, viewpoint and audience
- **Secondary skills:** developing using inference and detail; collating and summarising; text comparison; persuasive writing
- **Outcome:** summaries; interview; speech; *text comparison, *personal letter; magazine article / coursework assignment
- **Materials:** memoir; news articles; formal report structure handout; rhetorical devices handout
- **Texts:** Text 16A: Good for business; Text 16B: Medical aid; Text 16C: Student doubles as headteacher argument writing structure

Lesson plan

1 Ask students to read Text 16A and give the gist in one sentence. (5)

2 Ask students, in pairs, to re-read Text 16A to identify evidence of a) the attitude of the father to living in America, b) the attitude of the father to the son, c) the attitude of the son to living in America, and d) the attitude of the son to the father. Make a list on the board in four columns of the relevant points. (10)

3 Ask students where their sympathy lies, with the father or the son, and why. (5)

4 Choose two students to read out Text 16B, one as the reporter/narrator and the other as the voice of Panupong Lapsathien. (5)

5 Ask students to re-read Text 16B to identify the relevant material for planning and writing two paragraphs to a) describe what Panupong does and b) explain why he does it. Collect for assesment as summary. (15)

6 Ask students to read Text 16C and give the gist in one sentence. (5)

7 Ask students, in pairs, to script an interview with Babur Ali in Text 16C to answer three questions by a reporter about his life and its challenges. They need to expand the ideas in the text with inference and detail, and consider voice. (10)

8 Invite students, in pairs, to perform their interviews. Evaluate their selection and development of material and their use of voice to differentiate between the interviewer and the interviewee. (10)

9 Assign half the students the role of Panupong, and the other half that of Babur. Ask them to prepare a financial appeal of about 300 words which describes their work, why they need financial help, and how they would use it. The speeches should include explicit and implicit ideas from the texts. (15)

10 Invite students to deliver their speeches. Judge them according to their persuasiveness. (10)

Homework tasks

a Using the formal report writing structure, Texts 16B and 16C, and ideas from the speeches given in Task 10, plan and write a formal report. You are the president of an international charity which supports community aid, and you have been asked by Panupong and Babur for financial aid. Write a report of about 350 words to your committee, explaining what each of the young men do, evaluating their appeals, and recommending one of them for financial support from your charity.

b Use the material you collected in Task 2 to write a summary in answer to the questions a) What did the writer feel about his father and the way he adapted to life in New York? and b) What did the writer's father feel about his son and the way he responded to life in New York?

c Explain, giving supporting detail, a) the ways in which Text 16 B and Text 16C are similar, and b) the ways in which they both differ from Text 16A.

Additional tasks

a Ask students to write a letter from the father, in his hospital bed, to his son. The letter recalls the past, his treatment of his family and his employees, and refers to details and uses inferences from Text 16A. They must remember to make the voice and style different from Text 16A, and to show awareness of the change of audience and purpose.

b Ask students to plan and write an online article entitled 'Heroic helpers' which uses the material in Text 16B and Text 16C, and which gives their own views on the need for people to be socially conscious and willing to give up time to help others.

Text 16A

Good for business

Korean-American Henry Park reminisces about his father, who has just had a stroke and is in hospital in New York.

I thought his life was all about money. He drew much energy and pride from his ability to make it almost at will. He was some kind of human annuity. He had no real cleverness or secrets for good business; he simply refused to fail, leaving absolutely nothing to luck or chance or someone else. Of course, in his personal lore he would have said that he started with $200 in his pocket and a wife and baby and just a few words of English. Knowing what every native loves to hear, he would have offered the classic immigrant story, casting himself as the heroic newcomer, self-sufficient, resourceful.

The truth, though, is that my father got his first infusion of capital from a *ggeh*, a Korean 'money club' in which members contributed to a pool that was given out on a rotating basis. Each week you gave the specified amount; and then one week in the cycle, all the money was yours.

I know over the years my father and his friends got together less and less. Certainly, after my mother died, he didn't seem to want to go to the gatherings anymore. But it wasn't just him. They all got busier and wealthier and lived farther and farther apart. Like us, their families moved to big houses with big yards to tend on weekends, and they owned fancy cars that needed washing and waxing. They joined their own neighborhood pool and tennis clubs and were making drinking friends with Americans. Some of them, too, were already dead, like Mr. Oh, who had a heart attack after being held up at his store in Hell's Kitchen. And in the end my father no longer belonged to any *ggeh*; he complained about all the disgraceful troubles that were now cropping up, people not paying on time or leaving too soon after their turn of getting the money. In America, he said, it's even hard to stay Korean.

I wonder if my father, if given the chance, would have wished to go back to the time before he made all that money, when he had just one store and we rented a tiny apartment in Queens. He worked hard and had worries but he had a joy then that he never seemed to regain once the money started coming in. He might turn on the radio and dance cheek to cheek with my mother. He worked on his car himself, a used green Impala with carburetor trouble. They had lots of Korean friends that they met at church and then even in the street, and when they talked in public there was a shared sense of how lucky they were, to be in America but still have countrymen near.

What belief did I ever hold in my father, whose daily life I so often ridiculed and looked upon with such abject shame? The summer before I started high school he made me go with him to one of the new stores on Sunday afternoons to help restock the shelves and the bins. I hated going. My friends – suddenly including some girls – were always playing tennis or going to the pool club then. I never gave the reason why I always declined, and they eventually stopped asking. Later I found out from one of them, my first girlfriend, that they simply thought I was religious. When I was working for him I wore a white apron over my slacks and dress shirt and tie. The store was on Madison Avenue in the Eighties and my father made all the employees dress up for the blue-haired matrons, and the fancy dogs, and the sensible young mothers pushing antique velvet-draped prams, and their most quiet of infants, and the banker fathers brooding about, annoyed and aloof and humorless.

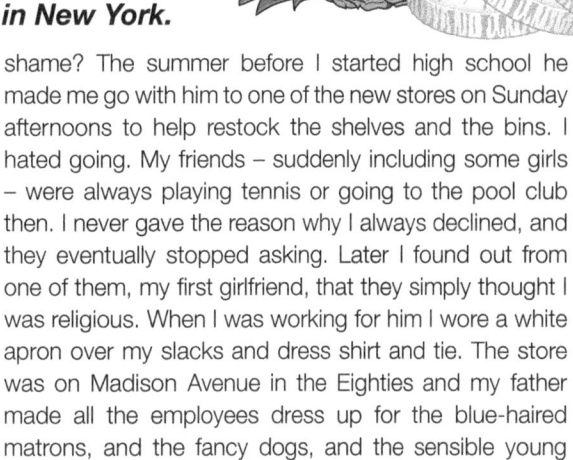

My father, thinking that it might be good for business, urged me to show them how well I spoke English, to make a display of it, to casually recite 'some Shakespeare words'. Mostly, though, I threw all my frustration into building those perfect pyramids of fruit. The other two workers seemed to have even more bottled up inside them, their worries of money and family. They marched through the work of the store as if they wanted to deplete themselves of every last bit of energy, every means and source of struggle. They peeled and sorted and bunched and sprayed and cleaned and stacked and shelved and swept; my father put them to anything for which they didn't have to speak. They both had college degrees and knew no one in the country and spoke little English. The men, whom I knew as Mr. Yoon and Mr. Kim, were both recent immigrants in their thirties with wives and young children. They worked twelve-hour days, six days a week for $200 cash and meals and all the fruit and vegetables we couldn't or wouldn't sell; it was the typical arrangement. My father, like all successful immigrants before him, gently and not so gently exploited his own. 'This is way I learn business; this is way they learn business.'

And although I knew he gave them a $100 bonus every now and then I never let on that I felt he was anything but cruel to his workers. I still imagine Mr. Kim's and Mr. Yoon's children, lonely for their fathers, gratefully eating whatever was brought home to them, our overripe and almost rotten mangoes, our papayas, kiwis, pineapples, these exotic tastes of their wondrous new country, this joyful fruit now too soft and too sweet for those who knew better, us near natives, us earlier Americans.

From *Native Speaker*, by Chang-Rae Lee.

Note: American spelling is used throughout this text.

Text 16B

Medical aid

Last year, Panupong Lapsathien from Bangkok in Thailand won a prize worth one million baht on a television game show. One month later, the 22-year-old had spent all the money – and it was far from enough.

For instead of buying a new car, Panupong bought an ambulance. It was an old van, newly equipped with emergency medical equipment. He switches on the lights and sirens and speeds off to help anyone who calls in an emergency, free of charge, for Panupong is a member of the volunteer rescue team of Vajira Hospital, founded in 1994. For six years he spent much of his time on his bicycle, roaming the streets of Bangkok to provide on-the-spot first aid to the injured and homeless. But then Panupong had to stop biking. He was pedalling at full speed to the scene of an accident when he lost control of the bike on a bend and his leg was so badly damaged that he could see the bone poking through the skin. Panupong spent two months in hospital, and his leg remained in a splint for another two months. He was no longer able to jump on his two-wheeled ambulance, though he would prefer to use his bicycle. 'Riding a bicycle is quicker to get to the scene, as the van is always stuck in a traffic jam. And of course it is much cheaper than driving, with petrol prices so high.'

His volunteering takes up his time from 9 p.m. to 6 a.m., and is unpaid. He lives on an allowance from his mother and his work as a part-time lecturer and guest speaker at some universities and organisations. But it's never enough, he admitted. 'I can't afford to volunteer every day, but if I don't go, I feel upset. I feel as if it's my responsibility, a lifetime commitment. What if one day there's a car crash and no one goes to help? What if someone's dying and your radio is switched off?'

Compared to some, the young volunteers may seem to live an extreme, hectic life. Many of them do not have the time for watching movies, partying or other leisure activities. Yet they say they feel fulfilled. 'When I do CPR and help someone start breathing again, I feel so proud. To save someone's life is the greatest honour for me,' says Panupong. 'It makes my life meaningful.' Every day there are stories of accidents and illnesses. Panupong and the team handle four to six cases a day. 'There are many out there who have to sleep in pain, soaked and cold in the rain, without any care and attention from state hospitals,' he said. 'Once I saw a homeless man with a badly injured arm, and I took him to the hospital and then we sped off to other cases. When we drove back to the area we saw the same guy, with the same wound, lying in the same place. Isn't he a human being like us, with a right to medical care? But it seems no one wants to help or get involved. I'm feeling discouraged as these issues are unlikely to be solved. I am just a volunteer, and can change nothing.'

But his enthusiasm, devotion and commitment have been recognised, and he has just been awarded the Best Youth of the Nation and Asian Award. He has also appeared in many magazines and TV programmes, sharing his experiences and his passion with others. He believes everyone should learn at least basic first aid techniques, to be ready in case of an emergency. 'Accidents can happen to anyone, and the bandages, cotton wool and antiseptic in your medicine chest might not be enough.'

Text 16C

Student doubles as headteacher

For his classmates the four o'clock bell means lessons are over, but for 16-year-old Babur Ali it is time to take off his uniform and start a new school day as probably the youngest headmaster in the world.

Since he was 11, Babur has been running his own school in a small village in West Bengal, passing on to the children of the poor families the knowledge he has acquired at his fee-paying school during the day. It began when children in his village of jute farmers started plaguing him with questions about what he learnt at the 1000 rupee (£12) a year school their parents could not afford. Five years later he is acknowledged by district education officials as 'headmaster' with ten volunteer teachers and 650 pupils desperate to learn.

The school began in the open air, but today it is housed in two bamboo, brick and tile huts, where children are rotated between indoor and outdoor lessons, often with 80 to a class. He rises at 5 a.m. for morning prayers, does household chores, then takes a bus to school in a village five kilometres away. From 10 a.m. to 4 p.m. he focuses on his own education, then he races back to his village to welcome his students at 5 p.m.

He teaches the state school curriculum – English, Bengali, History and Maths – until 8 p.m. and supervises his colleagues, mainly fellow pupils ranging from 16 to 19 years old. The schedule does not weary him: 'I never feel tired – in fact teaching gives me more strength.'

Babur's dream of official status for his school moved closer last week, when he was honoured for slashing illiteracy rates in his district by West Bengal's chief minister at a ceremony in Kolkata. His parents were bursting with pride. Babur has succeeded in attracting pupils to school where the West Bengal authorities, the central government and international aid agencies have all failed. At Babur's school the teachers work unpaid, the children wear their own clothes and the books and desks are financed through donations.

Babur believes he has found his vocation. He wants to qualify as a teacher so that he can develop his school and educate more poor children. His plan is to enrol for an open university degree so that he will be able to do so without deserting his pupils. The secret of his success, he said, is commitment. 'You have to be dedicated and determined. You need to create a learning environment. And there has to be goodwill between the teachers and the students.'

From article 'Hello class, I'm the 16 year old head', by Dean Nelson, *The Sunday Times*.

Answers – Unit 16

2 Text 16A: attitudes:

a Father's attitude to living in America:

- proud of being able to make money
- refused to fail or leave anything to chance
- saw himself as the classic immigrant who started poor but independently became rich
- actually relied on financial support from the Korean community
- became reclusive and disillusioned with his compatriots
- became busier and wealthier as time passed
- became more integrated into local society
- was strict with his employees

b Father's attitude to son:

- believed his son should work in his stores rather than have time off to spend with his American friends
- used him to show off to well-to-do customers
- thought he should be made to work as hard as his other employees
- believed that he should learn the hard way to be a successful businessman

c Son's attitude to living in America:

- resented having to work in the store on Sunday afternoons
- was too ashamed of his father to explain to his peers why he had to decline their social invitations
- channelled his frustration into displaying the fruit in his father's store
- felt sorry for the recent immigrants and their lonely children

d Son's attitude to father:

- thought his father only cared about money
- wondered whether wealth spoilt his father and his ability to feel joy
- regretted that his father lost his Korean friends
- rejected his father's beliefs and felt ashamed of him
- gave impression he believed his father was too harsh with his Korean employees
- thought that his father exploited his fellow immigrants

5 Text 16B: Summary of what Panupong does and why:

When he can afford it, he spends the night driving a medically equipped vehicle around the city of Bangkok in order to be able to come to the aid of victims of accidents after he receives an emergency call. He gives CPR to those whose hearts have stopped. He earns money for the cause by giving talks as a lecturer or speaker.

Although he receives no pay, Panupong feels responsible for the people in need of medical attention and is completely dedicated to the job, despite having been badly injured in the past when rushing to an emergency call. He is proud to be doing a useful service and says it gives value to his life. He feels sympathy for the suffering of fellow humans and believes they have the right to medical care. Sometimes he is discouraged by the thought that he alone can change nothing, but he cannot bear the thought of not being available in case someone is dying and he could save them.

9 Fundraising speeches (including inferences):

Panupong needs money: for petrol for the ambulance; to be able to afford to go on patrol every night; to provide shelter for the homeless; to run basic first aid courses for the public; to increase the number of people and vehicles in the team.

Babur needs money: for more staff to make classes smaller; for more books and furniture; to enable himself to become properly qualified; to extend the scheme to more Bengali villages.

Part 5: Descriptive Composition and Coursework 2

Unit 17: Close observation

Topic outline

- **Main skills:** descriptive writing; viewpoint
- **Secondary skills:** figurative language; inference
- **Outcome:** analysis of writers' effects; descriptive composition/coursework; *individual talk; *description of an image
- **Materials:** Worksheet for Unit 17: Prized possession; descriptive passage; descriptive writing structure handout; Presentation for Unit 17: Mona Lisa (see accompanying online resources)
- **Texts:** Text 17A: Miss Havisham; Presentation for Unit 17: Mona Lisa

Lesson plan

1. Show students an object which has an interesting colour, shape or texture (e.g. a plant, fruit, ornament). Ask them to say as many things about it as possible. (5)

2. Ask students to write phrases about the 'still-life' object which include adjectives and imagery (similes and metaphors), and words with sound effects (e.g. alliterative phrases, onomatopoeia). The descriptive language should be not clichéd and should contain polysyllabic or unusual words which are precise (e.g. colours should be specific – not just *green* but *metallic green, faded green, olive green* etc.). (10)

3. Invite students to offer their best descriptive phrases and write them on the board. Discuss what makes them effective. (5)

4. Give out the worksheet for Unit 17: Prized possession and ask students to complete it. (15)

5. Go through the worksheet and discuss student responses. (5)

6. Read Text 17A to students and ask them afterwards to say which phrases they remember. (5)

7. Give students Text 17A. Ask them to make a class checklist of success criteria for descriptive language, based on the phrases on the board and those they remembered from Text 17A. (10)

8. Show the presentation (12 slides) and ask students to comment on anything they found interesting. Leave slide 2 on the screen. (10)

9. Ask students to study the painting for a few minutes and then make notes for a) a description of her face, using as much detail and imagery as possible, b) their thoughts and feelings when they look at her, c) what she might have thought and felt as she was being painted. (15)

10. Invite students to read their responses and others to comment on them. (10)

Homework tasks

a. Write a response to Text 17B which describes the character and the room and explains how the atmosphere and mood have been created by the writer's language choices, using quotations as support.

b. Use your completed Worksheet 17 as the basis for the content and structure of a descriptive composition/coursework assignment entitled 'My most prized possession'. Add extra material and detail, and links between paragraphs, to make it at least either 400 (composition) or 600 (coursework) words. Think about expression and accuracy, as well as content. You may include references to events, people, thoughts and ideas, provided that the main purpose is descriptive.

Additional tasks

a Ask students to use their descriptive pieces to give an individual talk (perhaps with their possession, or a photograph of it, as a visual aid).

b Ask students to find a photograph or painting which moves or inspires them. They should write a detailed description of it and an explanation of why they respond strongly to it.

Text 17A

Miss Havisham

This was very uncomfortable, and I was half afraid. However, the only thing to be done being to knock at the door, I knocked, and was told from within to enter. I entered, therefore, and found myself in a pretty large room, well lighted with wax candles. No glimpse of daylight was to be seen in it. It was a dressing-room, as I supposed from the furniture, though much of it was of forms and uses then quite unknown to me. But prominent in it was a draped table with a gilded looking-glass, and that I made out at first sight to be a fine lady's dressing-table.

Whether I should have made out this object so soon, if there had been no fine lady sitting at it, I cannot say. In an arm-chair, with an elbow resting on the table and her head leaning on that hand, sat the strangest lady I have ever seen, or shall ever see.

She was dressed in rich materials – satins, and lace, and silks – all of white. Her shoes were white. And she had a long white veil dependent from her hair, and she had bridal flowers in her hair, but her hair was white. Some bright jewels sparkled on her neck and on her hands, and some other jewels lay sparkling on the table. Dresses, less splendid than the dress she wore, and half-packed trunks, were scattered about. She had not quite finished dressing, for she had but one shoe on – the other was on the table near her hand – her veil was but half arranged, her watch and chain were not put on, and some lace for her bosom lay with those trinkets, and with her handkerchief, and gloves, and some flowers, and a prayer-book, all confusedly heaped about the looking-glass.

It was not in the first few moments that I saw all these things, though I saw more of them in the first moments than might be supposed. But, I saw that everything within my view which ought to be white, had been white long ago, and had lost its lustre, and was faded and yellow. I saw that the bride within the bridal dress had withered like the dress, and like the flowers, and had no brightness left but the brightness of her sunken eyes. I saw that the dress had been put upon the rounded figure of a young woman, and that the figure upon which it now hung loose, had shrunk to skin and bone. Once, I had been taken to see some ghastly waxwork at the Fair, representing I know not what impossible personage lying in state. Once, I had been taken to one of our old marsh churches to see a skeleton in the ashes of a rich dress, that had been dug out of a vault under the church pavement. Now, waxwork and skeleton seemed to have dark eyes that moved and looked at me. I should have cried out, if I could.

From *Great Expectations*, by Charles Dickens.

Cambridge IGCSE First Language English — Descriptive Composition and Coursework 2

Worksheet for Unit 17: Prized possession

1. List your five most prized possessions. These may be things you are very proud of or feel sentimental about, or enjoy using or looking at.

   _____

   _____

2. Rank order them 1 to 5, putting a number next to each. Your number 1 should be the possession you would rescue first if your house were on fire.

3. Draw a rough sketch of your number 1 possession.

4. Write notes to describe your chosen possession, giving precise details of the object's size, shape, colour, texture and function. Include as many senses as possible, and create original similes.

   _____

   _____

   _____

   _____

   _____

   _____

   _____

   _____

   _____

© Cambridge University Press 2018 — Unit 17 **Close observation**

5 Explain how you came to possess your prized object: Who gave it to you and why? On what occasion? Where was it acquired? How long ago?

_____
_____
_____
_____
_____
_____
_____

6 Write notes on what the object makes you think about and feel, what you associate it with, and what memories are evoked by it.

_____
_____
_____
_____
_____
_____
_____
_____
_____

7 Write a paragraph arguing for the necessity or importance in your life of this possession, and why it would be worth rescuing more than anything else that you own.

_____
_____
_____
_____
_____
_____
_____
_____
_____

8 Decide on the order in which you will use the material above to form a descriptive composition, and number it accordingly.

Cambridge IGCSE First Language English — Descriptive Composition and Coursework 2

Presentation for Unit 17

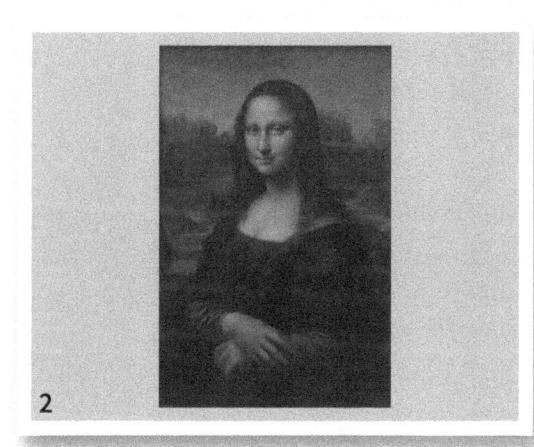

Slide 1

Mona Lisa
Renaissance woman to modern icon

Slide 2

(Image of the Mona Lisa painting)

Slide 3

La Gionconda
- Arguably the most famous painting in the world, it was begun by Leonardo da Vinci in 1503 but was not completed until shortly before his death in 1519.
- The subject is Lisa Gherardini, wife of Francesco del Giocondo, a wealthy Florentine silk merchant, hence the name 'La Gioconda'.
- Leonardo was living in Paris at the time he finished the painting, and its home has been the Louvre gallery since then.
- The painting was stolen in 1911. It was found in Florence two years later.

Slide 4

Leonardo da Vinci
- Born 1452 in Vinci near Florence, he was the illegitimate son of a public notary.
- He moved to Florence at the age of 17 and was apprenticed to the celebrated painter Andrea del Verrocchio.
- He became a celebrated polymath and 'Renaissance Man', a brilliant artist, sculptor, scientist, engineer and inventor.
- He worked in Florence, Milan and Rome before moving to Paris in 1516.
- Leonardo died in 1519 and was buried in France, his adopted home.

Slide 5

Mona Lisa's smile
- La Gioconda is painted in Leonardo's 'sfumato' style, in which the colours dissolve into each other, creating a softening of outlines and a subtle texture.
- The expression on Mona Lisa's face is often described as 'enigmatic' – literally, concealing a mystery.

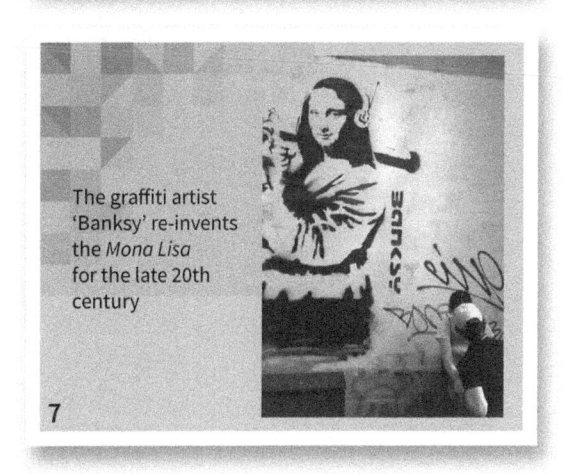

Slide 6

Marcel Duchamp's 1919 version with moustache

Slide 7

The graffiti artist 'Banksy' re-invents the *Mona Lisa* for the late 20th century

8 An interpretation of the *Mona Lisa* in grass

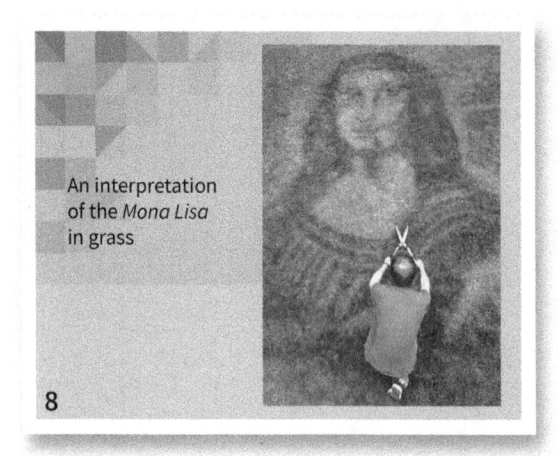

9 An interpretation of the *Mona Lisa* in Lego®

10 The *Mona Lisa* made out of slices of toast

11 The unveiling of the *Mona Lisa* in New York, 1961

How the Mona Lisa came to 'Camelot'

'Mona mania' changed the world in 1962 when Jackie Kennedy, the wife of the then president of the United States, received on December 19th the Christmas gift she had long dreamt of: the *Mona Lisa*. The painting was brought by ship from France, the first time *La Gioconda* had ever left the Louvre art gallery in Paris on loan, and was regarded by many in the art world as too fragile to travel, since the old lady was 500 years old and she needed a constant temperature and humidity. She was to be on holiday for three months to cement a Franco-American political alliance against communism. Two million people in Washington and New York queued to visit *Mona Lisa*. She was heralded as a symbol of freedom, but eight months later president John F. Kennedy was assassinated.

12

Answers – Unit 17

7 Text 17A: success criteria for descriptive writing:

   a Does the piece contain figurative language?

   b Is there at least one, and preferably more than one, adjective before each noun?

   c Are all five senses included, or at least implied, not just vision?

   d Are colour descriptions in precise shades, perhaps using compound adjectives?

   e Are the sentence lengths varied, with some complex sentences included?

   f Are there personal and imaginative elements, not just facts and statistics?

   g Is there some kind of logical framework giving the description form, dimension and progression?

   h Does the description contain vocabulary which is unusual, polysyllabic, interesting, or ambitious?

   i Is the description free from repetition of ideas or vocabulary?

   j Is the description free from clichés (overused and predictable expressions)?

   k Is the description free from everyday verbs like 'have' and 'got', and vague and immature adjectives like 'nice', 'good', 'big', 'small'?

   l Do the sentences begin in different ways, rather than always with 'It'?

   m Is an atmosphere evoked which engages the reader?

   n Is there a range of details which clearly define the ideas and images?

   o Does the piece have scope and variety?

   p Are the ideas developed and clearly sequenced?

   q Does the piece avoid becoming narrative-driven?

Unit 18: Seeing the future

Topic outline

- **Main skills:** figurative language; descriptive writing; imaginative writing
- **Secondary skills:** inference; structuring description
- **Outcome:** description of a house; descriptive composition/coursework; descriptive/imaginative/reflective blog
- **Materials:** Presentation for Unit 18: Houses of the Future? (see accompanying online resources); short story opening; photograph
- **Texts:** Presentation for Unit 18: Houses of the Future?; Text 18: Future past: City of the future; Picture 18

Lesson plan

1. Ask students to write and read out a sentence each describing the room they are currently in, creating interest by avoiding factual statements and using imagery to convey precise sizes, shapes, colours, and textures. (10)

2. Show the presentation on futuristic houses (see accompanying online resources). Invite students to describe each one as they are shown. Ask for a vote on which they consider the most desirable to live in, and why. (15)

3. Ask students to sketch and then write a description of about 250 words of their own vision of the exterior of a futuristic house. Select students to read out their descriptions while another student draws on the board what is being described. Judge which student gave the most precise and comprehensive description. (20)

4. Ask students how they think the future might be different from the present. Ask them to make suggestions for a collective mindmap on the board which includes ideas about the following: transport, clothing, education, leisure activities, family life. (15)

5. Read out Text 18 while students imagine the scene. (5)

6. Ask students what they can infer from the opening of the short story about a) life in 2026 in California, b) what happened in the past, and c) what is going to happen in the future. (5)

7. Ask students in pairs to look at Picture 18, and to collect phrases and images which effectively describe it. (A thesaurus may be useful.) (5)

8. Invite students to read out their best phrases. (5)

9. Ask students to use ideas from Text 18, Picture 18, and the mindmap for Task 4, to plan their descriptive opening for a setting for a futuristic story, beginning at breakfast time on a day in 2060. (10)

Homework tasks

a. Extend your collection of phrases and images in Task 7 into a plan and then write 400 words, or draft 600 words for a coursework 2 assignment, a description of the futuristic cityscape in the photograph. You can include references to what you imagine is happening within the vehicles and the buildings. Check your descriptive composition carefully against success criteria before submitting it.

b. Write a blog entry entitled 'Life can only get better/worse' in which you describe your vision of the lifestyle and society of the future, reflecting on why it will be better or worse than now. You can decide how far into the future you wish to look.

Additional task

Ask students to discuss the concept of a time capsule: who makes them, when, why, and what kind of things are put into them. Tell the class to imagine they are going to fill and bury a time capsule to mark a school or community anniversary. Allow one suggestion per student for what to put in it, with supporting description and reasoning about why a future generation would be interested in their object. Limit the number of objects there is space for (e.g. five) so that students have to vote on which ones to select and justify their choices.

Cambridge IGCSE First Language English — Descriptive Composition and Coursework 2

Presentation for Unit 18

Houses of the Future?

1
2
3
4
5

© Cambridge University Press 2018

Unit 18 **Seeing the future** 109

Cambridge IGCSE First Language English — Descriptive Composition and Coursework 2

6

7

8

9

10

11

110 Unit 18 **Seeing the future**

© Cambridge University Press 2018

Text 18

Future past

'Today is August 4, 2026,' said a second voice from the kitchen ceiling, 'in the city of Allendale, California.' It repeated the date three times for memory's sake. 'Today is Mr Featherstone's birthday. Today is the anniversary of Tilita's marriage. Insurance is payable, as are the water, gas, and light bills.'

Somewhere in the walls, relays clicked, memory tapes glided under electric eyes.

Eight-one, tick-tock, eight-one o'clock, off to school, off to work, run, run, eight-one!

But no doors slammed, no carpets took the soft tread of rubber heels. It was raining outside. The weather box on the front door sang quietly: 'Rain, rain, go away; rubbers, raincoats for today …' And the rain tapped on the empty house, echoing.

Outside the garage chimed and lifted its door to reveal the waiting car. After a long wait the door swung down again.

At eight-thirty the eggs were shriveled and the toast was like stone. An aluminum wedge scraped them into the sink, where hot water whirled them down a metal throat which digested and flushed them away to the distant sea. The dirty dishes were dropped into a hot washer and emerged twinkling dry.

Nine-fifteen, sang the clock, time to clean.

Out of warrens in the wall, tiny robot mice darted. The rooms were acrawl with the small cleaning animals, all rubber and metal. They thudded against chairs, whirling their mustached runners, kneading the rug nap, sucking gently at hidden dust. Then, like mysterious invaders, they popped into their burrows. Their pink electric eyes faded. The house was clean.

Ten o'clock. The sun came out from behind the rain. The house stood alone in a city of rubble and ashes. This was the one house left standing. At night the ruined city gave off a radioactive glow which could be seen for miles.

From 'August 2026: There will come soft rains', by Ray Bradbury, in *The Martian Chronicles*.

Note: American spelling is used throughout this text.

Cambridge IGCSE First Language English — Descriptive Composition and Coursework 2

Picture 18

City of the future

Unit 18 **Seeing the future**

© Cambridge University Press 2018

Answers – Unit 18

6 a life in 2026 in California – all functions are fully automated and robots perform all domestic tasks; technology dominates humans and treats them as children, inferior and stupid, who need to be reminded of everything; life is regimented by time, down to the exact minute, and routine governs everything; people are still expected to go out to work and to school

b what happened in the past – the city of Allendale, and presumably others, was destroyed by a nuclear explosion and all the inhabitants were killed by radioactivity

c what is going to happen next – nothing; the voices will continue to sing their repetitive rhymes in the 'one house left standing' for ever, or until the systems break down; even if there are still humans alive elsewhere, they will not be able to ever live in or visit the city

Note: Bear in mind that this story was written in 1950 and that some of these things may have already changed. For example, going out to work is now less common as so many people work from home. We have already far more electric and electronic gadgets and are more dependent on machinery and technology than was conceivable in the mid-20th century, even in the USA, when a vaccum cleaner was considered a luxury and dishwashers were almost unheard of. The future as envisaged by the writer does not seem futuristic to us, and could already have become the past.

Unit 19: Nightmare journeys

Topic outline

- **Main skills:** descriptive devices; figurative language; structuring description
- **Secondary skills:** creating atmosphere; conveying feelings; analysing writers' effects
- **Outcome:** descriptive continuation; descriptive composition; *diary entry

- **Materials:** novel opening; Worksheet and answers for Text 19A: Dream visit; novel extract; Descriptive writing structure handout
- **Texts:** Text 19A: Dream visit; Text 19B: Strange fancy

Lesson plan

1. Ask students to read Text 19A. (5)
2. Give out the worksheet for Text 19A for completion. (20)
3. Go through the worksheet answers. (15)
4. Give out the Descriptive writing structure handout. Explain how movement towards the object/place to be described or the passing of a brief period of time are frameworks which give shape to descriptive compositions. (5)
5. Ask students to use one of the two descriptive structures to plan a descriptive composition about revisiting a place from their childhood. (5)
6. Ask students to write and read out the first paragraph of Text 19A for their composition, beginning *Last night I dreamt I went to ...*, and invite comments on each one about how well they lead the reader into the composition by creating an atmosphere. (10)
7. Ask students to list vocabulary and imagery to use in their descriptive composition. Encourage the selection of unusual, powerful, precise, exotic-sounding, emotive words, figurative language (e.g. similes, personification), and sound effects (e.g. onomatopoeia, assonance). (10)
8. Read Text 19B to the class without students having a copy. Ask them which words or phrases they can remember. (5)
9. Give out copies of Text 19B to pairs and ask students to underline the most evocative uses of language. (10)
10. Elicit and discuss feedback. (5)

Homework tasks

a. Using your plan from Task 5 and your language notes from Task 7, complete your descriptive composition. Do not end with *And then I woke up* but with a more original final sentence, which could refer to movement away from the place, a sense of time having run out, or a statement of feeling about the experience.

b. Plan and write a continuation of Text 19B, of about 300 words, describing the room into which the visitor is taken and its occupant. Begin with the words, *The room in which I found myself was ...*

Additional tasks

a. Ask students to write an explanation in 200–300 words of how the writer uses language to convey meaning and to create effect in Text 19B. They should choose the three examples which they find the most evocative to support their answer, including some which use imagery.

b. Ask students to plan a descriptive composition about an empty or abandoned place, such as a theme park, sports stadium, factory, school. They should focus on the contrast with when it was full of life.

Text 19A

Dream visit

Last night I dreamt I went to Manderley again. It seemed to me I stood by the iron gate leading to the drive, and for a while I could not enter, for the way was barred to me. There was a padlock and a chain upon the gate. I called in my dream to the lodge-keeper, and had no answer, and peering closer through the rusted spokes of the gate I saw that the lodge was uninhabited.

No smoke came from the chimney, and the little lattice windows gaped forlorn. Then, like all dreamers, I was possessed of a sudden with supernatural powers and passed like a spirit through the barrier before me. The drive wound away in front of me, twisting and turning as it had always done, but as I advanced I was aware that a change had come upon it; it was narrow and unkempt, not the drive that we had known. At first I was puzzled and did not understand, and it was only when I bent my head to avoid the low swinging branch of a tree that I realised what had happened. Nature had come into her own again and, little by little, in her stealthy, insidious way had encroached upon the drive with long, tenacious fingers. The woods, always a menace even in the past, had triumphed in the end. They crowded, dark and uncontrolled, to the borders of the drive. The beeches with white, naked limbs leant close to one another, their branches intermingled in a strange embrace, making a vault above my head like the archway of a church. And there were other trees as well, trees that I did not recognise, squat oaks and tortured elms that straggled cheek by jowl with the beeches, and had thrust themselves out of the quiet earth, along with monster shrubs and plants, none of which I remembered.

The drive was a ribbon now, a thread of its former self, with gravel surface gone, and choked with grass and moss. The trees had thrown out low branches, making an impediment to progress; the gnarled roots looked like skeleton claws. Scattered here and there amongst this jungle growth I would recognise shrubs that had been landmarks in our time, things of culture and grace, hydrangeas whose blue heads had been famous. No hand had checked their progress, and they had gone native now, rearing to a monster height without a bloom, black and ugly as the nameless parasites that grew beside them.

On and on, now east now west, wound the poor thread that once had been our drive. Sometimes I thought it lost, but it appeared again, beneath a fallen tree perhaps, or struggling on the other side of a muddied ditch created by the winter rains. I had not thought the way so long. Surely the miles had multiplied, even as the trees had done, and this path led but to a labyrinth, some choked wilderness, and not a house at all. I came upon it suddenly; the approach was masked by the unnatural growth of a vast shrub that spread in all directions, and I stood, my heart thumping in my breast, the strange prick of tears behind my eyes.

The garden had obeyed the jungle law, even as the woods had done. A lilac had mated with a copper beech, and to bind them yet more closely to one another the malevolent ivy, always an enemy to grace, had thrown her tendrils about the pair and made them prisoners. Nettles were everywhere, the vanguard of the army. They choked the terrace, they sprawled about the paths, they leant, vulgar and lanky, against the very windows of the house.

A cloud, hitherto unseen, came upon the moon, and hovered an instant like a dark hand before a face.

From *Rebecca*, by Daphne du Maurier.

Text 19B

Strange fancy

The narrator returns with trepidation to a house he knew as a child.

When I again uplifted my eyes to the house itself, from its image in the pool, there grew in my mind a strange fancy – a fancy so ridiculous, indeed, that I but mention it to show the vivid force of the sensations which oppressed me. I had so worked upon my imagination as really to believe that about the whole mansion and domain there hung an atmosphere peculiar to themselves and their immediate vicinity – an atmosphere which had no affinity with the air of heaven, but which had reeked up from the decayed trees, and the gray wall, and the silent tarn – a pestilent and mystic vapour, dull, sluggish, faintly discernible, and leaden-hued.

Shaking off from my spirit what must have been a dream, I scanned more narrowly the real aspect of the building. Its principal feature seemed to be that of an excessive antiquity. The discoloration of ages had been great. Minute fungi overspread the whole exterior, hanging in a fine tangled web-work from the eaves. Yet all this was apart from any extraordinary dilapidation. No portion of the masonry had fallen; and there appeared to be a wild inconsistency between its still perfect adaptation of parts, and the crumbling condition of the individual stones. In this there was much that reminded me of the specious totality of old wood-work which has rotted for long years in some neglected vault, with no disturbance from the breath of the external air. Beyond this indication of extensive decay, however, the fabric gave little token of instability. Perhaps the eye of a scrutinising observer might have discovered a barely perceptible fissure, which, extending from the roof of the building in front, made its way down the wall in a zigzag direction, until it became lost in the sullen waters of the tarn.

Noticing these things, I rode over a short causeway to the house. A servant in waiting took my horse and I entered the Gothic archway of the hall. A valet, of stealthy step, thence conducted me, in silence, through many dark and intricate passages in my progress to the studio of his master. Much that I encountered on the way contributed, I know not how, to heighten the vague sentiments of which I have already spoken. While the objects around me – while the carvings of the ceilings, the sombre tapestries of the walls, the ebon blackness of the floors, and the phantasmagoric armorial trophies which rattled as I strode, were but matters to which, or to such as which, I had been accustomed from my infancy – while I hesitated not to acknowledge how familiar was all this – I still wondered to find how unfamiliar were the fancies which ordinary images were stirring up. The valet now threw open a door and ushered me into the presence of his master.

From *The Fall of the House of Usher,* by Edgar Allan Poe.

Cambridge IGCSE First Language English — Descriptive Composition and Coursework 2

Worksheet for Text 19A: Dream visit

1 Underline the words and phrases which create atmosphere in Text 19A.

2 Choose three words of your own to describe the atmosphere of the place.
   _____

3 Underline the words and phrases which convey feeling.

4 Choose three words of you own to describe the feelings of the persona.
   _____

5 a Give synonyms (using a thesaurus if necessary) for the following words from the passage:

   forlorn _____
   _____

   stealthy _____
   _____

   squat _____
   _____

   masked _____
   _____

   malevolent _____
   _____

   b Say what the difference in effect is, in each case, between the writer's choice of the words above and the synonyms you have suggested. Write your explanation of the different connotations on the line below each word.

6 Explain how the writer of Text 19A:

   a makes effective the description of the garden, in addition to the choice of vocabulary
   _____
   _____
   _____
   _____
   _____
   _____
   _____

© Cambridge University Press 2018   Unit 19 **Nightmare Journeys** 117

b conveys the feelings of the persona, in addition to the choice of vocabulary.

_____
_____
_____
_____
_____
_____
_____

7 Explain, using your own words, what the writer means by:

  a *cheek by jowl* (line 31)

  _____

  b *gone native* (line 44)

  _____

  c *the jungle law* (line 61)

  _____

  d *an enemy to grace* (line 64)

  _____

8 Quote the single words which show that:

  a No one looked after the house now. _____

  b The trees made it difficult to pass. _____

  c The bushes by the path had become dense and tangled. _____

  d The nettles were the dominant weed. _____

9 Explain the structure of the description in the passage (i.e. what governs the order of the content).

_____
_____
_____
_____
_____
_____

Answers to Worksheet for Text 19A: Dream visit

1 *rusted; uninhabited; narrow and unkempt; stealthy, insidious; long, tenacious fingers; menace; triumphed; crowded, dark and uncontrolled; squat; tortured; monster; choked; gnarled; like skeleton claws; black and ugly; nameless parasites; labyrinth; choked wilderness; masked; jungle law; malevolent ivy; enemy to grace; prisoners; army; vulgar and lanky; a dark hand before a face*

The use of the device of anthropomorphism (i.e. giving the vegetation human qualities), battle imagery, vocabulary associated with death and suffocation, the idea of denied entrance and hindered progress, and the repetition of certain powerful words (e.g. *choked*) all contribute to the atmosphere of a place growing out of control and threatening to humans. The choice of dark flowerless plants which are parasites or weeds (*ivy, nettles*) is also symptomatic of the sinisterness of the place.

3 *barred; forlorn; I was puzzled; trees that I did not recognise; none of which I remembered; I had not thought the way so long; my heart thumping in my breast; prick of tears behind my eyes*

These words add up to an overall feeling by the persona that she is lonely, excluded and unwelcome in this place; that the past is not accessible to her. Some of the words describing human feeling have been attributed to parts of the building (e.g. *forlorn*), and this transference of adjectives connects the persona and the place, making it more animate (alive) and her more inanimate (dead). The fusion of the atmosphere of a graveyard and the threat in the description of a sudden cloud covering the Moon and the simile of the dark hand, suggesting the extinguishing of light and life, adds to the emotional power of the passage.

5 a *forlorn* – lonely, abandoned, forsaken, desolate, bereft
stealthy – slow, undetectable, surreptitious, secretive, furtive
squat – short, thick, low, square, compact
masked – covered, hidden, unidentifiable, concealed, disguised
malevolent – hateful, ill-wishing, spiteful, vicious, evil

b The synonyms are likely to be more ordinary or less powerful or sinister words. The writer's choices build up a sense of the garden having evil intentions and posing a threat to the unwelcome visitor.

6 a The dream seems to be set in late winter, creating a bleak mood: the trees are naked and there is mud in the ditch. The garden is padlocked, making it seem a forbidden place and that trespassers will be punished. The personfication of all aspects of the garden, controlled by over-arching nature, makes the dream visitor seem helpless and outnumbered in the face of a united and huge enemy army. The trees are embracing each other, but the visitor is entirely alone and exposed. What had been beautiful, like the hydrangeas, has become ugly and attacked by parasites; nature has become unnatural; everything is decaying yet has the strength to strangle, choke and imprison its neighbours in the battle for space and light. There are no references to sound or smell in the description, which makes it dream-like and divorced from the sense perceptions which would exist in reality if walking through a garden.

b The persona feels overawed by the proximity of the vegetations and disorientated that nothing is as it used to be, as shown by the comparisons. The sizes, quantities and distances seem unreal. She feels enclosed and encroached upon, and, as she enters deeper into the garden, we wonder how or if she will find her way back to the iron gate. She is reduced to tears when she finally sees the house, which is at the mercy of the invading garden. The image of the 'dark hand before a face' conveys her trepidation as the Moon is eclipsed by cloud and she is now in darkness.

7 a *cheek by jowl* – very close together; in close proximity

b *gone native* – become primitive/untamed; adapted to rest of surroundings.

c *the jungle law* – the survival of the fittest (is the only law)

d *an enemy to grace* – devoid of elegance; without dignity

8 a no one looked after the house now – *unkempt*

b the trees made it difficult to pass – *impediment*

c the bushes by the path had become dense and tangled – *labyrinth*

d the nettles were the dominant weed – *vanguard*.

9   Structure of the passage: the description is given in order of what the persona sees and feels as she moves through the gate and along the path towards the house. This gives the passage a spatial structure of closing in on the object of interest, and instils suspense into the description as the reader does not know if she will get there or what she will find if she does. The winding nature of the path (now east now west) means she can suddenly come upon new things to describe, previously not seen from her perspective at the gate. The passage ends with a reference to 'the very windows of the house', which brings her as close as she can get without going inside.

Cambridge IGCSE First Language English — Descriptive Composition and Coursework 2

Unit 20: City portraits

Topic outline

- **Main skills:** descriptive writing; analysing writer's effects
- **Secondary skills:** imagery; travel writing
- **Outcome:** tourist guide entry; introduction to guide book; travel writing; *blog post
- **Materials:** travel article; travel blog; tourist guide
- **Texts:** Text 20A: A year in Tokyo; Text 20B: A walk through Kuala Lumpur; Text 20C: Temple of Heaven Park in Beijing

Lesson plan

1. Ask students to jot down without thinking what comes to mind when they hear the name Tokyo. Elicit their responses. Discuss why places are linked to particular images. (5)

2. Tell students to look at the image in Text 20A and say how this compares with their own impressions. (5)

3. Ask students to skim-read Text 20A. (5)

4. Ask students, in pairs, to scan Text 20A for examples of the features and content of travel writing. Collect feedback and list on board. (10)

5. Ask students to scan Text 20A and underline words evoking a sensory response, putting them under the headings of the five senses. (10)

6. Collect feedback in columns on board; ask students to explain why the choices effectively evoke the mood and atmosphere of the place. (10)

7. Explain iceberg diagrams (layers of meaning widening downwards from denotation to connotation to association). Write two words from Text 20A, *Mosquitoes* and *Wedding,* on the board, and ask students to call out words and phrases to complete an iceberg diagram for each. (10)

8. Ask students to read Text 20B and comment on its voice and style. (5)

9. Ask students to identify and bracket the parts of Text 20B which are the writer's opinion or reflection about Kuala Lumpur rather than informative fact. (5)

10. Ask students to read Text 20C and list the features of guide book style and content. (5)

11. Ask students to change the remaining text (outside the brackets) of Text 20B into informative style and write a guide book entry for Kuala Lumpur, employing the features listed for Task 10. Collect for assessment. (20)

Homework tasks

a. You are the writer of the airline magazine article in Text 20A and you have been asked to write the descriptive introduction to a new guide book to Tokyo. You need to select and generalise ideas from your magazine article and adapt the style for a new purpose, making it less personal and more formal. Write about 400 words.

b. Using the format of Text 20B, in about 400 words, write a walking tour of your own city. It should be a mixture of factual description and your thoughts and feelings about the places on your tour.

Additional task

Ask students to imagine that they are each a resident of Kuala Lumpur and they do not agree with some of the things said about their city in Text 20B. They should write a blog post to add to the website which points out the misrepresentations and justifies their own views.

Text 20A

A year in Tokyo

Westerners still arrive in Tokyo hoping to find an old Japan of shrines and paper houses, of shy women and inscrutable men. They leave after a week, puzzled and disappointed. Others expect a technological wonderland and find something of that in the department stores of Akihabara, but find something else too, something unexpected, resonant, mysterious.

In my first weeks in Tokyo, impression succeeded impression with a rapidity that made assimilation impossible. Other than knowing I was in the capital city of Japan and one of the great concentrations of humanity on the planet, I didn't really know where I was. As time passed, I seemed to be travelling away from any understanding of the place, to be more and more bewildered, as though I had wandered into a stranger's dream. Much initial effort went into trying to avoid getting lost or, having become so, into trying to find something – anything – that looked familiar. Each time I left my little apartment in the city's western suburbs I was never quite sure I would see it again. I would pause at street corners and look back at the way I had come, memorising landmarks but somehow not quite believing in them, as though that blue-tiled roof, or the rattling, pinging pachinko parlour, might have drifted away like incense smoke before I returned.

Summer, hot and humid, is not an easy season in Tokyo. The locals carry little folded cloths to mop the sweat from their faces but staying cool was a struggle. Nights were not much easier. I would lie on my little roll-out mattress, an electric fan whirring beside my head, mosquitoes flying tirelessly above. Some days the air was thick as soup. I longed to escape to the country, to the mountains or the coast, but could hardly be bothered to put on my sandals. Anyway, I was working, moving through the looping guts of the Tokyo transport system, arriving at hard-to-identify places to sing alphabet songs with pre-school children or, in the evenings, to teach English to their older brothers and sisters.

When I wasn't teaching, I was training. The world headquarters of aikido – 'the way of harmony', a martial-art cousin of judo and jujitsu – was in downtown Shinjuku, and by getting off my futon at some unlikely hour of the morning, I could get down there in time for the 8 a.m. class or, more heroically, the 6 a.m. Some of my happiest hours in Tokyo were spent in the training hall being hurled around by people who had spent 20, 30, 40 years in the art. The oldest practitioners I called the 'grey belts' as their black belts, won so long ago, had faded to a ragged pearl colour. Among them were men – and the occasional woman – in their 70s or 80s. I was terrified at first of accidentally killing one of them but soon learnt that I was the one likely to need rescuing.

On days off from teaching, pleasantly weary after my exertions on the mat, I would wander in the curling alleyways of Shinjuku revelling in the ordinary business of the people who lived and worked there: the bar owners, the housewives, schoolgirls in tartan skirts, a monk in saffron. There was a barber's shop I used to visit where the barber, wearing a surgical mask over his mouth (for his protection or mine?) would shave me – the hairy foreigner – with a thoroughness that included scraping his razor over my forehead, clipping my nasal hairs and plucking the hairs from my ears with tweezers. Hot flannels were laid over my face, then unguents out of curious bell jars were rubbed vigorously into my skin while the man's daughter used her cupped hands to massage my shoulders. It was not an expensive indulgence – Japan can be surprisingly good value …

September means typhoons, and a certain historic nervousness. Days of warm swirling rain, inescapable rain. Everything rots. Then, quite suddenly, the fug of summer is blown away by the first cool breezes of the autumn. As the mornings turned chilly, I would buy a can of hot sweet coffee from the vending machines by my local station, sipping it between the swaying and dozing salarymen on the Toei-Shinjuku line.

When did the snow come? December? February? I cannot quite remember, but have a vivid recollection of walking home one afternoon through the grounds of the Shinto shrine in Motoyawata and seeing a winter wedding, the bride in her silken hood, the groom sombre in his hakama. To keep off the snow, the wedding party carried umbrellas of lacquered paper. The couple, shy and serious, paused for photos then, on wooden sandals, everyone tottered off, while behind them, on the frozen water of the purification trough, the snow continued its soft descent. I could have stayed forever (I almost did), feeding on the city's casual poetry – a creature lost in translation, but perfectly content to be so.

From an article by Andrew Miller in *High Life Magazine*, British Airways.

A walk through Kuala Lumpur

Of all the cities in the world that have a Chinatown, Kuala Lumpur is probably the one where it's unmissable. That probably has a lot to do with the fact that Kuala Lumpur is more of a glitzy shopping destination than a cultural one with lots of sights and attractions. We were just aching to do something beyond strolling through malls.

Kasturi Walk
Walk is possibly the oddest word for this stretch of trinket shops under a covered area outside the Central Market. We passed under a gigantic pewter butterfly (Pewter, thanks to the Royal Selangor company, is a pretty big deal in Kuala Lumpur). A couple of sleepy vendors swatted flies off their collection of exotic fruits while displays of batik clothes and woven bracelets sat unattended. Charles pointed out a magnet kiosk selling magnets with Denmark, ILoveNY and every destination apart from KL branded across it. We shuffled on quickly, and entered the Central Market through the first door we found.

Central Market
We'd been warned, but we ventured in anyway. So it probably serves us right for getting bored out of our minds at Central Market. An air conditioned market with lanes for different Asian countries – Little India, Little-China, Malay street and more stocked a whole bunch of handicrafts and souvenirs. Which is great if you're not from Asia and all of it is exotic to you. We walked past stores selling toys, key chains, wooden masks, soaps, tiny models of the Petronas Towers and other knick knacks, pausing only to click pictures and check out a couple of antique stores.

Sri Mahamariamman Temple
Walking on, we passed another point on the map that we weren't incredibly interested in. The Sri Mahamariamman Temple seemed far too similar to the zillions of temples we have back in India. That said, I must admit we did stop and stare in awe at the massive five-tiered Gopuram with its over 200 deities carved out in intricate detail.

Kuan Ki Chinese Temple
Just as we were wondering if we'd be able to find any of the Chinese temples, we saw a flash of red that caught our attention. Sitting inconspicuously by the side of the road, was a beautiful cherry red Chinese temple. From where we stood outside, we could look through, past the stone guards flanking the entrance, into a smoke filled courtyard. The stone guards are Chinese lions, the male with a ball in his mouth, and the female with a baby serving to ward off negativity. Past columns with snake/dragon like creatures wrapped around them, we saw the colourful *men shen* (the door Gods) Walking in, we paused as our eyes began to water fiercely. An entire curtain made of incense coils were burning over the entryway, sending a sweet smell and a thick haze of smoke all around. Light streamed in from above, catching the lazy spirals of smoke as they wafted towards the heavens. This was the strangest of all temple experiences we've ever had. No, there was no hush of silence that spoke of God's presence. There were no chants or devotees sending themselves into a trance. Everything was very matter of fact. Yes worshippers were maintaining a respectful decibel level, but there was no hush of reverence. They walked about in their shorts and jeans, lighting incense sticks and flags, bowing their heads to the Taoist God of war and going about their day. Just seeing this temple alone made our otherwise "meh" day worth it.

Petaling Street
Once again, a massively hyped up "Must See" attraction in Kuala Lumpur that definitely did not live up to the expectations. A walking street, lined with old crumbly buildings, shops selling tee shirts and fake branded bags spilling out on the street. Street food vendors and cold drinks in hand carts. Looking back, it was just like Khao San road in Bangkok (minus the bars and semi-naked backpackers dancing on table tops). I don't know if the difference in our experience was alcohol or the fact that backpacker streets just don't appeal to us anymore. It made me wonder for a while, if being a frequent traveller tends to de-sensitize you towards new experiences that are somewhat similar? Would this have been exciting for us a couple of years ago? We pondered this, keeping our heads up, looking

at the beautiful old pre-war buildings and rows of Chinese lanterns looming above us as we manoeuvred an obstacle course of tourists and touts.

Sin Sze Si Ya Temple

Finally glad to have escaped the rather claustrophobic Petaling Street, we saw a little sign on the road that I almost missed. Charles took my hand and led me into what seemed to be the parking lot of a building. I looked at him quizzically, wondering what he was up to. Great call on that tiny yellow sign by Charles, because he had led us into another Chinese temple. Hidden away from the street, the Sin Sze Si Ya temple is a shrine to two illustrious personalities of Chinese history. Rumoured to be the oldest Taoist temple in Kuala Lumpur, there's a strange ritual practised here. There I was standing entranced, staring at all the idols on the altar, as Charles walked around trying to take a few pictures without disturbing any of the worshippers. When suddenly, a girl crawled out from under the altar beside me. I read later on, that crawling under the altar 3 times is said to bring good luck. I also read about the caretaker who is one of the few who can decipher *chim* (fortune sticks) today. Wish I'd known this while still in KL.

Old China Cafe

We looked at the watch, realising it was well past lunchtime. This was where I jumped into navigator mode, leading Charles down a deserted ghost town kind of street, in the pursuit of a very special cafe. The highlight of our trip to Chinatown, Kuala Lumpur. The Old China Cafe is less restaurant, more institution. Dating back to the mid 1800s when Chinese settlers mined for tin in the area, it used to serve as a guild hall. One of the last remnants of this area's rich history, we were thrilled to find out a lot of the original construction had been maintained. Two large mirrors on opposite walls lit up the otherwise dingy room beautifully. But they weren't only aesthetic. They're *Feng Shui* mirrors, believed to reflect good luck. We took our time, taking in the artwork, old photographs, calligraphy and other adornments on these old walls, the latches on the wooden doors, all of it really giving us a sense of this old place. We even overheard a writer interviewing the grandson of one of the old inhabitants at the next table. Eavesdropping on his tale only heightened our sense of curiosity of what life would have been like in the area back then.

From *Chinatown, Kuala Lumpur: A Walking Tour and Long Lunch,* by Revati Victor.

Text 20C

Temple of Heaven Park in Beijing

When you enter the Temple of Heaven site, the first thing you notice is the space. This was designed to be an open and spacious enclosure, with the central temples surrounded by open land and trees, enhancing the exclusiveness of the location. Many of the trees here are several hundred years old. Much of the area was planted with cypress trees, with the deep green color traditionally symbolizing respect. Such trees are often found at temple, altar, and mausoleum sites in China. It is claimed there are some 20,000 such trees in the Temple of Heaven grounds; 3,600 of them are more than 100 years old, and the oldest ones close to the main altars date back to the Jin dynasty, being some 800 years old. The landscaping, flower gardens, and mown grass have been added in more modern times. Much of the area is now used as parkland, forming one of the largest public parks in Beijing. You can see many people here exercising, practising *tai chi* or dance routines, or just walking and chatting. With its location now in a busy residential suburb of the city, this has become a popular area. It is particularly active with local residents early in the morning and later in the afternoon; it is well worth lingering here after your temple visit to enjoy some of this relaxed atmosphere. People will gather to sing, play instruments, or perhaps challenge each other to games of chess. It is a magnificent setting for relaxation with the temple buildings in the background.

From 'The Beijing Tour Guide', www.wanderstories.com.

Answers – Unit 20

4 Text 20A: content and style of travel writing:
Although superficially a purely informative genre of writing, there is usually also a poetic/figurative element of language in travel writing to make the place seductive – or at least to convince the reader that the writer did actually visit the place – even though there is no reason why the writer needs to persuade readers to visit these places, there being no financial incentive involved.

The typical features and content of travel writing are:
references to the permanent cultural and landscape features which can be visited; appositional phrases and avoidance of 'and' for concision; alternatives to regular word order to avoid monotony; references to food, restaurants; use of sounds and other senses; use of words in the local language; mixing facts with inferences, opinions and personal reponses; use of the first person; multiple adjectival usage; use of imagery and poetic language (e.g. alliteration) to evoke atmosphere, but not so much that it ceases to be informative and becomes purely descriptive writing.

5 Sensory description:
Sight – *blue-tiled roof; the mountains or the coast; the looping guts of the Tokyo transport system; hurled around; faded to a ragged pearl colour; curling alleyways; schoolgirls in tartan skirts, a monk in saffron; wearing a surgical mask over his mouth; the hairy foreigner; curious bell jars; seeing a winter wedding; umbrellas of lacquered paper; the snow continued its soft descent*

Sound – *rattling, pinging; an electric fan whirring; mosquitoes flying; sing alphabet songs; typhoons; wooden sandals*

Note also how sound is conveyed through the use of alliteration which is also onomatopoeic (e.g. *pinging pachinko parlour; snow continued its soft descent*).

Smell – *like incense smoke; unguents*

Taste – *the air was thick as soup; hot sweet coffee*

Touch – *hot and humid; folded cloths to mop the sweat from their faces; scraping his razor over my forehead; plucking the hairs; hot flannels; rubbed vigorously into my skin; massage my shoulders; warm swirling rain; cool breezes; chilly*

6 Many of the above imply more than one sense. For example, *drifted away like incense smoke* (also sight), *an electric fan whirring* (also touch), *the air was thick as soup* (also touch), *hurled around* (also touch) and *saffron* (also taste). The verb *rots* conjures up both sight and smell, and *fug* fuses several senses, as do *snow* and *rain* and *frozen*.

This is called synaesthesia and is a poetic device which can also be used in descriptive writing generally to strengthen the sensuous effect of words and images. What makes the description of this text particularly striking is that it contains many touch images, which is the most intimate and evocative of the senses.

Note also how sound is conveyed through the use of alliteration which is also onomatopoeic (e.g. *pinging pachinko parlour; snow continued its soft descent*).

7   Text 20A: example of iceberg diagrams for *mosquitoes* and *wedding*.

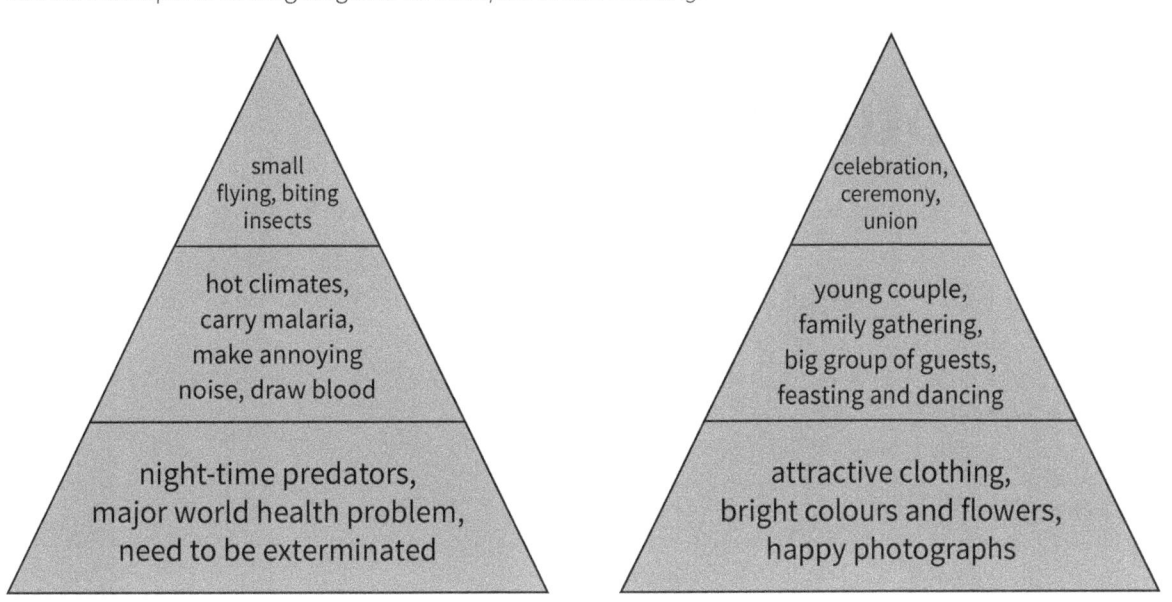

Mosquitoes pyramid (top to bottom):
- small flying, biting insects
- hot climates, carry malaria, make annoying noise, draw blood
- night-time predators, major world health problem, need to be exterminated

Wedding pyramid (top to bottom):
- celebration, ceremony, union
- young couple, family gathering, big group of guests, feasting and dancing
- attractive clothing, bright colours and flowers, happy photographs

8   Text 20B is written in a personal chatty voice and colloquial style, containing the second person plural pronoun, idioms, slang, contractions, compound sentences and non-sentences. The style contrasts with the informative content.

10 Text 20C has the typical features of informative style: use of impersonal 'you'; passive verb forms; lists; participle phrases.

Part 6: Narrative Composition and Coursework 3

Unit 21: Crucial decisions

Topic outline

- **Main skills:** narrative writing; narrative viewpoint
- **Secondary skills:** narrative planning; *narrative openings
- **Outcome:** narrative composition/coursework assignment
- **Materials:** accounts of mountaineering accident; aspects of narrative handout; worksheet for Unit 21: Narrative openings
- **Text:** Text 21: The final choice

Lesson plan

1. Ask students to consider stories they have recently read and say what needs to be considered before embarking on the writing of a story. (See the aspects of narrative handout). (5)

2. Ask two students to read the two voices and viewpoints of Text 21. (5)

3. Ask class to vote on which account is more exciting and why. Ask how it would have been different as a third-person narrative by someone who was in the climbing party and a witness to the event. (5)

4. Ask students, in pairs, to identify and list the ways in which the accounts have been made engaging for the reader in terms of a) content and b) style. (10)

5. Collect feedback in two columns on board. (5)

6. Ask students to decide how they think Text 21 could end and to write a final paragraph as a third-person narrative, relating what happened in the morning and reconciling both viewpoints. (10)

7. Invite students to read out their endings and comment on their credibility and predictability. (5)

8. Ask students to think of a different situation and to plan a narrative with the title of 'A matter of life and death'. They should refer to the lists on the board and include in their planning how the crisis will be resolved. (15)

9. Ask students to complete Worksheet for Unit 21: Narrative openings and feed back their responses. (20)

10. Ask students to decide on the type of opening for their own story and write the opening sentence. Some can be read to the class for an opinion on their power to engage. (10)

Homework task

Write the narrative composition you have planned and started in Tasks 8 and 10. It should be either 350–450 words or 500–800 words, depending on whether it is a practice composition or a coursework assignment.

Additional tasks

a. Ask students to practise the other types of opening for their story, and to judge which one works best and what difference it makes to the level of reader engagement.

b. See the additional activities at the end of the worksheet.

Text 21

The final choice

As experienced mountaineers, Joe and Simon attempt the West Face of the Siula Grande in the Peruvian Andes. The climb goes according to plan until, on the descent, Joe falls and breaks his leg. Simon then has to lower him down from ledge to ledge, and this is when disaster strikes.

Joe's account

The sense of weight on my harness increased, as did the speed. I tried braking with my arms but to no effect. I twisted round and looked up into the darkness. Rushes of snow flickered in my torch beam. I yelled for Simon to slow down. The speed increased and my heart jumped wildly. Had he lost control? I stifled the rising panic and tried to think clearly. No, he hadn't lost control, because although I was going down fast, it was steady. But there was still something wrong.

It was the slope. It was now much steeper, and that could mean only one thing – I was approaching another drop. I screamed out a frantic warning but he couldn't hear me. I shouted again, as loud as I could, but the words were whipped away into the snow clouds, and he couldn't have heard me even five metres away. I had no idea how far I was from the half-way knot. Each lowering became timeless. I slid for ever through the boiling snow without any sense of time passing – just a barely endurable period of agony.

A sense of great danger washed over me. I had to stop. I had to stop myself. If Simon felt my weight come off the rope he would know there must be a good reason. I grabbed my ice axe and tried to brake my descent. I leant heavily over the axe head, burying it in the slope, but it wouldn't bite. The snow was too loose. I dug my left boot into the slope but it, too, just scraped through the snow.

Then abruptly my feet were in space. I had time to cry out, and claw hopelessly at the snow, before my whole body swung off an edge. I jerked on to the rope and toppled over backwards, spinning in circles from my harness. I was hanging free in space. I could see an ice wall two metres away from me every time I completed a spin. I shone my torch up the wall, following the line of rope, until I could make out the edge I had gone over. The wall was solid ice and steeply overhanging. I could see it dropping below, angled away from me, then snow flurries blocked my view.

There was no chance of Simon hauling me up. It would be suicidal for him to attempt it.

Simon's account

It had been nearly an hour since Joe had gone over the drop. I was shaking with cold. My grip on the rope kept easing despite my efforts. The thought overwhelmed me that I could not hold the rope or stop the descent. The snow slides and wind and cold were forgotten. I was being pulled off. I slipped a few inches more. Then I thought of the knife. It was in my sack. It took an age to let go a hand and slip the strap off my shoulder, and then repeat it with the other hand. I braced the rope across my thigh and held on to the plate with my right hand as hard as I could. Fumbling at the catches on the rucksack, I could feel the snow slowly giving way beneath me. Panic threatened to swamp me. I felt in the sack, searching desperately for the knife. My hand closed round something smooth and I pulled it out. I put it in my lap. I had already made the decision. There was no other option left to me. The metal blade stuck to my lips when I opened it with my teeth.

I reached down to the rope and then stopped. I had to clear the loose rope twisted round my foot or it would rip me down with it. I carefully cleared it to one side, reached down again, and this time I touched the blade to the rope. It needed no pressure. The taut rope exploded at the touch of the blade and I flew backwards. Leaning back in the snow, I listened to the furious hammering in my temple as I tried to calm my breathing. I was alive, and for the moment that was all I could think about. Where Joe was, or whether he was alive, didn't concern me in the long silence after the cutting. His weight had gone from me. There was only the wind and the avalanches left to me.

When at last I sat up, the slack rope fell from my hips. Had I killed him? I didn't answer the thought, though some urging in the back of my mind told me that I had. I felt numb: freezing cold and shocked into silence, I stared bleakly at the faint torch beam cutting through the swirling snow and felt haunted by its emptiness. Another avalanche swept over me in the darkness. Alone on a storm-swept mountain face, and becoming dangerously cold, I was left with no choice but to forget about Joe until the morning.

Adapted from *Touching the Void*, by Joe Simpson.

Worksheet for Unit 21: Narrative openings

There are six basic types of narrative openings:

1. setting
2. character
3. action
4. dialogue
5. reflective comment
6. shocking admission
7. intriguing statement

In small groups, study the following, well-known opening sentences (A–Z) to published novels or short stories.

a Decide which of the six types of opening sentence you think is being used (using the numbers above). Some of them may be combinations.

b Give each opening a mark out of 10, based on your desire to continue reading.

c Discuss which type of opening seems to be the most engaging for the reader.

d Report your choice, giving reasons, of the best five openings to the rest of the class and compare responses with those of other groups.

e Write a continuation of your favourite opening sentence to complete a first paragraph, and read it to the class.

		Type	Mark
A	It was a bright cold day in April, and the clocks were striking thirteen.		
B	Robert Cohn was once middleweight boxing champion of Princeton.		
C	It was the coldest winter in the Alps in living memory.		
D	As Gregor Samsa awoke one morning from uneasy dreams he found himself transformed in his bed into a gigantic insect.		
E	True! – nervous – very, very dreadfully nervous I had been and am!		
F	'Not that horse, mister.'		
G	So, the dreadful old woman was dead at last.		
H	There was nothing special about number Forty-Seven.		
I	Lonely and boring the hours stretched endlessly ahead.		
J	When Floyd Anselmo saw the purple cow grazing on a hillside of his dairy range one cold morning in October he thought his mind must be hallucinating.		
K	He was never called Ekky now, because he was getting to be a real boy, nearly six, with grey flannel trousers that had a separate belt and weren't kept up by elastic, and his name was Eric.		
L	Andrea looked out through the curtains as soon as she woke.		
M	Once upon a time and a very good time it was there was a moocow coming down the road and this moocow that was coming along the road met a nicens little boy named baby tuckoo.		
N	Hale knew they meant to murder him before he had been in Brighton three hours.		
O	An arbitrary choice then, a definitive moment: October 23, 1990.		

P	'Attention,' a voice began to call, and it was as though an oboe had suddenly become articulate.		
Q	Only the steady creaking of a flight of swans disturbed the silence, labouring low overhead with outstretched necks towards the sea.		
R	When Bill Simpson woke up on Monday morning, he found he was a girl.		
S	'Lizzy!' she exclaimed, flinging open the door. 'Are you okay?'		
T	Peter was crammed onto a narrow ledge which sloped down towards a terrible abyss.		
U	It wasn't a human.		
V	A moment's silence, and then a whistle blew and the garden became filled with moving shadows and running footsteps.		
W	The Iron Man came to the top of the cliff.		
X	Fugu is a fish caught off the Pacific shores of Japan.		
Y	'How did that alligator get in the bath?' demanded my father one morning at breakfast.		
Z	The house shook, the windows rattled, a framed photograph slipped off the shelf and fell into the hearth.		
[Write a continuation here of your favourite opening from those above.]			

Additional activities:

a Choose another of the openings in the table and complete a paragraph.

b Collect five more examples of opening sentences from published works and comment on them.

c Create six new narrative opening sentences, one of each type.

Cambridge IGCSE First Language English — Narrative Composition and Coursework 3

Answers – Worksheet for Unit 21: Narrative openings

A 7	**H** 1 + 4	**O** 7	**V** 1 + 3 + 7
B 2	**I** 5	**P** 3	**W** 3
C 1	**J** 2 + 3 + 7	**Q** 1	**X** 5
D 2 + 6	**K** 2	**R** 2 + 6	**Y** 4
E 5	**L** 3	**S** 4	**Z** 1 + 3
F 4	**M** 3	**T** 3 + 1	
G 6	**N** 2 + 7	**U** 7	

Answers – Unit 21

3 Text 21 viewpoint:

The first-person accounts can be judged to be equally exciting, because both characters are in severe danger which could prove fatal, and although Joe's physical predicament is worse by the end, Simon's terrible decision has left him in an impossible position.

A third-person account would not have been as effective as either of these first-person accounts because the reader would not have been able to empathise as much with the intense and agonising thoughts and fears.

However, although a third-person account would be less gripping and immediate, first-person narrators must have survived in order to be telling the story, so this reduces tension.

4 Text 21 features:

a Content – Speed of movement, poor visibility, and inability to communicate are always dramatic devices to create suspense. Natural hazards, weather and terrain (*avalanche*), are being used to add to the already dangerous situation. The events are stretched out to add tension so every movement, however inessential, is mentioned, and the narrative includes the thought processes of the characters to delay the action and intensify the emotional effect.

b Style – Short sentences create a feeling of panic and provide a change of pace to signify the climax of the story. Alarming vocabulary, such as *agony, yelled, screamed* and *hopelessly*, conveys the feelings of pain and fear.

Unit 22: Incredible tales

Topic outline

- **Main skills:** narrative writing; narrative structure
- **Secondary skills:** detecting irony; summarising; inference; using dialogue in narrative; creating humour; creating tension
- **Outcome:** narrative composition/coursework assignment; mini-saga synopsis; narrative continuation; *news report; *dialogue; *formal report
- **Materials:** short story extracts; Worksheet for Text 22A: Crossed wires; narrative writing structure handout
- **Texts:** Text 22A: Crossed wires; Text 22B: Out in the cold

Lesson plan

1. Elicit definitions on the board for tale, fable, myth, legend, allegory. Discuss the purpose of each genre. (5)
2. Ask four students to do a dramatic reading of Text 22A, one taking the part of the narrator and three speaking as the characters. (5)
3. Check understanding of vocabulary and ask for a) a summary of the action and b) comment on the type of ending. (5)
4. Ask students to give rules for dialogue layout. (5)
5. Ask students to complete the Worksheet for Text 22A and then feed back their answers to the class. (20)
6. Ask students to read Text 22B. (5)
7. Ask students to suggest a suitable moral for the tale and then decide on the best. (5)
8. Ask students, in pairs, to identify and list the devices used in Text 22B to create narrative tension, providing examples for each. (10)
9. Elicit feedback and write up a list for students to copy. (5)
10. Ask students, in pairs, to identify the narrative structure of Text 22B, labelling the stages in the margin of a copy of the text. (5)
11. Elicit answers, then give students the narrative writing structure handout. (5)
12. Ask students to think of a film or novel they know, comedy or tragedy, and to turn it into a mini-saga (a synopsis of exactly 50 words.) (10)
13. Ask students to read out their synopses, while the others guess which book or film they refer to. (5)

Homework tasks

a. Ask students, in pairs, to script and perform the dialogue which takes place between Tom Vincent and a prospector at Cherry Creek on his arrival. (Note that inverted commas are not needed in playscript dialogue or interview format.)

b. Write a story of between 350 and 450 words which is a modern version of a fable or a well-known tale. (For a coursework Assignment 3, write either a longer version or two separate stories.) The piece should be humorous and/or ironic. Try to use some of the devices identified in Task 8, and follow the Narrative writing structure handout. Take care to set out dialogue correctly.

Additional tasks

a. Plan and write the American's journal for this day, as he is on the plane going home. Give your view of what happened, your opinion of Muni and the other locals, and your reasons for wanting the statue. Use supporting details and examples from the passage. (Refer to the journal writing handout.)

b. Ask students to plan and write a report by a police officer on the disappearance of the statue, to Include details of the crime and when it took place, what you have discovered and been told, and what you intend to do about it.

c. Ask students to plan and write a report by a police officer on the disappearance of the statue, to Include details of the crime and when it took place, what you have discovered and been told, and what you intend to do about it.

Text 22A

Crossed wires

This is the ending of a short story set in a remote village in southern India. A poor goatherd is sitting by a life-size clay statue of a horse when an American tourist, whose car has run out of petrol. stops on the highway. He assumes that Muni owns the statue – which is in fact a Hindu totem – and decides to buy it from him to take back to America. They 'converse' in different languages, neither of them understanding what the other is saying.

'Lend me a hand and I can lift off the horse from its pedestal after picking out the cement at the joints. We can do anything if we have a basis of understanding.'

At this stage the mutual mystification was complete, and there was no need even to carry on a guessing game at the meaning of words. The old man chattered away in a spirit of balancing off the credits and debits of conversational exchange, and said in order to be on the credit side, 'O honourable one, I hope God has blessed you with numerous progeny. I say this because you seem to be a good man, willing to stay behind an old man and talk to him, while all day I have none to talk to except when somebody stops by to ask for a piece of tobacco. Noting the other's interest in his speech, Muni felt encouraged to ask, 'How many children have you?' with appropriate gestures with his hands.

Realising that a question was being asked, the red man replied, 'I said a hundred,' which encouraged Muni to go into details. 'How many of your children are boys and how many girls? Where are they? Is your daughter married? Is it difficult to find a son-in-law in your country also?'

In answer to these questions the red man dashed his hand into his pocket and brought forth his wallet in order to take immediate advantage of the bearish trend in the market. He flourished a hundred-rupee currency note and asked, 'Well, this is what I meant.'

The old man now realised that some financial element was entering their talk. He peered closely at the currency note, the like of which he had never seen in his life; he knew the five and ten by their colours although always in other people's hands, while his own earning at any time was in coppers and nickels. What was this man flourishing the note for? Perhaps asking for change. His eyes travelled to his goats nosing about, attempting to wrest nutrition from minute greenery peeping out of rock and dry earth.

The foreigner followed his look and decided that it would be a sound policy to show an interest in the old man's pets. He went up casually to them and stroked their backs with every show of courteous attention. Now the truth dawned on the old man. His dream of a lifetime was about to be realised. He understood that the red man was actually making an offer for the goats.

He had reared them up in the hope of selling them some day and, with the capital, opening a small shop on this very spot. While he was reflecting thus, the red man shook his hand and left on his palm one hundred rupees in tens now. 'It is all for you, or you may share it if you have a partner.'

The old man pointed at the station-wagon and asked, 'Are you carrying them off in that?'

'Yes, of course,' said the other, understanding the transportation part of it.

The old man said, 'This will be their first ride in a motor car. Carry them off after I get out of sight, otherwise they will never follow you.' He brought his palms together in a salute, turned round and went off, and was soon out of sight beyond a clump of thicket.

The red man looked at the goats grazing peacefully. Perched on the pedestal of the horse, as the westerly sun touched the ancient faded colours of the statue with a fresh splendour, he ruminated, 'He must be gone to fetch some help, I suppose,' and settled down to wait. When a truck came downhill, he stopped it and got the help of a couple of men to detach the horse from its pedestal and place it in his station-wagon. He gave them five rupees each, and for a further payment they siphoned off gas from the truck and helped him to start his engine.

Muni hurried homeward with the cash securely tucked away at his waist in his *dhoti*. He shut the street door and stole up softly to his wife as she squatted before the lit oven wondering if by a miracle food would drop from the sky. Muni displayed his fortune for the day. She snatched the notes from him, counted them by the glow of the fire, and cried, 'One hundred rupees! How did you come by it? Have you been stealing?'

'I have sold our goats to red-faced man. He was absolutely crazy to have them, gave me all this money and carried them off in his motor car!'

Hardly has these words left his lips when they heard bleating outside. She opened the door and saw the two goats at her door. 'Here they are!' she said. 'What's the meaning of all this?'

He muttered a great curse and seized one of the goats by its ears and shouted, 'Where is that man? Don't you know you are his? Why did you come back?' The goat only wriggled in his grip. He asked the same question of the other too. The goat shook itself off. His wife glared at him and declared, 'If you have thieved, the police will come tonight and break your bones. Don't involve me. I will go away to my parents …'

Abridged from the short story 'A Horse and Two Goats', by R.K. Narayan.

Text 22B

Out in the cold

When travelling, a companion is considered desirable. In the Klondike, as Tom Vincent found out, a companion is essential. 'Never travel alone' is a saying in the north. He had heard it many times and laughed, for he was a sturdy young fellow, with faith in himself and in the strength of his head and hands.

It was a bleak January day when he learnt respect for the frost. He had left Calumet Camp on the Yukon River to go to Cherry Creek, where his party was prospecting for gold. The frost was sixteen degrees below zero, and he had nearly fifty kilometres of lonely trail to cover, but he did not mind. In fact, he enjoyed it, swinging along through the silence, his blood pounding warmly through his veins, and his mind carefree and happy.

He had set off at 7 a.m., and by eleven had covered half the distance. Seated on a fallen tree, he unmittened his right hand, reached inside his coat and fished out a biscuit. He had barely chewed the first mouthful when his numbing fingers warned him to put his mitten on again. This he did, surprised at the bitter swiftness with which the frost had bitten. He could feel himself beginning to chill, so he leaped to his feet and ran briskly up the trail. This made him warm again, but the moisture he exhaled crusted his lips with ice crystals and formed a miniature glacier on his chin. Now and again sensation abandoned his face, and he rubbed it till it burned with the returning blood.

After an hour, he rounded a bend and came upon one of the most formidable dangers of northern travel. The creek itself was frozen solid, but from the mountain came the outflow of several springs. These never froze, being protected from the frost by the blanket of snow, and the water formed shallow pools, their unbroken surface giving no warning of the lurking danger beneath. The instant he broke through, Tom felt the cold water strike his feet, and he struggled to the bank. He was quite cool and collected. The only thing to do was build a fire. For another precept of the north runs: 'Travel with wet socks down to seven below zero; after that build a fire'.

It is impossible to build a fire wearing heavy Alaskan mittens, so Tom bared his hands, gathered a number of twigs, and knelt down to kindle his nest of fire. From a pocket he drew out his matches and a strip of thin birch bark. He separated one match from the bunch and scratched it on his trousers. The bark burst into bright flame, which he carefully fed with the smallest twigs, cherishing it with the utmost care, gently nurturing it. His feet had started to grow numb, but the fire, although a very young one, was now alive.

However, at the moment he was adding the first thick twigs to the fire, a grievous thing happened. The pine boughs above his head were burdened with months of snowfall, and collecting the twigs had disturbed its balance, causing an avalanche which blotted out his fire. He realised how great his danger was and immediately started to rebuild it, but his fingers were now so numb that he could not bend them, and when he lit a match it burnt his fingers and he had to drop it.

He stood up, now desperate. He could not feel his feet, although his ankles were aching painfully, and he feared that frostbite had set in. His hands were worthless. If only he had a comrade to start the fire that could save him! He was thinking quickly. What if the match did burn his hands? Burned hands were better than dead hands. When he came upon more twigs, he got his last match into place on his palm and forced his nerveless fingers down against it. At the second scratch the match caught fire, and he knew that if he could stand the pain he was saved.

An anxious five minutes followed, but the fire gained steadily. Then he set to work to save himself. Alternately rubbing his hands with snow and thrusting them into the flames, he restored their circulation sufficiently to be able to get dry socks and boots out of his pack. Then he cut away his moccasins and bared his feet, rubbing them too with snow. He rubbed until his burned hands grew numb. For three hours he worked, till the worst effects of the freezing had been counteracted. All that night he stayed by the fire, and it was late the next day when he limped pitifully into the camp at Cherry Creek.

Adapted from the short story 'To Build A Fire', by Jack London.

Worksheet for Text 22A: Crossed wires

1   Look at the end of the story. Explain the double twist.

2   Explain the allegorical moral or message of the story.

3   Explain the ironies contained in the passage.

4 Explain the humour contained in the passage.

5 Explain the role and viewpoint of the narrator in the passage.

6 If the story were turned into an animal fable, which animals could be used to represent the stereotypical human characters of the American and the Indian, and why?

Answers for Worksheet for Text 22A: Crossed wires

(Example answers)

1   The two men both think they have got the best of the deal.

   Muni has been successful in acquiring some money for once, and expects to be praised, but his wife doesn't believe where he got it from and is threatening to leave him.

   The goats have come home, so Muni will still have to look after them and his life isn't going to change.

2   The story is saying that communication fails not only because of a lack of a shared language but because of a difference of culture and expectation. This is an example of an East–West clash between spiritual and consumer values that could have serious political consequences and not be only a matter of horses and goats. The story warns against the dangers of guessing what you think someone else is saying. The two men have nothing in common and are as much different species, with different ways of thinking, seeing, experiencing and processing the world, as the different species of animals in fables.

   Alternatively, the message could be that however different the background, all humans are acquisitive and want what they don't yet have, and are motivated by money, which can 'talk' even when no other language can.

3   Muni thinks he has got an amazing deal from the American, but it wasn't the worthless goats that he sold.

   Muni believes the American is stupid for wanting to buy the goats, but the American thinks the Indian is stupid for selling the statue so cheaply.

   Muni will think that the American didn't get his side of the bargain because the goats came back.

   The American may be rich but he is so incompetent in this country he is visiting that he has run out of petrol and is at the mercy of the locals.

   The American has acquired something which signifies the spiritual values of Indian religion, which is against his own 'religion' of capitalism.

   The horse belongs to the local people and should not be transported to an alien and environment where it will be without meaning or history.

   The Hindu horse statue wasn't Muni's to sell and the village may not be too pleased when they find out that it has gone and that Muni made a lot of money from it.

4   The humour is created by the failure to realise that the other hasn't a clue what each is saying, and their guesses being totally wrong. The content of Muni's speech shows his complete lack of understanding of the country and social context that the red-faced man comes from. The reader enjoys the comedy created by the answers being a complete mismatch to the questions (e.g. that the American has a hundred children).

5   The narrator is omniscient, knowing what each character is thinking, but also neutral, so that no comment or evaluation is made or implied about their intentions and actions. This narrative stance is typical of fables that leave it to the reader to judge right and wrong, and what it to be learnt. By calling them 'old man' and 'red man', a distance is created between narrator and character. This device shows, however, how the protagonists see each other in a superficial and stereotypical way.

6   Students' own answers.

Answers – Unit 22

1 Definitions for tale, fable, myth, legend and allegory:

All of these narrative genres, often delivered orally, serve the purpose of entertainment, but with a different focus.

A tale can be any short imaginative story, about something out of the ordinary or extreme, with the focus on plot rather than character, to evoke amusement, fear or wonder.

A myth uses the supernatural to explain aspects of creation and nature in a simple, non-scientific way.

A legend is a traditional, historical narrative concerning a famous real person or group which exaggerates their exploits to create cultural identity and cohesion.

A fable is a short, succinct narrative which usually features talking animals to make a moral point about human behaviour memorable and more universally applicable. Fables usually contain an ironic twist at the end, so that someone is taught a lesson by the unexpected outcome.

An allegory uses animals, gods or human stereotypes to embody beliefs or attitudes in order to convey a warning about some aspect of society.

3 a Muni thinks he is selling his goats to an American, who thinks he is buying a statue of a horse and takes it away. Muni's wife believes he has stolen the 100 rupees because the goats are still there, and she tells him she is leaving him.

  b The ending uses dialogue to create a 'cliffhanger': we don't know whether or not she will carry out her threat to leave him, and the story ends in an ellipsis so that she doesn't even finish her speech.

7 (Example answers)

- Listen to those who know.
- Better not to learn the hard way.
- Give nature respect.
- Never give up.
- Fire is the gift of life.
- Don't tempt fate.

8 Text 22B creates tension by:

- previewing disaster (*as Tom Vincent found out*)
- the use of irony to create expectation (*he was carefree and happy*)
- words relating to speed (*barely*; *swiftness*; *briskly*)
- contrast (references to heat and cold, life and death, and the battle between them)
- threatening diction (*formidable*; *lurking*; *struggled*; *grievous*; *blotted*; *worthless*)
- alarming imagery (*warned*; *miniature glacier*; *abandoned*)
- time references to show pressure (*after an hour*; *now*; *five minutes*; *three hours*)
- repetition of same action, but with increasing urgency and desperation (trying to get warm, lighting a fire)
- repetition of key vocabulary (*pain*; *numb*; *burn*; *save*)
- suspense (*had to drop it*; *he feared that …*; *he knew that if …*; *anxious*).

10 Text 22B narrative structure:
- setting (time and place)
- main character introduced and described, plus reference to others and relationship
- events/creation of unexpected situation
- problem intensifies / crisis created
- climax/remedy required
- solution and resolution

Unit 23: Framed

Topic outline

- **Main skills:** narrative writing; narrative framing
- **Secondary skills:** narrative style; setting and atmosphere; prediction; descriptive writing
- **Outcome:** news report; short story; descriptive composition; *narrative continuation
- **Materials:** short story; novel opening; Worksheet and answers for Text 23B: Doorway to the past
- **Texts:** Text 23A: The wall; Text 23B: Doorway to the past

Lesson plan

1. Read Text 23A to class. Ask students to comment on its ending and explain the irony. (5)

2. Ask students, in pairs, to underline words and phrases which convey the power of:

   a. the water in paragraphs 1, 2 and 3

   b. the fire in paragraphs 4 and 5.

   c. the falling wall in paragraphs 1, 3 and 5. (5)

3. Elicit answers and comments on the atmosphere, mood and expectation the imagery creates. (5)

4. Ask students to look at and comment on the effect of:

   a. the four simple sentences at the beginning of paragraph 4

   b. the four simple sentences in the final paragraph. (5)

5. Ask students to plan and write a news report of the event, including statements by an eyewitness and an official. Tell them to create additional 'factual' details, such as place and people's names and ages, and give their report a headline and a sub-heading. Collect for assessment (500–800 words). (20)

6. Read Text 23B to class. Elicit a response about its effectiveness as a novel opening (i.e. did it make them want to read on?). (5)

7. Give out copies of Text 23B and the Worksheet for Text 23B for students to complete in pairs (20)

8. Discuss responses and give answers to the worksheet. (15)

9. Ask students to plan a prologue as a short story opening which introduces a flashback to a previous time. (10)

Homework tasks

a. Finish the short story started in Task 9. Consider whether you end the story by returning to the frame and 'bookending' the narrative. The story will need to be longer if it is for a coursework assignment.

b. Write a story which continues from the opening of the diary at the end of Text 23B.

Additional task

Ask students to write a detailed description of a building on fire, using imagery, multiple adjectives and senses. Use a spatial (movement towards) or chronological (time passing) structure for your writing.

Text 23A

The wall

Firemen are fighting a blaze in a London warehouse caused by a bomb in the second world war.

I remember it was our third job that night, and it was 3 a.m. And there we were – Len, Lofty, Verno and myself, playing a fifty-foot jet up the face of a tall city warehouse and thinking nothing at all. You don't think of anything after the first few hours. You just watch the white pole of water lose itself in the fire and you think of nothing. Sometimes you move the jet over to another window. Sometimes the orange dims to black, but you only ease your grip on the ice-cold nozzle and continue pouring careless gallons through the window. You know the fire will fester for hours yet. However, that night the blank, indefinite hours of waiting were sharply interrupted by an unusual sound. Very suddenly a long rattling crack of bursting brick and mortar perforated the moment. And then the upper half of that five-storey building heaved over towards us. It hung there, poised for a timeless second before rumbling down at us. I was thinking of nothing at all and then I was thinking of everything in the world.

In that simple second my brain digested every detail of the scene. New eyes opened at the sides of my head so that, from within, I photographed a hemispherical panorama bounded by the huge length of the building in front of me and the narrow lane on either side. Blocking us on the left was the squat pump, roaring and quivering with effort. Water throbbed from its overflow valves and from leakages in the hose. A ceaseless stream spewed down its grey sides into the gutter. To the other side of me was a free run up the alley. A couple of lengths of dead, deflated hose wound over the darkly glistening pavement. A needle of water fountained from a hole in a live hose.

Behind me, Len and Verno shared the weight of the hose. They heaved up against the strong backward drag of water pressure. All I had to do was yell 'Drop it!' and then run. We could risk the live hose snaking up at us. We could run to the right down the free alley – Len, Verno and me. But I never moved. That long second held me hypnotized, rubber boots cemented to the pavement. Ton upon ton of red-hot brick hovering in the air above us numbed all initiative.

The building was five storeys high. The top four storeys were fiercely alight. The rooms inside were alive with red fire. The black outside walls remained untouched. And thus, like the lighted carriages of a night express train, there appeared alternating rectangles of black and red that emphasized vividly the extreme symmetry of the window spacing. Orange-red colour seemed to bulge from the black framework like boiling jelly that expanded inside a thick black squared grill.

Three of the storeys, thirty blazing windows and their huge frame of black brick, a hundred solid tons of hard, deep Victorian wall, pivoted over towards us and hung flatly over the alley. The night grew darker as the great mass hung over us and the moonlight was shut out. The picture appeared static to the limited surface sense, but beyond that there was hidden movement. A wall will fall in many ways. It may sway over to the one side or the other. It may crumble at the very beginning of its fall. It may remain intact and fall flat. This wall fell as flat as a pancake. It clung to its shape through ninety degrees to the horizontal. Then it detached itself from the pivot and slammed down on top of us, cracking like automatic gunfire. The violent sound both deafened us and brought us to our senses. We dropped the hose and crouched. Afterwards Verno said that I knelt slowly on one knee with bowed head, like a man about to be knighted. Well, I got my knighting. There was an incredible noise – a thunderclap condensed into the space of an eardrum – and then the bricks and mortar came tearing and burning into the flesh of my face.

Lofty, by the pump, was killed. Len, Verno and myself they dug out. There was very little brick on top of us. We had been lucky. We had been framed by one of those symmetrical, rectangular window spaces.

Adapted from 'The Wall', by William Samsom, in *Fireman Flower*.

Text 23B

Doorway to the past

THE PAST is a foreign country: they do things differently there. When I came upon the diary, it was lying at the bottom of a rather battered red cardboard collarbox, in which as a small boy I kept my Eton collars. Someone, probably my mother, had filled it with treasures dating from those days. There were two dry, empty sea-urchins; two rusty magnets, a large one and a small one, which had almost lost their magnetism; some negatives rolled up in a tight coil; some stumps of sealing-wax; a small combination lock with three rows of letters; a twist of very fine whipcord; and one or two ambiguous objects, pieces of things, of which the use was not at once apparent: I could not even tell what they had belonged to. The relics were not exactly dirty nor were they quite clean, they had the patina of age; and as I handled them, for the first time for over fifty years, a recollection of what each had meant to me came back, faint as the magnet's power to draw, but as perceptible. Something came and went between us: the intimate pleasure of recognition, the almost mystical thrill of early ownership—feelings of which, at sixty-odd, I felt ashamed. It was a roll-call in reverse; the children of the past announced their names, and I said "Here." Only the diary refused to disclose its identity. My first impression was that it was a present someone had brought me from abroad. The shape, the lettering, the purple limp leather curling upwards at the corners, gave it a foreign look; and it had, I could see, gold edges. Of all the exhibits it was the only one that might have been expensive. I must have treasured it; why, then, could I not give it a context? I did not want to touch it and told myself that this was because it challenged my memory; I was proud of my memory and disliked having it prompted. So I sat staring at the diary, as at a blank space in a crossword puzzle. Still no light came, and suddenly I took the combination lock and began to finger it, for I remembered how, at school, I could always open it by the sense of touch when someone else had set the combination. It was one of my show-pieces and, when I first mastered it, drew some applause, for I declared that to do it I had to put myself into a trance; and this was not quite a lie, for I did deliberately empty my mind and let my fingers work without direction. To heighten the effect, however, I would close my eyes and sway gently to and fro, until the effort of keeping my consciousness at a low ebb almost exhausted me; and this I found myself instinctively doing now, as to an audience. After a timeless interval I heard the tiny click and felt the sides of the lock relax and draw apart; and at the same moment, as if by some sympathetic loosening in my mind, the secret of the diary flashed upon me. Yet even then I did not want to touch it; indeed my unwillingness increased, for now I knew why I distrusted it. I looked away and it seemed to me that every object in the room exhaled the diary's enervating power and spoke its message of disappointment and defeat. And as if that was not enough, the voices reproached me with not having had the grit to overcome them. Under this twofold assault I sat staring at the bulging envelopes around me, the stacks of papers tied up with red tape—the task of sorting which I had set myself for winter evenings, and of which the red collar-box had been almost the first item; and I felt, with a bitter blend of self-pity and self-reproach, that had it not been for the diary, or what the diary stood for, everything would be different. I should not be sitting in this drab, flowerless room, where the curtains were not even drawn to hide the cold rain beating on the windows, or contemplating the accumulation of the past and the duty it imposed on me to sort it out. I should be sitting in another room, rainbow-hued, looking not into the past but into the future; and I should not be sitting alone. So I told myself, and with a gesture born of will, as most of my acts were, not inclination, I took the diary out of the box and opened it.

From the prologue of *The Go-Between,* **by L.P. Hartley (Hamish Hamilton Ltd, 1953).**

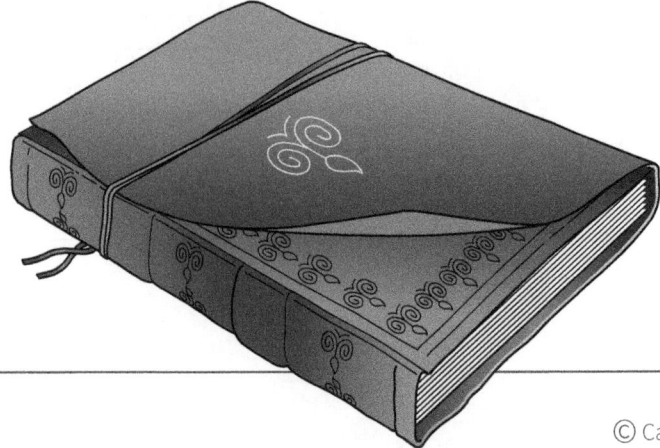

Cambridge IGCSE First Language English — Narrative Composition and Coursework 3

Worksheet for Text 23B: Doorway to the past

1. Explain the context of the prologue.

2. Describe the atmosphere of the passage and the mood this creates.

3. How has the character of the narrator been conveyed?

4. What is the role of the diary in the passage?

5   Describe the structure of the passage.

6   What does the reader expect to happen in the rest of the novel?

7   How have the reader's expectations been created?

Answers for Worksheet Text 23B: Doorway to the past

1   A man in his sixties is sorting through things from his past when he finds a box filled with childish treasures from his schooldays, which stir up memories. He does not immediately recognise the diary, which surprises him, but, having forced open its lock, he remembers that it has unpleasant associations and is reluctant to go further. However, he dutifully faces the challenge and opens the diary, which is connected to events which changed his life and are responsible for his present drab and miserable existence.

2   The cold and rainy atmosphere outside and the 'drab, flowerless room' create a mood of loneliness, sadness and sterility associated with 'disappointment and defeat'. It prepares the reader for a switch to a hot summer and being outdoors when the narrator goes back to his past through means of opening the diary. The rain 'beating on the windows' could be interpreted as the past demanding readmittance, and the undrawn curtains could imply that at least subconsciously the narrator wants to remember, as his past was less solitary and more exciting and 'rainbow-hued' than the grey present, and he has no future to look forward to.

3   The character of the narrator is conveyed by reference to his mother and his private school, suggesting that they were major features in his life, and his answer of 'Here' shows that he was obedient to higher authorities when summoned. He was a hoarder, or he would not still have the box and its contents after half a century, and this indicates his desire for ownership. He is curious and likes to experiment, and is drawn to secrecy and mystery, as to a magnet. His being proud of his memory shows that he likes to excel and impress his 'audience' through performance and also pretence. He cannot resist a challenge, which suggests he will be guilty of hubris as some stage. The 'self-pity' suggests he will become a victim, and the 'self-reproach' shows that he will punish himself if he fails in some way. References to duty and willpower show that he desires to please and to conform, to achieve at the highest possible level, and that failure and rejection would be devastating to him.

4   The diary represents the secrets of the past, his memories, and is the receptacle of his childhood self, whom he is about to meet again. It is everything that his present is not. Something happened 50 years ago which determined how he would live his life thereafter. It is a 'magnet' whose pull he cannot resist, though he fears the emotions, repressed for a lifetime, that it will stir up in him again.

5   The prologue consists of only one paragraph, as time, place and subject are all fused and heightened. It starts with mention of the diary, but only as one thing in the box and the other objects are described first, neutrally. Once the narrator has revealed that it is 50 years since he handled the items in the box, and references have been made to his school days, then we have an interest in the diary as containing a record of his childhood experiences, and the diary becomes the narrator's focus as there is a move from the other items to this main object in the box. The diary contains a secret, so there is a further move to unlock it and gain access to its interior, to begin the journey from the present to the past. Suspense is created for the reader, as we do not know whether he will be able to remember the combination after half a century (although we also know that he will, as there would be no point in its existence otherwise) and we also want to know what it contains, and why he is reluctant to read it again, especially as we know he blames it for ruining his life. When he finally opens it, he and the reader go through the doorway to the foreign country of the past.

6   The reader expects the story to end in tragedy, otherwise there would be no explanation for why he is now a miserable and lonely old man. Whatever happened when he was a child, however, was far more dramatic and exciting than anything that happened to him afterwards: at least he felt alive then, and wanted to keep a record of his experience in a diary.

7   The reader expects that what went wrong when he was a teenager will have a lot to do with the personality established in this passage (pride, will-power, showing-off, possessiveness, obedience, curiosity, duty, guilt), otherwise they would not have been mentioned. They are all characteristics that can lead to an unfortunate outcome in certain circumstances. As he was only a child 50 years ago, we know that he will not have been in control of his life then, but was at the mercy of others.

Answers – Unit 23

1. It is ironic that the only one of the firemen who was killed was the one to the side of the building and not in the path of the falling wall. It is an amazing coincidence that the heads of the other three firemen all fitted into the empty window spaces in the falling wall.

2. **a** Power of the water in Text 23A:
   - *fifty-foot jet* – height of water and the pressure implied by *jet*
   - *pole of water* – height of water and its rigidity
   - *careless gallons* – amount of water, as if it was inexhaustible
   - *water throbbed* – describes pulsing effect of the bursts of water and the action of the pump
   - *ceaseless stream spewed* – emphasises unending quantity and the way it was gushing out
   - *fountained* – shows height and pressure
   - *strong backward drag of water pressure* – force of water in the hose
   - *the live hose snaking up* – like a dangerous reptile capable of rising up and striking because of the power of water inside; it sustains the metaphor begun by *live*, *dead* and *wound*

   b Power of the fire in Text 23A:
   - *fiercely alight* – makes it clear that the fire is violent and threatening
   - *alive with red fire* – fire has animated the building, making it dangerous and unpredictable
   - *a night express train* – the building has been turned into an unstoppable force
   - *bulge* – unpleasant word depicting how the fire moves and distorts
   - *like boiling jelly* – refers to both its extreme heat and its capacity to melt things in its path
   - *thirty blazing windows* – the fire can light up a huge expanse of building at the same time

   c Power of the falling wall in Text 23A:
   - *a long rattling crack of bursting brick and mortar perforated the moment* – the noise of the wall breaking up is like gunfire; the verb is a destructive one of making holes
   - *building heaved over towards us* – as if alive, it moved its gigantic weight to threaten the men
   - *Ton upon ton of red-hot brick hovering in the air* – an inordinate weight of fiery bricks were just hanging, like a bird of prey, waiting to plunge and kill those below
   - *pivoted over towards us* – had the power to twist itself and pursue the target
   - *a hundred solid tons* – emphasises weight and density
   - *the great mass hung over us and the moonlight was shut out* – the sheer size of the falling wall created a fearful darkness overhead
   - *slammed down on top of us* – the verb is one of destructive force
   - *cracking like automatic gunfire* – noise is again mentioned; the simile again equates the wall with a deadly weapon
   - *a thunderclap* – compares the noise of the falling wall to the deafening noise of a storm overhead (sustaining the metaphor of rumbling in paragraph 1)
   - *the bricks and mortar came tearing and burning* – shows the wall's violent movement and speed, and the damage it is about to inflict

3. The story's setting, action, violent diction and imagery, including all the senses, creates an atmosphere of danger and impending death, and a mood of inevitability and hopelessness against the odds that the fire or the building, or even the hoses, will get the better of the firemen. There is indeed a death, but the build-up and tension created through the descriptive language make the survival of the other three firemen seem like a miracle. (We know, however, that the persona must have survived to be telling the tale, and this is the drawback of using a first-person narrator.)

4. **a** The use of simple sentences makes the tone matter-of-fact, stresses cause and effect, and speeds up the narrative pace.

   b It also contributes to the voice and social class of the narrator, adding to the authenticity of the persona and the credibility of his account.

Unit 24: Just walking

Topic outline

- **Main skills:** narrative dialogue; narrative settings; narrative structure; narrative endings
- **Secondary skills:** imagery for atmosphere; identifying irony; inference; prediction
- **Outcome:** narrative composition; *analysis of writers' effects; *journal entry
- **Materials:** futuristic short story
- **Text:** Text 24: The pedestrian

Lesson plan

1. Assign the roles of narrator, character and police car and read Text 24 aloud in three suitable voices. (10)

2. Ask students to say what they think is going to happen to Leonard Mead, and why. (5)

3. Ask students to explain the effect of the extended dialogue in Text 24. (5)

4. Ask students to first underline all the words or phrases in paragraphs 1, 2 and 3 which describe the environment and atmosphere, and then to write a sentence which gives an overview of the combined overall effect of their choices. (10)

5. Give answers while students check their own. Choose students to read out their statements of overall effect. (5)

6. What can we tell about the narrator's feelings in Text 24? Ask students to make inferences, giving evidence to support them. Ask students to infer his attitudes to a) television and those who watch it, b) the police, and c) life in 2053. (5)

7. Ask students to identify and explain the effect of all the uses of irony in the text. (5)

8. Ask students, in pairs, to identify the different stages in the story. (5)

9. Invite answers and list stages on board. Discuss how each change adds tension. (5)

10. Ask students to write an opening paragraph to a story called 'The pedestrian', using the same devices of giving location, season, weather, time of day, and using mood images. They can choose whether to set it in the past, present or future. (10)

11. Tell students, in pairs, to swap paragraphs and comment on each other's, saying why they would or would not wish to read further in the story. Students should improve their openings where necessary. (10)

12. Ask students to plan the rest of their story started in Task 10, paying particular attention to the ending, which will affect the atmosphere and mood of everything that comes before. They should try to create a cliff-hanger ending as in Text 24, where the outcome has been prepared for and can be predicted, but is not narrated. (15)

Homework task

Write your story, for exam practice or coursework assignment, and check it carefully before you submit it. Make sure that everything in the story adds something to it and is specific not vague or general.

Additional tasks

a. Ask students to select three words or phrases from paragraph 4 and three from paragraph 6 of Text 24, and to write an explanation of the writer's effects.

b. Write Leonard Mead's final journal entry, using material from the story. It should reveal what has happened to him in the psychiatric centre and what he thinks is going to happen to him.

Text 24

The pedestrian

To enter out into that silence that was the city at eight o'clock of a misty evening in November, to put your feet upon that buckling concrete walk, to step over grassy seams and make your way, hands in pockets, through the silences, that was what Mr Leonard Mead most dearly loved to do. He would stand upon the corner of an intersection and peer down long moonlit avenues of sidewalk in four directions, deciding which way to go, but it really made no difference; he was alone in this world of 2053 A.D., or as good as alone, and with a final decision made, a path selected, he would stride off, sending patterns of frosty air before him like the smoke of a cigar.

Sometimes he would walk for hours and miles and return only at midnight to his house. And on his way he would see the cottages and homes with their dark windows, and it was not unequal to walking through a graveyard where only the faintest glimmers of firefly light appeared in flickers behind the windows. Sudden gray phantoms seemed to manifest upon inner room walls where a curtain was still undrawn against the night, or there were whisperings and murmurs where a window in a tomb-like building was still open.

Mr Leonard Mead would pause, cock his head, listen, look, and march on, his feet making no noise on the lumpy walk. For long ago he had wisely changed to sneakers when strolling at night, because the dogs in intermittent squads would parallel his journey with barkings if he wore hard heels, and lights might click on and faces appear and an entire street be startled by the passing of a lone figure, himself, in the early November evening.

On this particular evening he began his journey in a westerly direction, toward the hidden sea.

There was a good crystal frost in the air; it cut the nose and made the lungs blaze like a Christmas tree inside; you could feel the cold light going on and off, all the branches filled with invisible snow. He listened to the faint push of his soft shoes through autumn leaves with satisfaction, and whistled a cold quiet whistle between his teeth, occasionally picking up a leaf as he passed, examining its skeletal pattern in the infrequent lamplights as he went on, smelling its rusty smell.

'Hello, in there,' he whispered to every house on every side as he moved. 'What's up tonight on Channel 4, Channel 7, Channel 9? Where are the cowboys rushing, and do I see the United States Cavalry over the next hill to the rescue?'

The street was silent and long and empty, with only his shadow moving like the shadow of a hawk in mid-country. If he closed his eyes and stood very still, frozen, he could imagine himself upon the center of a plain, a wintry, windless Arizona desert with no house in a thousand miles, and only dry river beds, the street, for company.

'What is it now?' he asked the houses, noticing his wrist watch. 'Eight-thirty P.M.? Time for a dozen assorted murders? A quiz? A revue? A comedian falling off the stage?'

Was that a murmur of laughter from within a moon-white house? He hesitated, but went on when nothing more happened. He stumbled over a particularly uneven section of sidewalk. The cement was vanishing under flowers and grass. In ten years of walking by night or day, for thousands of miles, he had never met another person walking, not one in all that time.

He came to a cloverleaf intersection which stood silent where two main highways crossed the town. During the day it was a thunderous surge of cars, the gas stations open, a great insect rustling and a ceaseless jockeying for position as the scarab-beetles, a faint incense puttering from their exhausts, skimmed homeward to the far directions. But now these highways, too, were like streams in a dry season, all stone and bed and moon radiance.

He turned back on a side street, circling around toward his home. He was within a block of his destination when the lone car turned a corner quite suddenly and flashed a fierce white cone of light upon him. He stood entranced, not unlike a night moth, stunned by the illumination, and then drawn toward it.

A metallic voice called to him:

'Stand still. Stay where you are! Don't move!'

He halted.

'Put up your hands!'

'But–' he said.

'Your hands up! Or we'll shoot!'

The police, of course, but what a rare, incredible thing; in a city of three million, there was only one police car left, wasn't that correct? Ever since a year ago, 2052, the election year, the force had been cut down from three cars to one. Crime was ebbing; there was no need now for the police, save for this one lone car wandering and wandering the empty streets.

'Your name?' said the police car in a metallic whisper. He couldn't see the men in it for the bright light in his eyes.

'Leonard Mead,' he said.

'Speak up!'

'Leonard Mead!'

'Business or profession?'

'I guess you'd call me a writer.'

'No profession,' said the police car, as if talking to itself. The light held him fixed, like a museum specimen, needle thrust through chest.

'You might say that,' said Mr Mead.

He hadn't written in years. Magazines and books didn't sell anymore. Everything went on in the tomb-like houses at night now, he thought, continuing his fancy. The tombs, ill-lit by television light, where the people sat like the dead, the gray or multi-colored lights touching their faces, but never really touching them.

'No profession,' said the phonograph voice, hissing. 'What are you doing out?'

'Walking,' said Leonard Mead.

'Walking!'

'Just walking,' he said simply, but his face felt cold.

'Walking, just walking, walking?'

'Yes, sir.'

'Walking where? For what?'

'Walking for air. Walking to see.'

'Your address!'

'Eleven South Saint James Street.'

'And there is air in your house, you have an air conditioner, Mr Mead?'

'Yes.'

'And you have a viewing screen in your house to see with?'

'No.'

'No?' There was a crackling quiet that in itself was an accusation.

'Are you married, Mr Mead?'

'No.'

'Not married,' said the police voice behind the fiery beam. The moon was high and clear among the stars and the houses were gray and silent.

'Nobody wanted me,' said Leonard Mead with a smile.

'Don't speak unless you're spoken to!'

Leonard Mead waited in the cold night.

'Just walking, Mr Mead?'

'Yes.'

'But you haven't explained for what purpose.'

'I explained; for air, and to see, and just to walk.'

'Have you done this often?'

'Every night for years.'

The police car sat in the center of the street with its radio throat faintly humming.

'Well, Mr Mead,' it said.

'Is that all?' he asked politely.

'Yes,' said the voice. 'Here.' There was a sigh, a pop. The back door of the police car sprang wide. 'Get in.'

'Wait a minute, I haven't done anything!'

'Get in.'

'I protest!'

'Mr Mead.'

He walked like a man suddenly drunk. As he passed the front window of the car he looked in. As he had expected, there was no one in the front seat, no one in the car at all.

'Get in.'

He put his hand to the door and peered into the back seat, which was a little cell, a little black jail with bars. It smelled of riveted steel. It smelled of harsh antiseptic; it smelled too clean and hard and metallic. There was nothing soft there.

'Now if you had a wife to give you an alibi,' said the iron voice. 'But–'

'Where are you taking me?'

The car hesitated, or rather gave a faint whirring click, as if information, somewhere, was dropping card by punch-slotted card under electric eyes. 'To the Psychiatric Center for Research on Regressive Tendencies.'

He got in. The door shut with a soft thud. The police car rolled through the night avenues, flashing its dim lights ahead.

They passed one house on one street a moment later, one house in an entire city of houses that were dark, but this one particular house had all of its electric lights brightly lit, every window a loud yellow illumination, square and warm in the cool darkness.

'That's my house,' said Leonard Mead.

No one answered him.

The car moved down the empty riverbed streets and off away, leaving the empty streets with the empty sidewalks, and no sound and no motion all the rest of the chill November night.

From the short story 'The pedestrian', by Ray Bradbury, in *The Golden Apples of the Sun*.

Note: American spelling is used throughout this text.

Answers – Unit 24

3 Text 24: effect of extended dialogue:

The extended dialogue in Text 24 is the main method of establishing the lifestyle of the culturally, spiritually and physically arid city, the dangerous situation the pedestrian is in, and the character of Leonard Mead. It reveals how non-conformist he is, and how unacceptable this is to the controlling forces and those in charge of curing 'regressive tendencies'. He is not an equal participant in the dialogue. The multiple repetitions of the word 'walking' hammer home the irony and surrealism of walking being a crime. The contrast of speech styles conveys the different and irreconcilable ideologies of the human and the robotic car. The dialogue is in the form of an interrogation and it prefigures further, and worse, interrogations to come. The monosyllabic or very brief utterances make it clear that no real communication is taking place and that there is no understanding between the two 'speakers'. Finally, the robot does not bother to answer him.

4 Text 24: phrases conveying sense of environment and atmosphere:

The words *silence, misty, November, frosty, dark, graveyard, gray phantoms, tomb-like* and *lone* convey an overall effect of an environment which is colourless, empty and silent. The atmosphere is barren and lifeless because it lacks light and warmth. This imagery links with the cold, hard, metallic words used later in the story, and contrasts with Leonard's bright yellow and illuminated house. It is stressed that Leonard, the only visible human in the story, is alone whereas other living beings – those in groups inside houses and the dogs in *squads* – are plural, which suggest that he would have no chance of defeating his possible enemies, especially in such a harsh and unfeeling place.

6 Text 24: inferences:

a We can infer that the writer (as well as the persona) of the story does not approve of mindless viewing of whatever happens to be on television. We can infer this because the hostile police car does approve of 'viewing screens' and so the reader is positioned to disagree with it. Leonard refers to the trivial, valueless programmes which everyone but himself watches in their dim, tomb-like houses, having become lifeless 'grey phantoms', and which keep everyone captive in the evenings so that the city is silent and dead. There isn't even any crime any more because that requires initiative and non-conformity, and these qualities have died out because of the mind-numbing nature of television.

b The police are presented as unreasonable and tyrannical, since they arrest Leonard unnecessarily and are suspicious of all the things which make him different and interesting. Crime has been eradicated but at the expense of deadening the human spirit. He is interrogated in staccato questions and exclamations which are threatening and make the reader realise he will not be given a fair hearing when he arrives at the detention centre he is being taken to.

c Life in the cities of 2053 will be unattractive. Machines will rule by day and by night and there will be nothing to enjoy looking at, nothing creative being produced, and nothing soft to the touch or brightly lit: there will be total sensory deprivation. People will not go out or socialise but will sit in their concrete boxes every evening watching endless, pointless TV. Packs of dogs will roam the streets at night. There will be no place for individuals and anyone who doesn't conform will be regarded as a threat and removed from society. Everyone is expected to get married and no one lives alone.

7 Text 24: effect of the uses of irony:

Leonard stumbles and this indicates he is not going to survive. He is a pedestrian in a world which does not allow walking. The simile *not unlike a night moth, stunned by the illumination, and then drawn toward it* prefigures that he will be destroyed because of his preference for freedom, air and light. References to tombs, graveyards and the impaling of insects all imply that Leonard is going to die, and that he is an extinct species (*like a museum specimen, needle thrust through chest*). His association with soft and bright means that he cannot survive against the stronger elements of metallic hardness and universal greyness.

8 Text 24: stages in the story:

1. General scene-setting which moves into a particular evening creates expectation that something unpleasant/significant is going to happen on this occasion
2. He is nearly home when he is caught – irony of being almost safe before the danger appears
3. Introduction of another 'character' – dialogue is in the form of an interrogation, and the harsh voice and unreasonable questions and responses make it clear that there is a serious threat
4. He is physically trapped, drawn to the harsh light, then removed – he is no longer able to act freely and is being taken somewhere frightening
5. 'Cliff-hanger' device leaves the story open-ended to make reader infer what will happen next – doom-laden last sentence recaps the previous negative imagery

Argument writing structure

1 Introduction

State the topic and explain its current relevance.

2 Alternative view

Give the main arguments for the opposite viewpoint from the one you intend to argue.

3 Criticism of alternative view

Expose the weaknesses and fallacies of the alternative viewpoint.

4 Your view

Present a series of arguments to support your viewpoint, and support each with evidence in the form of statistics, examples, analogies, details, quotations or references to personal experience.

5 Conclusion

Conclude with a prophecy or warning of what you think future developments might be if the issue is not addressed urgently.

Aspects of narrative

a   Viewpoint

Occasionally writers employ the second person when writing narrative, but this is not advisable for exam students as it is hard to manage successfully and does not normally fit the composition title. The choice (if you are given one), therefore, is between a first-person and third-person narrator: they both have advantages and disadvantages which you need to be aware of before you start your story.

- First-person narrators can only know what they know themselves, and cannot say what other characters are thinking and feeling; they cannot end the story with their death, and it is a cliché to end with their becoming unconscious. On the other hand, a sense of authority and credibility can be conveyed by first-person narration.

- Third-person narration has the advantage of having an all-knowing narrator who can tell us what is going on in the heads of any of the characters (though it is still safer to stick to one perspective), but it loses the sense of directness which can be conveyed by the use of a first person who was allegedly involved in the action. The most important thing is for you to make a decision and stick to it, and not switch between different types of narration.

b   Voice

Whether the narrator is first or third person, the voice can be that of a character or witness to an event or sequence of events, and the persona or narrator may adopt a style different from that of the student's own style. This can be an effective means of characterisation, but you must be careful not to adopt a style which includes slang or swearing, or which uses overly simple language and sentence structures, however realistic, because these will be penalised in the assessment of complexity of style and maturity of vocabulary.

c   Characters

It is advisable to have either two or three characters in an exam-length story. More than three makes it hard for them to be adequately characterised and distinguished. It is necessary to explain the relationship between the characters. It is usual to give their name, age (roughly), some clue about their physical appearance and their personality, and their job if they have one and if it is relevant. These details allow the reader to picture the characters and engage with them.

d   Storyline

It is not really possible to think of a totally original story, nor do examiners expect it. All writers recycle, with differences of setting and character, a basic set of plots. It is acceptable for students to use an idea from a book or film, or to pretend that something which happened to someone else happened to them, provided that the detail is their own and the story has not just been lifted without adaptation or elaboration. Real historical events, as in the case of Text 21: The final choice, can also be turned into fiction-type narratives. You should not attempt a story which is too long or complex to be delivered in the time available: one event or a short series of events is all that can be managed effectively. A sequence of events should not be linked by 'And then' and treated as being equally important; they should be connected by a chain of cause and effect. Less important occurrences can be skipped over so that the focus is on the major event, which is the one causing the crisis.

e   Tense

Although it is possible to write an effective narrative in the present tense, it is not advisable for exam purposes. So often the student forgets they have begun in the present and switches to the past, or keeps switching between the two, since it is unnatural to write about something which is supposed to have already happened in the present, and therefore difficult to remember and sustain.

Aspects of narrative (cont.)

f Structure

The ordering of events is normally, and more safely, chronological. However, an ambitious and capable student who wants to do well will need to consider using devices such as time lapses, flashbacks, and starting at the end. Some writers start with the climax and then fill in the back story leading to that point, so the story has a circular structure. Another narrative device, used for the opening and the ending, is to frame the story within another story. For instance, finding a diary many years later and putting it back in its secret place at the end of the narrative could frame the reading of it and the story it contains. In any case, characters have to be introduced before their problem can be explained, which precedes the climax which is followed by the resolution. The climax should come about three quarters of the way through the narrative: too soon and insufficient tension will have been created; too late and the ending will seem rushed and unprepared.

g Openings

First sentences have to grip the reader and engage their curiosity from the beginning. If readers cannot place themselves in a setting, they will feel unable to visualise the scene and relate to what is happening. Although the rest of the narrative is likely to have a logical/chronological structure, there is a choice of types of narrative opening:

- the setting gives location, surroundings, time, place, weather, season
- one or two main characters can be described as an introduction to an event or action involving them
- a shocking or intriguing opening statement provokes immediate interest
- starting in the middle of an event engages the reader's attention
- starting in the middle of a conversation makes the reader curious about the speakers and topic.

h Description

Narratives need some description as well as action. Unless the reader can always visualise the scene and the characters, they will become disengaged. However, too much description slows down the pace and reduces the tension. Details should be given where they are necessary to create a sense of character, place and atmosphere, and to convey originality and credibility. For instance, it is better to say exactly what someone ate or where they walked, rather than just that they had a meal or went for a walk.

i Dialogue

Dialogue should be used, but only sparingly, for dramatic effect or for significant exchanges between characters. It is safer for dialogues to be between only two characters at a time, and probably only two of the characters in a short story need to speak directly to each other. It is difficult to manage more than that, or to create distinctive voices for them. When direct speech is used, it should be set out correctly within double quotation marks, with a new line for every change of speaker, otherwise it becomes impossible for the reader to follow and marks will be lost for inaccuracies of punctuation.

j Endings

Endings have to satisfy the reader by being both slightly unpredictable and yet credible in the way they have been foreshadowed. Sometimes a twist can be used to catch the reader off-guard and provide humour, irony or surprise, but this must be believable in the context and not a sudden turn of events which is not consistent with the previous characterisation or situation. It is possible not to conclude a story but leave it at the climactic point of greatest tension as a 'cliff-hanger'. This has to be managed carefully so that it is clearly deliberate and does not give the impression that the student has run out of time or is avoiding having to provide a resolution.

Descriptive writing structure

1	**Setting**
	Descriptive compositions need some kind of framework to give them a shape and logical progression to involve the reader. If you are describing a place, it is appropriate to set the general scene: location, surroundings, atmosphere, season, weather, time of day. Either time (a short period only) or distance can be used as the structure for a descriptive composition.

2	**Positioning**
	The observer takes up a position with regard to the object or place being described, e.g. they are standing outside a room or walking towards a market. This arouses interest in what will be revealed on closer inspection, e.g. when the gate into the secret garden or the chest in the attic is opened. Visual and acoustic images are used in this section to draw the reader in. If time is the framework, then this must be established, e.g. daylight is beginning to fade at dusk or storm clouds are gathering.

3	**Approaching**
	The observer moves towards the object or place being described, which gives the description logical progression. New details can be revealed because of the closer proximity, e.g. as the view of the beach becomes clearer. At this stage the sense of smell can be added to sight and sound. Alternatively, time has moved on, e.g. darkness is creeping into the sky and changing the landscape.

4	**Arriving**
	The observer is now part of the scene, e.g. in the heart of the street market, paddling in the sea, or in contact with the object in the chest. Close-up details of sight and sound can be used here, as well as the sense of touch, and taste can also be implied, e.g. food smells, the salty water. Alternatively, time has moved on, e.g. it is now night and the new sky and atmosphere can be described, or the storm reaches its climax.

5	**Leaving**
	The observer leaves the scene or the object, with or without a backward glance. The initial scene may be restored at the end of the description, or alternatively it may be going home time for the people on the beach or at the market, so that the final scene is the opposite of the opening one. Reference to either time or distance can be used as closure.

Formal letter structure

1	**Opening**
	Address your letter to *Dear + the name or job title of the person you have been asked to write to*, followed by a comma, then start a new line for the opening paragraph under the comma. (*Note:* in examinations you are not required to put an address, date or valediction).

2	**Paragraph 1: Introduction**
	Why are you writing? Give the general purpose and context only (e.g. to complain, apply, request, disagree) and an indication of what you are responding to (e.g. a recent holiday or a letter in last week's newspaper)r.

3	**Paragraph 2: Details of situation**
	Give previous history of the relevant event, or your background or experience for an application. Say what happened exactly if you are making a complaint, or focus directly on the text you are arguing with. This section should include specific factual data, such as numbers and other details.

4	**Paragraph 3: Further development**
	Give further support to your claim or request, including evaluative comments. Summarise the current situation and give reasons why your letter should be given consideration (e.g. other problems which occurred with your holiday accommodation, or how well you fulfil the job-requirements).

5	**Final paragraph: Future action**
	Say what you wish to happen next (e.g. that you look forward to being called for interview, or expect to receive some compensation as soon as possible). Suggest, firmly but politely, what may happen if you do not receive a response to a complaint, or if your views are not agreed with.

Formal report structure

1 Context

Indicate in the introduction what you are reporting on, whom and for what purpose the report is being written. The person(s) receiving the report, as well as the writer of it, is likely to be someone in an official position, and the formal and factual style must reflect this.

2A Type A report (examination and judgement of competitors)

If bullet points or names are provided to help you structure a formal report, each should be addressed and extended into a paragraph which uses ideas and details from the text to support your evaluation of the choices (e.g. to examine the qualifications of different candidates for a job). You should select both favourable and unfavourable information for each choice to show that you are capable of arriving at a fair judgement.

2B Type B report (record and evaluation of one subject)

If the report requires a chronological structure (e.g. if it is a witness statement or account of an experience or series of events), then the information must be presented in paragraphs in the order in which it occurred, with the timings made clear throughout. Your style will be factual and objective.

3 Recommendation

Whichever type of report you are writing, you will be producing evidence for the forming of a final judgement by yourself or by your audience. A witness statement will not end with a personal opinion – though the evidence should speak for itself – but most reports will take a final position on the topic and reach a conclusion either by giving a preference for one of the candidates or a recommendation for a future course of action.

Journal content

An informative and entertaining journal entry contains a mixture of the elements below.

1 Narration	
Say what happened on the occasion you are recording in your journal, and explain who was involved.	

2 Description	
Make the setting clear by giving details of time and place. Indicate mood and atmosphere, perhaps using imagery. Characters also need to be briefly described with a few telling details of appearance and behaviour.	

3 Reflection	
Say what thoughts the incident or scene provoked in your mind. Memories or comparisons may be appropriate. Consider why the occasion was significant and worth recording.	

4 Emotion	
Say what your participation in the occasion made you and others feel. Which aspects evoked an emotional response?	

5 Quotation	
Someone may have said something memorable or otherwise significant. You can record it as direct speech for dramatic or humorous effect, or to establish character.	

Magazine article structure

1 Topic

The article introduces the issue, which may be something topical and in the news or recently published research, a proposal which has been put forward by a government or other agency, or the description of the person that the article will concern. Unlike a news report, which is purely informative, and a speech, which is argumentative, a magazine article is mainly a form of discursive writing.

2 Background

The article is likely to fill in the past history of the person or event which the article concerns, so that readers are fully aware of the necessary facts and reason why the article has been written and what has led to the current state of affairs.

3 Discussion

The article is likely to return to the present-day situation at this point, discussing and giving different viewpoints of the person or event, with details, examples and quotations, and making comparisons with the past or with similar topics. Though the writer's own viewpoint may be inferred, alternative views must be given equal weight and other voices heard.

4 Prediction

At this point the article may deal with the future developments or predicted outcome of the present situation (e.g. that a person will go on to become even more famous and successful, or that a current situation will develop in a particular direction).

5 Conclusion

The article needs a neat conclusion, which may be an ironic reference or humorous comment, an evaluation of the different viewpoints, a reference back to the beginning of the article, or an apt quotation.

Narrative writing structure

This is a simple chronological structure. More complex structures involve flashbacks, forward time jumps, dual narration, starting in the middle of dialogue or action, or a cliffhanger or ambiguous ending.

1	**Setting**
	Describe the location, surroundings, atmosphere, time of day, season, weather.

2	**Characters**
	Introduce up to three characters by describing their appearance and behaviour. Make their relationships with one another clear.

3	**Problem**
	Create a situation requiring decision or action. Build up conflict, perhaps using dialogue and disagreement between characters.

4	**Climax**
	Narrate an event or series of events leading to a crisis. Time pressure may be a factor in causing suspense and tension.

5	**Resolution**
	Describe the outcome, which may involve an ironic twist or comment.

News report structure

News reports follow a unique structure of referring first to the present, then to the past and finally to the future.

Headline

1 News event

What has just happened? When exactly did it happen? Where did it happen? Who was involved?

2 Background

Why did it happen? Give the history and lead-up to this event and mention its supposed causes.

3 Account of event

How did it happen? Give the details of the stages of the actual event and say what is still happening now.

4 Quotations

In a mixture of direct and indirect speech, give the relevant statements of participants, witnesses, police officers, medical workers, etc.

5 Predictions

What will happen next? Explain the likely consequences of the event, refer to future investigations, and mention any procedures that will be put in place.

Rhetorical devices

A rhetorical device is a technique of using language in a way that increases the persuasiveness of a piece of text by evoking an emotional or intellectual response in the audience.

The following devices are commonly used in argumentative writing. The reader should be aware of them, as they manipulate them into agreeing with the writer or speaker and may distract attention from the poor quality of the actual arguments.

addressing reader as 'you' – for intimacy and presupposition that the reader will agree; also use of inclusive 'we', and reference to opposition as 'they'

antithesis – to make it seem a simple, two-sided issue

aposiopesis (…) – unfinished utterance to make the audience imagine and supply that which has not been said

colloquialisms – to create conversational effect to invite reader trust

double structures – to strengthen the point

emotive vocabulary – language used to evoke a strong feeling (e.g. guilt, pity or revulsion)

exclamations – to create the impression that the writer feels passionate or shocked about the issue

euphemisms – language which avoids directly naming something unpleasant or undesirable

hyperbole – to increase the apparent power of the argument or evidence

imperatives – to sound authoritative and superior

insulting vocabulary – to ridicule opponents

irony – to create humour and appreciation

juxtaposition – to make a stark contrast which forces a comparison to be made

lists – to give the impression that a lot of data exists to support the writer's view

litotes – to express a positive in a negative (often double negative) form (e.g. 'not displeasing')

meiosis – to understate in order to draw attention to its opposite (e.g. 'it cost a few pennies')

modern idioms and fashionable phrases – to show the writer is up-to-date

non-sentences – to make the content stand out and sound decisive

repetition – to emphasise point to make it memorable, using same or different words (tautology)

rhetorical questions – to engage and involve the reader

sarcasm – to mock opponents so that the reader will not wish to identify with them

short categorical statements – to give the impression that there can be no argument

triple structures – to make the content striking and effective; third element is often climactic (i.e. longest or most serious word or point of the three).

Success criteria

Tick that you have fulfilled the following list of criteria after completing a piece of work. You need to be familiar with this checklist before you plan and/or draft a response. If there is something here that you didn't do and can't tick, try to put it right before submitting your work for assessment. It is possible to improve responses, even after writing the final version, by crossing out and replacing words and by using asterisks (*) and caret (^) marks to add material.

Reading

Content

Did you…

- skim and scan the passage before answering? ☐
- answer the whole question? ☐
- use different material in different answers? ☐
- focus fully on the question? ☐
- use the structure and content support provided? ☐
- develop ideas where required? ☐
- refer closely to the passage? ☐
- give details where appropriate? ☐
- select only relevant material from the passage? ☐
- demonstrate understanding of implicit meaning? ☐
- show awareness of the writer's style? ☐
- evaluate the effectiveness of the writer's style? ☐
- follow the length guidelines? ☐

Expression

Did you…

- answer the question concisely? ☐
- answer the question in full sentences? ☐
- use own words when required? ☐
- write in the appropriate style for the response genre? ☐
- organise your material into a sequence? ☐
- give overall structure to your response? ☐
- check your responses for clarity? ☐

Success criteria (cont.)

Writing

Content

Did you…

- convey understanding of the ideas in the passage? ☐
- evaluate the ideas in the passage? ☐
- refer closely to points in the passage? ☐
- avoid repetition of ideas? ☐
- stay within the length guidelines? ☐
- show awareness of audience? ☐
- show awareness of purpose? ☐
- stay focused on the task? ☐

Expression

Did you…

- order response material effectively? ☐
- link ideas within and between paragraphs? ☐
- use a range of vocabulary? ☐
- use a variety of sentence structures? ☐
- use the characteristics/devices of the response genre? ☐
- choose precise words? ☐
- use the appropriate register of vocabulary? ☐
- adopt a suitable tone of voice? ☐
- sustain an appropriate viewpoint? ☐
- avoid repetition of vocabulary? ☐
- avoid lifting phrases from the passage? ☐
- use clear and concise language? ☐
- use fluent and mature expression? ☐
- use correct spelling, grammar and punctuation? ☐
- use paragraphs in continuous writing? ☐
- put quotations or speech into inverted commas? ☐
- check your work for mistakes? ☐

Summary writing process

1 Skim-reading

Read passage for gist of time, place, genre and topic, identifying unknown words to be worked out using one of the four methods: syllabic breakdown; similarity to another English word; similarity to a word in another language; guessing from context.

2 Scan-reading

After reading the summary question and underlining its key words, return to passage and highlight the relevant material for each part of the question. Select only the essential word or phrase. Examples, repetitions, direct speech, figurative language and trivial details should be excluded.

3 Transfer to plan

Transfer the highlighted material to make a list of all the relevant points, changing some of the words and phrases into your own words at the same time. Some technical words cannot be changed and some individual words from the passage may be used, but long phrases should not be copied.

4 Structuring the plan

The points in the plan should be grouped logically and reordered – to make it possible to combine more than one point per sentence – using brackets and arrows. This will make it possible to get all the points into a response within the word limit.

5 Writing the summary

The summary should be written in an informative style, in complex sentences (avoiding 'and'). Check afterwards for clarity and concision, and for unnecessary repetition, all of which affect the writing mark. The summary should be purely objective and without narrative, comment, introduction or conclusion.

Writers' effects process

1	**Skim-reading**
	Read the passage or paragraph to get a sense of time, place, topic, genre, tone and atmosphere.

2	**Scanning and selecting**
	After reading the question on writers' effects, and underlining the key word in each part of the question, return to the passage and highlight or underline all possible relevant language choices. Identify and highlight only the key word or phrase which is particularly effective, not a large 'chunk' of text (e.g. *fox-like face*, *pearly*).

3	**Transferring to a plan**
	Transfer the best of the chosen quotations to a list (depending on how many you have been asked to give), dividing them between the two sections (if you have been asked to look at more than one section). Choose those which are unusual or particularly powerful and figurative, so that there is something to say about them. Against each choice explain its meaning and the effect it conveys in this context. Treat each short choice separately and avoid 'clumping' (i.e. giving a list and treating them as a group). Explore the similes and metaphors. You may use literary terms if they are relevant and accurate, but you still need to explain the precise effect of the example you have chosen and how it works in this particular context. For example, 'fox-like' suggests that he has a thin face and pointed nose; 'pearly' conveys the idea of the opaque and shiny whiteness found in oyster shells.

4	**Developing the response**
	Look again at the relevant paragraphs of the passage, this time at the use of such devices as repetition, contrast, question marks or exclamation marks, sentence lengths, sound effects and what these convey to the reader. Comment at the beginning or end of each section of your response on how the vocabulary choices link and combine to create a sustained overall effect. For example, 'The combined effect of these references to cold and dark is to create an uncomfortable and tense atmosphere'. Remember to include non-linguistic features as well. For example, in the sentence 'Perhaps one of the most weird and fascinating characters I met during my travels was the Rose-beetle Man', the delayed object creates suspense.

5	**Writing the response**
	The response should be written in continuous prose, putting one of the selected quotations in inverted commas within each sentence and explaining its effect, and not repeating unnecessarily the words 'the effect is …'. The whole response is expected to be no more than 300 words, expressed concisely but exploring fully the connotations and associations for the reader.

Answers to coursebook questions

Note: In some cases more than one correct answer is possible, or students have been asked to write their answers in their own words. Some examples are supplied but they are not prescriptive.

All sample answers in this title were written by the author. In examinations, the way marks are awarded may be different.

Unit 1

A Identifying paragraph topics

1 and 2 Students' own answers.

3 Reading task.

4
  a The most noticeable features of the scenery are the volcano, the ravines/valleys and the coastline/beaches.
  b Tourists can spend their time on the beach, walking/hiking, shopping or sight-seeing.
  c The temperature is mild, all year round.
  d The economy relies on tourism and there is some fruit and flower export.
  e There are archaeological sites, ancient and modern buildings, wildlife centres and scenic villages.

5 *Tenerife*; *landscapes*; *climate*; *tourism*; *activities*; *agriculture*; *sites*; *sight-seeing*

6 and 10 Cape Town

(With its majestic Table Mountain backdrop), Cape Town is one of the most beautiful cities in the world. A harmonious blend of architectural styles reflects the tastes of the past as well as today's more functional requirements. (Between the high-rise office blocks, Edwardian and Victorian buildings have been meticulously preserved, and many outstanding examples of Cape Dutch architecture are found). Narrow, cobblestone streets and the strongly Islamic presence of the Bo-Kaap enhance the cosmopolitan ambiance of the city. //

(Cape Town's shopping options invite you to endlessly browse). Elegant malls, (such as the Victoria Wharf at the V & A Waterfront), antique shops, craft markets, flea markets and art galleries abound. Specialist boutiques offer an enticing array of unusual items (not readily obtainable elsewhere). One of Cape Town's biggest tourist attractions, the Waterfront, (evokes images of the early activities of the harbour. Much of its charm lies in the fact that this busy commercial harbour) is set in the midst of a huge entertainment venue with pubs, restaurants, shops, craft markets, theatres and movies. //

Table Mountain is undeniably the biggest tourist attraction in South Africa, (drawing local holidaymakers as well as tourists from the four corners of the globe. The summit can be reached by trails or cable-car, but mountaineers do it the hard way. On a clear day, the spectacular views from the summit (1,086 m above sea level) stretch across the mountainous spine of the Cape Peninsula and beyond Table Bay and Robben Island.//

(Robben Island, which lies about 11 kilometres north of Cape Town, has, over the years, become synonymous with the anti-apartheid struggle in South Africa). It was here that activists, such as Nelson Mandela and Walter Sisulu, among many others, were imprisoned because of their opposition to apartheid. (The historical importance of Robben Island (meaning 'Seal Island') can be gauged by its designation as a cultural heritage site). //

(Stretching away from Table Bay Harbour), the Atlantic seafront features virgin beaches along undeveloped frontages to the north, and the densely populated Sea Point to the south, (leading on to the Clifton, Camps Bay and Llandudno beauty spots, among others). The western coastline is characterised by rocky outcrops (and beautiful beaches). Major (national and international) windsurfing competitions are held at Bloubergstrand. Seal watching is an amusing diversion. Boat trips (around the harbour and along the coast) are always popular.

7   The five paragraphs each reflect a change of topic.

8   Atmospheric centre; Relaxing by the harbour; View from Table Mountain; Mandela's island; Coastal activities

9   Cape Town has beautiful natural features of rock and sea, and a range of leisure activities and pastimes to suit everyone.

10 The material you would not use in a summary about the city is underlined in the text for Task 6 above. The excluded material consists of repetition, examples and minor details.

11 The typical features of guide books are: dates and statistics; lists; place names; references to agriculture, architecture, landscape, industry, transport, and local crafts; use of the impersonal 'one' or 'you'; adjectives before nouns; passive voice; compound and complex sentences.

B Selecting summary points

1   Reading task.

2   *monumental*: imposing, impressive
    hieroglyphic: symbols, signs
    incorporating: encompassing, including
    debris: rubble, litter
    devour: consume, swallow

3   a *cluster of mud buildings* (the assonance creates an effective picture of the primitiveness of the dwellings); *gigantic quarry* (this suggests huge and deliberate excavation works over a long period of time)

    b *rich paintings* (the description conveys the colourfulness and preciousness of the decorations); *complex inscriptions* (this reveals that there are words as well as pictures, of an unexpectedly intricate kind)

    c *rich golden brown of the lower sky spills onto the surface of the Nile*; *intense amber*; *glow* (the sustained image conveys the spread of a golden orange colour from sky to water to land, encompassing the whole landscape)

4 and 5

Key phrase	Point
barren, rubble-strewn desert	wasteland
in upper Egypt	south of capital
Luxor station is tastefully monumental	has elaborately decorated station
we drive along the river to find our boat	is on the Nile
on the West Bank opposite the city	is on the East Bank

6   The Luxor passage has some of the features of guide books and is similar in content, but it is a personal account and belongs to the genre of travel writing, which aims to entertain as well as inform. Among the factual information, there are references to people, the use of direct speech, and feelings are described. The pronouns 'I'/'me' and 'we'/'us' are used. The structure of the piece is the chronological journey taken by the writer.

7   a Tenerife, the largest of the Canary Islands, has a rocky landscape and moderate climate. It is a tourist destination offering a range of leisure activities, interesting sites and opportunities for sight-seeing.

    b The southern Egyptian city of Luxor, situated on the East Bank of the Nile, is surrounded by desert. It has an impressively grand station.

C Summary technique

1 Students' own answers.

2 Reading task.

3 Robinson Crusoe is stranded on what he calls the Island of Despair in autumn 1659, after his ship sinks in a storm and he manages to swim ashore as the only survivor.

4 **(Example answer)**

Robinson Crusoe <u>needs</u> shelter, tools and a means of light, and he faces the <u>difficulties</u> of protecting himself from wild animals and natives, and of finding enough food to survive. His is <u>afraid</u> of being attacked, and is <u>disappointed</u> by his efforts to hunt goats, and by how much work is involved in building a strong barricade around his shelter.

5 **(Example answer)**

He may: run out of food; be attacked by something or someone; lose his dog; become weak/ill and unable to work; become lonely/despairing.

Unit 2

A Writing style choices

1 Students' own answers.

2 Reading task.

3 a Book reviews are published to give guidance to readers about books they might enjoy or find interesting.

   b Reviews are written by specialist book reviewers employed by the newspaper to inform the readership of the latest books that have been published.

   c People who enjoy books read the reviews to learn which books might suit them.

   d The newspaper benefits by retaining readers who like this feature; readers benefit by discovering books they might wish to acquire; publishers benefit in having their latest publications publicised and, hopefully, recommended to increase sales; writers benefit from the royalties they'll received on the resulting sales.

   e Someone who enjoys historical non-fiction accounts of dramatic and dangerous expeditions.

4 (Example answer)

This book tells the dramatic story of the disastrous voyage of the *Karluk*, the unsuitable ship that led a foolhardy expedition to the Arctic in 1913 with its naive passengers and Captain Bob Bartlett. Chief of the scientists on board was the anthropologist Vilhjalmur Stefansson, who was convinced that he would discover a lost continent beneath the ice and became world-famous.

When the ship predictably becomes trapped in the Alaskan ice fields with the coming of winter, the fear and tension mount as the passengers realise they are doomed and the conflict deepens between the uncaring and treacherous Stefansson and the dedicated ship's captain.

There are horrific descriptions of the atmosphere on board the tiny stricken vessel and of their final attempts to cross the deadly ice after hunger and disaster force them to abandon ship and try to reach land and safety.

5

Event	Date/time
The *Jeanette* crushed	1881
Last of the *Jeanette* crew dies	140 days later
Amundsen reaches the North Pole	1912
Scott dies near the South Pole	1912
The *Karluk* sets out from Canada	17 June 1913
The *Karluk* trapped in ice near the North Pole	Winter 1913
The *Karluk* crushed and abandoned	10 January 1914
Shackleton dies on board the Quest	1922

6 Reading task.

7 a tense: present/present perfect/past simple

   b register: generally formal

   c vocabulary level: mixture of colloquial and sophisticated

   d sentence length: mixed, but mainly short

   e sentence type: simple/compound

   f content: facts and feelings

8 (Example answer)

November 3rd 1913

The inevitable has happened. The sea has begun to freeze and is closing in on the ship. It will not be able to withstand the pressure in the end. It is not the kind of ship, that we should ever have set out in for this expedition, being only a wooden whaler too old and small for the job, but Stefansson did not listen to my advice on this matter, as indeed he does not on any matter. He completely disregards my professional expertise and experience. The man is consumed by a fantasy. There is no lost continent beneath the ice. How I wish we had never left our homes in British Columbia!

December 5th 1913

We are now in a perilous situation, running out of supplies. The morale of the crew and passengers is very low. Everyone feels that we are doomed. This unforgiving place at the end of the Earth has claimed many brave lives already, so we are unlikely to survive. The day is spent in the library, gloomily reading through accounts of previously failed expeditions to this cruel region. We are having great difficulty in keeping warm. Stefansson has become impossible, arguing aggressively with me whenever I make a suggestion and treating us all with contempt, as if he does not care at all about the terrible danger he has brought us into. He insists we shall stay on board the ship and wait for the spring thaw to continue our voyage.

January 10th 1914

Stefansson has gone. He lost his nerve. The supplies have run out and he went with a dog-sledge and a few men to try to find or hunt for food. It is no surprise that he has not returned. This morning what we had been fearing and waiting for finally happened: with a terrible groaning and shuddering of the *Karluk*, the ice broke through the hull and we are being slowly crushed, just like the *Endurance* and the *Jeanette*. We must all leave now, and hope that fate will be kind to us. We cannot wait 140 days to die of cold and starvation. My concern is only for my crew, whom I feel responsible for leading into this horrible place.

I must try to make amends by making whatever sacrifices are necessary to preserve their lives, to make up for Stefansson's treachery. I do not feel that Stefansson deserves a good end.

B Comparing texts

1 Students' own answers.

2 Reading task.

3 **Similarities:** the temperature and the ice were the enemies; a decision had to be taken; the motivation was to achieve fame; the main characters changed their minds; the main characters seemed obsessed and willing to take risks; both were controversial figures.

Differences: the sea and the mountain were different natural challenges; the crew of the *Karluk* were inexperienced, innocent victims; Hargreaves achieved her goal, but Stefansson did not; Hargreaves perished, but Stefansson lived and continued to explore; one was a man and one a woman with family; she was charming and likeable and he was charmless and disliked.

4 (Example answers)

    a talkative, sometimes extrovert, sometimes introvert, emotional, selfish, driven, inconsistent, indecisive, affable, insecure, determined, brave, foolish, tormented, irresponsible, ambitious

    b contractions, colloquialisms, simple and compound sentences, questions and exclamations, everyday vocabulary, long paragraphs

5 (Example answer)

Dear Mum and Dad

I know you are anxiously waiting to hear what is happening here at K2 base camp and what I have decided to do. It was deeply disappointing to have trained for so long and come so far to discover that the conditions here are not suitable to make the attempt to get to the summit. I have waited six weeks for the rain, wind and cloud to disappear, and failed twice already to get to the top. But there must be a break in the weather soon, and you will no doubt think I'm crazy, but I have decided to stay another week, in the hope that the weather will clear and I can give it another try. Third time lucky! I really need to prove to myself that I can do this, and I may not get another chance. I have thought very long and hard about this, but I just can't bear to give up now, when I am so close to achieving my life's ambition.

I am giving this letter to Celsi, who is now leaving. Celsi has been such a good comrade and I am sorry to see him go. I was intending to leave with him, and I packed my things last night, but when I woke up this morning the decision I made last night felt wrong.

Please try to understand, and to help Tom and Kate to understand, too. I miss them so much and half of me desperately wants to come home to them. And to you. But I also want them to be proud of their mother, and for all women to realise what is possible and see me as an inspiration. I live to climb, and I know I can do this. I must not be defeated by my own weakness; I must pursue my dream, whatever the outcome.

My love to you all,

Alison

6   a   The blog contains colloquial language, such as shortened forms (*it's*, *he's*) and fashionable idioms (*ended up in tragedy*, *this historic undertaking*, *plugged*), casually sexist language (*lady*), repetition (*story* at the beginning) and hyperbole (*legendary*, *greatest… ever*, *incredibly*). There are several non-sentences (second and third 'sentences' and beginning of final paragraph), missing commas (*Alison's son Tom Ballard*), grammar errors (*it almost seems like he's chasing her*) and comma-splicing (*Tom Ballard is young, he's now 26 years old*). There is generally an economy of expression (long list of mountains, shortage of verbs and connectives (use of colons instead).

The article contains polysyllabic vocabulary (*supplementary*, *monumental*, *inevitably*), uncommon vocabulary (*ardent*, *paradigm*, *mercurial*), imagery (*wind-tossed*, *plucked*, *racked*), adverbs (*bitterly*, *utterly*, *desperately*) and rhetorical questions (first and last paragraphs). There ia a range of sentences structures, including some that begin with *And*, *But* and *So*. The paragraph transition phrases are time references (*At 6.30 p.m.*, *An hour later*).

   b   The blog does not follow a chronological structure. It introduces the mother and briefly refers to what happened to her, then moves to her son and continues to focus on him. It finishes in the author's own words, with a long quotation in colloquial diction and style, in the form of an interview response.

The article gives a mainly chronological account of the final days of the climb and its outcome, followed by an evaluation of Hargreaves' character. It gives facts, details and statistics (*12,000 ft*, *15 minutes*), includes many short, integrated quotations (*She was going home*, *one more try*) and includes references to the other climbers.

   c   The blog is not governed by expectations of formality or accuracy. It appeals to a younger audience that wants to know what is happening instantly, without a build-up of suspense but with a focus on the personal angle of feelings and relationships, which are given more prominence than facts. Brevity, immediacy and modernity are the priorities, not correctness of expression.

The article is a formal publication which must be accurate in its use of language and which is aimed at a mature, educated audience. It attempts to create drama and tension through the structure by delaying information until the end of the sentence, through the multiple use of dramatic adverbs to evoke emotion and by using compound connectives as sentence openers for impact (because these are rarely used in formal writing). The opening sentence is intended to engage the reader through the creation of suspense.

C Audience awareness

1   Reading task.

2   **(Example answer)**

Hello everyone.

I'm here to tell you about an exciting programme of outdoor pursuits which gives you opportunities to stretch yourself physically, to acquire leadership skills and to have amazing adventures. It will also give you a foundation of practical skills and a set of friends for the rest of your life.

It's called the International Award and has three levels – bronze, silver and gold – depending on your age. All of them are character-building and involve helping in the community, taking part in physical activities and going on expeditions.

You'll meet lots of people of your age, from many different backgrounds, and join them in challenging and rewarding activities. Not only will you enjoy yourself doing things like playing sport and camping, but you will also get a sense of confidence, satisfaction and reward from being in the programme. And you'll end up with something valuable to put on your CV to impress future educational institutions and employers. Everybody likes a team player!

3 Presentation task.

4 Reading task.

5 **(Example answers)**

- imperative verbs: *take us up on our offer*; *witness complete peace*; *sit out…*, *relive…*, *walk along… transfer…*
- questions: *Dare you try it?*
- exclamations: *The most exciting experience you'll ever have! …; unexpected surprises for the unwary! …; so you need to be fit! ….; conquering the mighty Zambezi River!*
- clichés: *breathtakingly beautiful*; *unexpected surprises*; *plenty of opportunity*; *relive the memories*
- short/non-sentences: *Something to suit everyone*; *A chance for you to explore…*
- repetition: *dramatic*; *pristine*
- superlatives and intensifiers: *The most*; *the first*; *the best*; *at the forefront*; *very*; *really*; *directly*; *exclusively*.
- personal pronouns: <u>you</u> *need to be fit*; *take us up on* <u>our</u> *offer*; <u>your</u> *day's rafting*
- evocative/emotive adjectives: *amazing*; *clear*; *intrepid*; *dramatic*; *successful*; *famous*; *scenic*; *glittering velvet*
- alliterative phrases: *breathtakingly beautiful*; *watch the wildlife*; *peace and privacy*
- rhyme: *splash and dash*; *beaches of the Zambezi*; *amazing day*; *complete peace*
- numbers: *$132*, *5 days*, *minimum of 4 required*

6 **(Example answers)**

Hi Karim

I've just come across an internet ad for white water rafting courses at Victoria Falls. I've been hoping for ages we could do something like this and now I think we're finally old enough for our parents to let us go. They know how keen we are on water sports!

The company has been running these courses for 28 years – it was the first one in the country to offer rafting trips – so I'm sure they are reliable. They give you a certificate at the end of the course! It would give us something to look forward to for when we've finished our exams. It's not just the action that sounds exciting, but apparently the setting is really amazing, too, so we can take loads of photos and maybe do some exploring.

There are lots of different options: I fancy one of the overnight trips because then we get to do some camping, and camping is always fun – remember the last time, on the school trip? This time it would be on a beach and our group would be the only people there, sitting around a campfire and having a party after our day's rafting; we can even do without a tent and sleep under the stars – I've always wanted to do that. This option needs a minimum of four but I'm sure we can think of another couple of people who'd be interested in such a special experience. You get to walk back after breakfast next morning. It is quite a demanding hike but we're both fit and like a challenge.

Do you think your parents will let you go? Tell them it's not that expensive, and we'd really like to prove we can do something on our own. Let me know asap and I'll arrange the booking.

Denzel [301 words]

7 and 8 Students' own answers.

Unit 3

A The language of description – using adjectives

1 A narrative tells a story through a series of events (plot) involving characters. Description is a detailed account of something witnessed or experienced. Both may or may not be fictional.

2 **a** Descriptive writing must be based on the truth. False

   b You need a wide vocabulary to be good at descriptions. True

   c It is difficult to make descriptive writing interesting. True

   d Descriptive writing is the easier choice. False

   e You should use only the sense of sight when describing something. False

   f Descriptive writing doesn't need a structure. False

   g You don't need to write in full sentences for description. False

   h Descriptions are often written in the present tense. True

3 (Example answers)
   - loneliness: grey, chilly, empty, blank
   - decay: dark green, rusty, mouldy, damp, smelly
   - celebration: gold, bright, glittering, loud, joyous, vibrant, lively
   - tranquillity: white, soothing, serene, gentle, relaxing
   - fear: black, suffocating, terrifying, petrifying, palpitating
   - love: red, warm, embracing, glowing, reassuring, cosy

4 Students' own answers.

5 (Example answers)

   a The students went on a stimulating/beneficial/productive/enjoyable day trip.

   b The weather yesterday was so cataclysmic/stormy/windy/foggy/freezing that the match was cancelled.

   c I think your new track suit is very attractive/becoming/well-designed/flattering.

   d The flight to Madagascar was uncomfortable/turbulent/understaffed/overcrowded/noisy/alarming.

   e What a stupendous/breathtaking/magnificent/astounding view!

6 a and b   (Example answers)

   i They circumspectly navigated round the dilapidated, rambling house on the overgrown, shady corner of the littered, ill-maintained street.

   ii The melancholic, serious-looking girl with the oversized, stripy cat in the symmetrically-designed, sloping garden precipitately fled.

   iii The mud-covered, neglected-looking car in the unsupervised, poorly-lit car park by the polluted, swollen river spontaneously ignited.

   iv They ecstatically relished the unforgettable festive meal in the exhorbitantly priced, fashionable restaurant in the bustling, atmospheric city centre.

   v The troublesome, attention-seeking toddlers demanding to be put on the brightly coloured plastic swings in the popular suburban park were screaming lustily.

Cambridge IGCSE First Language English — Answers to coursebook questions

7   (Example answers)

   dawdle, saunter, strut, swagger, tiptoe, slink, crawl, creep, stride, skip, stumble, march, stroll, plod, hobble, flounce, glide, sneak, lumber, prance, trudge, amble, toddle, race, traipse, slog, waddle, mince

8   Reading task.

9   a   The underlined phrases (the ship's great black side; raging, frothing and boiling; frightened and incredulous and ignorant; dangerous wild animals; terrified, out of control, berserk; dumbstruck and amazed) are multiple adjectival phrases. They are strong and evocative of fear and turmoil.

   b   The italicised phrases (*a thrilling show*; *an earthquake of the senses*; *like a riotous crowd*; *as unbelievable as the moon catching fire*; *the monstrous metallic burp*) are images, both similes and metaphors. They convey the abnormal and sensational.

   c   The words in bold (**orchestrate**, **hotfooted**, **nailed**, **crafted, exploded**, **thundered**) are verb forms with a figurative meaning. With the exception of **crafted**, they are strongly physical and suggestive of noise and pain.

   d   The narrator starts off naively rather enjoying the spectacle, then starts to be alarmed, but not unduly, by the angle of the ship. The narrator then feels cold and wants to leave; the noises begin. Incredulity and panic take hold and the water rises. The narrator experiences real fear and realises the ship is sinking. Things move faster and chaos ensues, conveyed by the questions. The animals are loose and increase the level of noise, movement and surrealism.

   e   An effective atmosphere of fear is created by a combination of darkness, shrieking, the rising water and the sinking ship. This is compounded for the narrator by his being cut off from his family and his feelings of isolation. He seems to be alone with the crazed zoo animals.

10 Ensure that students' answers are approximately 150 words and include a range of strong, interesting adjectives and verbs.

11 Students' own answers.

B Using imagery and literary devices

1   Reading task.

2   a   The adjectives used are mainly of size, number, shape and colour.

   b   Compound adjectives have a double value in description, conveying two ideas with one word in a condensed way. Subtleties of colour can be conveyed in compounds.

   c   Sound effects are created by the descriptive vocabulary (*soothing whisper*, *murmur of insects*) and by assonance (*wound laboriously round*, *shaggy tangle*, *low growth*). They give the description a poetic, lyrical quality.

   d   Adverbs are used for personification (*laboriously*, *sorrowfully*, *expectantly*). They add an animation to the garden, along with the other human references to *pink-faced*, *ballerina*, *parents*, *run wild*, *quivered* and *whisper and murmur*.

   e   The repeated words are *leaves* and *flowers*, making the garden seem abundantly and completely filled with plants in every direction.

   f   The sentences are of various types and lengths. The final short, simple sentence has a climactic and conclusive effect in contrast to the mostly longer rambling sentences, which convey the sprawling growth of vegetation in the garden.

3   The sentence containing an image is the more effective in each pair (the first in sentence in a, c and e and the second in b and d).

4   a, c and d are metaphors; b, e and f are similes.

   Students' own answers.

5 (Example answers)

  a The baby's skin was as soft as <u>cotton wool</u>.

  b He leaped across the stream like <u>a gazelle pursued by a lion</u>.

  c The train <u>threaded</u> its way through the mountain pass.

  d She is as dangerous as a <u>cornered rattlesnake</u>.

  e The soldiers marched as if they <u>had been turned into robots</u>.

6 (Example answers)

  a The child's crying was ear-splitting.

  b The house looked as empty as a nest robbed of eggs.

  c Rain startled to hurtle down as if trying to perforate the pavement.

  d The stadium was as densely packed as a jar full of sweets.

  e The woman's fury suddenly ignited.

7 **a and b** Students' own answers.

  c Original poem without the gaps:

  The winter evening settles down
  With smell of steaks in passageways.
  Six o'clock.
  The burnt-out ends of <u>smoky</u> days.
  And now a <u>gusty</u> shower wraps
  The <u>grimy</u> scraps
  Of withered leaves about your feet
  And newspapers from vacant lots;
  The showers beat
  On <u>broken</u> blinds and chimney-pots,
  And at the corner of the street
  A <u>lonely</u> cab-horse steams and stamps.

  And then the lighting of the lamps.

8 **a** Descriptive devices: personification (*settles down*); alliteration (*smell of steaks in passageways*, *beat on broken blinds*, *steams and stamps*, *lighting of the lamps*); metaphor (*burnt-out ends*); assonance (*leaves/feet*). There are references to all the senses.

  b The effect of the poem is to create the mood of the end of the working day, as night falls and the lamps are lit. The atmosphere of the poem is a depressing one of dirtiness, emptiness and decay, evoked by *smell*, *burnt-out*, *smoky*, *grimy scraps*, *withered*, *newspapers*, *vacant*, *broken*, *lonely*, and the setting of a rainy winter evening in a city street. The monosyllabic diction and use of *And* give the poem the feelings of the everyday routine experience ('your' is used) of coming home from work: monotony, repetition and resignation.

9 and 10 Students' own answers.

C Planning and structuring: Openings and endings

1   The first sentence gives the immediate necessary information: the subject is the villa, we are told its size, shape and colour, and an evocative personified image is used to convey character. The last sentence switches from the observed to the observers: their reaction is given to what they are looking at, and strong feeling has been created. The final sentence is highly emotive (despite or because of being a cliché) and a bond between person and place has been established, with all the more impact because the utterance is so short and absolute.

2   a   It was the summer of 1996 and there had been a heatwave in Brasilia for over a week. <u>Opening</u>

   b   As far as I'm concerned, the future is not something to look forward to. <u>Ending</u>

   c   The impression will stay in my mind for the rest of my life. <u>Ending</u>

   d   The trip to Africa was all my grandmother's idea. <u>Opening</u>

   e   I hadn't really noticed the garden before the afternoon when my ball went over the wall. <u>Opening</u>

3   The likely rank order is:
   1 = b   (flat statement in dull language)
   2 = c   (a little interest created by the detail)
   3 = e   (sustained metaphor, although a cliché)
   4 = d   (child's viewpoint; evocative simile)
   5 = a   (imperative to engage; air of mystery; descriptive detail)
   There may be debate about the relative merits of a, d and e.

4   Students' own answers.

5   Students' own answers. Ensure their plans reflect the bullet points in the Planning box next to the task.

6   Students' own answers. Ensure their plans reflect the same bullet points. They should note that the definite article defines a specific place that should be the focus of the piece; the use of the plural expects the piece to describe more than one mountain.

Unit 4

A Reading for factual information

1. Reading task.

2. **a** A *whiz-kid* is someone clever whose career progresses rapidly; they achieve success at a young age through being ambitious, decisive and efficient. The onomatopoeic word *whiz* represents a very fast movement creating a rush of air and a sound effect.

   b

progenitor	originator
potential	future prospects
philanthropist	supporter of humanitarian causes
foundation	charitable organisation
superlatives	words expressing highest degree
innovation	change
entrepreneur	speculator in business
accolade	recognition of merit

3 and 4

Childhood & early life:	Boston USA; divorced parents; lived in poverty; employed from age of nine
Education & career	studied art; dropped out of college; lived on welfare; employed by Google 2003–05; co-founded Twitter in 2006; produced films and books; won many awards; successful businessman; worth $200 million
Beliefs & opinions	supports causes to help people and the environment; thinks society is important; values the visual; believes creativity should be part of technology

5. **a and b** Students' own answers.

6. Reading task.

7. (Example answers)

   a Making your mind up; How to make that big choice; Considering college?; Making the next move; Approaching uni.

   b The genre of the text is a factual guide or educational brochure – essentially an informative article, as the heading suggests.

   c The audience is prospective university students. It is they and not their parents who are addressed as 'you', and the interests of students are examined, including their social lives.

   d The sub-headings are in the form of basic questions that would be in the minds of university applicants, and therefore designed to engage the audience. They create a question and answer format which is easy to follow and, like the use of bullets, breaks up the information into manageable chunks.

8. (Example answers)

   a i You need to ask about the university's record in catering for and dealing with overseas students and their problems, and how many students there are from your country and other countries.

   ii The factors to be budgeted for are not only the basic necessities of food, accommodation and bills, but also books and equipment, clothes and entertainment, as well as the cost of travelling to and from college and home to your own country.

   iii Ask questions about work experience opportunities, employment percentage for graduates, the reputation of the degree course and the university's league table position in your subject. Other issues concern staff qualifications and achievements, and the amount of teaching they do.

iv It is important to consider whether the town is friendly and attractive, and whether it has a railway station and a range of shops. The cultural opportunities available should also be taken into account.

b

Do	Don't
– have some idea of what you are looking for	– collect too many prospectuses
– have an idea which subject you want to study; know which universities have the best reputation for your subject	– assume all degree courses cost the same
	– assume all cities are equally expensive to live in
– ask the university representative about living costs	– limit yourself to only one possibility
– find out which universities specialise in your subject	– make your application decision quickly
– contact anyone who has personal experience	– necessarily accept the first offer made to you
– consider the social aspects of the place	

B Inferring writers' attitudes

1   Reading task.

2   a   The old woman's working life consists of continual walking, carrying and cooking; she is the sole carer of the house, six grandchildren, a goat and the crops; she has to make enough money for them to survive and has little time to rest or sleep.

    b   The distances are long; she is the only adult; she has many responsibilities; she is 60 years old; she is worn out.

    c and d   (Example answerd)

    We have sympathy for her because her physical tasks are arduous, especially for a woman her age, and she is very tired and anxious. Pathos is created by *at night she thinks of/Tomorrow*, and the list of tasks in the second verse, ending with an ellipsis, which shows how unending her labours are. We are sorry for the fact that she walks so far each day that she had developed a limp.

    e   (Example answer)

    The poet presents the old woman as being selfless and suffering, and gives the impression that she admires her by the way that she details so many different tasks and tells us that she has no one to help her. The poem structure indicates a progressively worsening situation for the old woman (she sings, then fails to sleep, then limps), which leaves the reader thinking that the next stage will be even worse, when she is no longer able to walk and work. The first and last lines of each verse implicate the reader and show the poet's concern for and understanding of her plight. The fact that she has no name and is just a generic *old woman* suggests that she represents all elderly African women, and that their lives have always been, and may always be, this harsh.

3   Reading task.

4   a   **frolicking:** playing [present participle]
        plied: crossed [past simple]
        annals: logs, records [plural noun]
        poignant: moving [adjective]
        squalid: dirty [adjective]
        ravaged: devastated, damaged [past participle]
        mutilated: maimed, disfigured [past participle]
        virulent: powerful, pernicious, malignant, toxic [adjective]
        afflicted: sufferers, diseased, victims [person noun]
        emulated: imitated, strove to equal [past simple]

    b   Students' own answers.

    c   are a testament to: give witness to; give proof of; are official confirmation of
        a legend among: well-known and admired
        on the offensive: making attacks
        live in a bubble: are cut off from the world; live in an isolated community
        inspirational hub: the source of stimulating ideas

Cambridge IGCSE First Language English — **Answers to coursebook questions**

5 (Example answer)

The occupants of the *Africa Mercy*, which number 450, consist of an international crew and doctors, along with their families – including 50 children – and the patients who are operated on and cared for on the ship. Additional paying volunteers, some of whom live in Freetown, the nearest port, work as nurses, mechanics and teachers.

The difficulties they face are caused by the squalor of the living conditions in Freetown, the terrible injuries inflicted by the war in Sierra Leone and the threat of malaria. There is a huge demand for medical care on the ship and not every case from the surrounding trading posts can be accommodated. Being confined to the ship makes it difficult for the children to find things to do and the turnover of occupants makes long-lasting friendships impossible. [131 words]

6 **a** *creaks and blisters*: The verbs of noise and appearance give the ship a run-down, ailing character.

   b *plunging headlong*: This suggests a reckless and dramatic movement to escape the sun.

   c *gleaming vessel*: The ship is compared to a jewel reflecting the light, in contrast to the dark grime of the shanty town, symbolising the hope it represents to the natives on shore.

   d *no house, no car, no life savings and no pension*: The quadruple negative stresses how much Parker has sacrificed to work on the *Africa Mercy* – all the things a person normally acquires during their working life – and therefore how unusual and selfless he is.

   e *Can you imagine … Can you imagine … Can you imagine …;* This triple structure is a rhetorical device to insist that the reader appreciates how dire the state of the local hospital is very different from what it should be.

7 Reading task.

8 **a** vexations: annoyances, worries; contrary: in the opposite/wrong direction; squall: sudden strong wind, short storm; fast: stuck, unable to move; molestation: harassment, being pestered

   b *hove* – past tense of heave (used only nautically); *ere* – before; *asoak* – wet, drenched; *sallied forth* – set out, departed; *green* – inexperienced

   c *ploughing through the gentle Pacific*: metaphor – suggests the ship travelled at speed through the light waves.

   the joy of our hearts & the relief of our hands: antithesis, balanced construction – the double phrase of two nouns each balanced by 'and' explains that both the mind and the body were equally gratified.

   shining metal: metonymy, substitution – the use of this descriptive poetic phrase instead of the factual word conveys the visual attraction and excitement of finding gold.

   leave their bones: euphemism – this phrase sounds more poetic and less shocking than the verb 'die'.

   disappointments, disease & death: triple alliteration – the reducing length and strength of meaning of the three words beginning with 'd' leads to the climactic monosyllabic 'death' as an inevitable conclusion.

9 **a** The letter is in effect a journal: it is a record of a momentous journey and series of events, in chronological order. The contractions (the ubiquitous use of *&* and *Capt.*) are typical of diaries/journals as well as letters, which are often written quickly and use space-saving devices. In the 19th century, letters were usually lengthy and detailed. As they were kept by the recipient, they served the purpose of a journal in addition to being a way of communicating with family in another town or country.

   b The writer appears to be young and/or uneducated. He uses simple and repetitive vocabulary (*many, very, good, bad*), misses out necessary commas between clauses and around phrases (*at high tide at midnight*) and his sentence structures are nearly all compound, linked with *and* (or rather ampersands), *but* and *so*.

   c (Example answer)

   unable to return home because of lack of money **11**
   contracting fatal disease **12**
   having so much baggage **7**
   long voyage to America **2**
   perilous sleeping conditions **6**

delay before ship sets sail **1**

threat of thieves and murderers **8**

running aground in the river **4**

limited success in finding gold **10**

bad weather at sea **3**

long walk through dry, barren land **9**

danger of drowning **5**

C Sequencing facts and ideas

1 Reading task.

2 a and b (Example answer)

I was born close to the Qinling Mountains, where our project is working to conserve giant pandas and their habitat. [1] Qinling is called the biological gene bank of China, with a large number of rare plants and animals, including the giant panda, crested ibis, takin, snub-nosed golden monkey, and many more. [2]

I had a wonderful childhood, living close to nature and having fun and adventures in the woods. [3] Those memories and experiences are important to my own philosophy of life. [4] I believe man has to respect nature, to live in harmony with it. [5]

Now I'm lucky enough to work for WWF (World Wide Fund for Nature) to help the giant panda conservation in Qinling. [6] The giant panda is not only the well-known icon of WWF and international conservation, it's also an umbrella species. [7] So by saving the forests for pandas, we also save other plants and animals. [8]

A trip to a remote field site can last three or more days, depending on the distance and conditions. [9] In the field, we visit project sites, doing interviews, giving presentations, conducting surveys, organising discussions, taking photos and gathering news. [10] In the office, I spend my time organising communication and awareness events and activities, collecting and editing news information, and preparing press statements and magazine articles. [11]

The panda is a very special animal and it's an honour for me to work for it, and to see the difference that the support from panda adopters is making. [12] Although the Chinese government and the public are aware of the need for conservation, there's still much more to be done. [13]

3 **a** the Plaza de Mayo to the Teatro Colon: At the northern end of the Plaza, take the fifth fork and proceed until you reach the Obelisk; turn into Cerrito on the opposite side of the roundabout and you will find the Teatro Colon on the left-hand side, three blocks along.

  b the Congress Building to the Plaza San Martin: Head south along Avenue de Mayo until you reach the Café Tortoni. Go along the road parallel to Florida (which is closed to cars) for 11 blocks and you will arrive in the Plaza.

  c the Obelisk to the Parque Colon: Drive along Avenue Corrientes to the end, almost as far as the port, then turn right at the T-junction into Avenue Eduardo Madera; the park starts immediately on the right and covers four blocks.

  d Café Tortoni to Montevideo St: Head north on the street the café is on for nine blocks. You will cross Carlos Pelegrini and Cerrito Streets in the centre. You will know you are on Montevideo St when you see the Plaza de Congresso on your left.

  e the Shopping Hall to the port: Take either Avenue Cordoba or Viamonte Street southwards until you have to turn onto Avenue Eduardo Madera. Turn right onto Avenue Eduardo Manero and you'll see the port on the other side of Avenue Antahtida, which runs parallel to Eduardo Manero.

Unit 5

A Respond using a range of genres

1 Reading task.

2 (Example answers)

a **hubbub:** loud commotion, din, clamour
smirking: smiling smugly, self-satisfiedly
ranks: rows
writhing: squirming, wriggling
hollowly: echoing, emptily
tittered: giggled, sniggered
immersed: submerged, absorbed, engrossed, engaged
subdued: dispirited, muted
crimsoned: flushed, blushed, turned red
jeering: mocking, taunting
ignominious: humiliating, shameful
faltering: hesitant, wavering
pert: cheeky, jaunty
deferred: submitted, yielded, surrendered
oblivious: unaware, unconscious, unheeding
squadron: a unit of soldiers, tanks or aircraft
bewildered: befuddled, confused, puzzled
disembarked: got out of or down from, emerged from
malevolent: malicious, malign, spiteful
bondage: enslavement, servitude

b *staring*; *tittered*; *smirking*; *their accusation*; *watching her*; *hostile*; *ready to jeer*; *A grin went over the faces of the class*; *hated*; *resented*

c *as if she were in torture over a fire of faces*; *she was naked to them*; *uncertain*; *suffering*; *exposed to the children*; *The children were her masters*; *She deferred to them*; *this inhuman number of children*; *she was always at bay*; *she must suffocate*; *They were a squadron*; *they were a collective, inhuman thing*

3 a and b (Example answers)

- *thundered/roared*: conveys the loudness of voice and bad temper of Mr Harby, and the fear he evokes
- *Ursula's heart hardened*: shows how much she was feeling and suffering
- *rapid firing of questions*: adds to the sustained metaphor of battle and facing an army, and makes Ursula seem like an unarmed victim of a shooting
- *in torture over a fire of faces*: she feels she is being roasted alive by the faces, which resemble flames
- *she was naked to them*: she feels she cannot hide from the exposing gaze of the children
- *hands shot up like blades*: the raised arms seem to threaten Ursula like knives in combat
- *Like a machine*: the other teacher asks questions monotonously and continuously, in a mechanical, inhuman way which is the opposite of Ursula's faltering delivery
- *always at bay*: like a trapped animal about to be devoured by a pack of hounds
- *she must suffocate*: she feels surrounded and deprived of air
- *They were a squadron*: the massed children are like enemy soldiers drawn up in ranks and facing her in battle
- *everything was as in hell*: she feels as though she has become trapped in some dark, noisy underworld of torture and punishment
- *like some bondage*: she dreads going back to class for the afternoon session as it feels to her like being in prison

c The words *smirking*, *jeer*, *grin*, *block*, *inhuman*, *torture* and *horrible* are repeated, most of them more than once. These words are key to the feeling of being humiliated by a group of schoolchildren and how she felt they were aligned en masse against her as a joint foe rather than as individual pupils. Her imprisonment is represented by the repeated actions described, from which there is no escape during the long, unpleasant day at the school.

4 (Example answer)

Dear Mr Harby

My daughter has told me about her new class teacher and I am writing to tell you that I am not satisfied that she was an appropriate appointment to the post. My son/daughter has told me that the new teacher is very young, lacks disciplinary skills, and is not sufficiently experienced or assertive to be able to control a class of more than 50 pupils. She apparently behaves as if she is afraid of the children and is clearly not suited to the job of teacher. She seems to suffer embarrassment in the classroom and gives the impression that she would rather be anywhere else.

According to what I have heard from other parents of children in the class, she does not have a satisfactory relationship with her colleagues and does not share their teaching methods. She winces when the voices of the two male teachers come through the classroom wall, and refuses to use her voice in the same way to drill the pupils mechanically. Mental arithmetic is a matter of constant practice and the questions must be delivered in a quick and confident way. Since you humiliated her on her first day by criticising her way of leading her charges into the assembly hall, you presumably agree that she is not a fit person for the job.

If she is not replaced as soon as possible with someone who is suited to the job and willing to impose their will on the pupils, the children will continue to mock her and dominate her, with the result that nothing will be learnt. Furthermore, the teacher might lash out at a child or suffer some kind of breakdown, which will leave our children without a teacher.

Yours sincerely, [291 words]

5 a Text A is a website article – informative; short paragraphs and sub-headings.
Text B is from a novel – first person narrative/fake autobiography; characters and events; tension; dialogue.

b i voice: Text A is mainly objective and dispassionate but with some informality (humorous asides and exclamation marks); the last paragraph gives an opinion and uses the inclusive 'you'. Text B is a young female, distraught by cruel treatment and helplessness.

ii purpose: Text A is mainly to inform. Text B is to entertain, and, specifically in this passage, to create a dramatic effect and to evoke pathos for the child characters.

iii audience: Text A is for researchers seeking information on this historical topic on the internet. Text B is for people who enjoy romance novels and/or 19th-century fiction (mostly female adults).

iv structure: Text A is organised (although not in a particular order), it uses frequent sub-headings and changes topic frequently. Text B is chronological, with interspersed, single speeches.

6 a vocabulary: Text A is factual and uses statistics. Text B is descriptive, making use of many adjectives; it uses terminology from school subjects and sewing, as well as archaisms (*&c* for etc.).

b punctuation: Text A has capital letters for proper nouns and short quotations in single inverted commas. Text B used colons, semi-colons and double inverted commas for speech.

c syntax: Text A uses simple sentences (occasional compound ones and parentheses, and is written in the passive voice. Text B has long complex sentence structures, inverted word order and lists.

7 (Example answer)

How schools have changed!

How would you like to be in a class of 100? That's how it used to be in some schools in 19th-century England, all lined up in rows of desks. Many schools were single sex, and even when they were mixed, boys and girls were kept as separate as possible, entering by different doors and doing different subjects – needlework for the girls and more serious subjects for the boys. The subjects they all did in the restricted curriculum were reading, writing and maths. Many of the subjects studied today were not available then, like artistic subjects, and there was no project or group work, just a teacher at the front firing questions at the class.

Another big difference from today was the discipline. Teachers used whistles to order pupils around, and they had to march into assembly. Their learning was by rote and if they failed the constant tests, they were punished by having to write out hundreds of lines or in more humiliating ways. A favourite punishment was to make a pupil wear a Dunce's cap and sit on a stool to be mocked by the others.

This barbaric attitude to discipline would be impossible nowadays, as it amounted to physical assault, and beatings left marks on the children. It's true that learning by heart has its benefits, but not everyone has a good memory so it's an unfair way to assess students. Everything then was about your rank, and how to avoid being bottom of the class and get to the top, which must have been emotionally stressful.

A lot of what pupils had to memorise were lists of facts and dates, many of them useless and irrelevant to their lives, and I don't think parents or pupils nowadays would accept that this could be called education. It's bad enough now when we are asked to just copy out of a textbook (in those days it was copying onto slates from a chalkboard) because that isn't learning and is very tedious, but back then they did little else. And if we hate tests now – which also don't test real learning only cramming, which is forgotten straight after the test – can you imagine what is was like to have one every day and get punished if you made any mistakes at all? What's more, you were also judged on how clean you looked and whether you stood up straight!

I think one of the hardest things for modern pupils to accept would be the shortness of the holidays; they only had a few days off for religious festivals and a summer break in which to help their families with the harvest. So, school was no fun and holidays were work too. Not exactly the best days of your life!

B Genre analysis

1 Reading task.

2 Paragraph 1 = c
Paragraph 2 = d
Paragraph 3 = d
Paragraph 4 = c
Paragraph 5 = d
Paragraph 6 = c
Paragraph 7 = c
Paragraph 8 = f
Paragraph 9 = f
Paragraph 10 = e
Paragraph 11 = e
Paragraph 12 = a
Paragraph 13 = b

3 See Task Tip B3 next to the task.

4 **a and b**

   i *17 aliens held*: 17 immigrants are in custody.

   ii *500-year-old child found*: The body of a child who died 500 years ago has been discovered.

   iii *Squad helps dog bite victim*: An army unit gave aid to someone bitten by a dog.

   iv *Miners refuse to work after death*: A group of miners has refused to continue to work underground following the death of a colleague.

   v *Wage rise bid defies ban*: A claim for higher wages has been made, despite such claims being forbidden.

5 **a** The Spiderman headline uses assonance, alliteration and quotation/cliché. Headline **i** in Task B4 uses pun and **v** uses assonance and alliteration.

   b Students' own answers.

6 Robert, who has gained fame – and notoriety – for scaling some of the world's tallest skyscrapers without permission, climbed the 191-metres-tall TotalFinaElf building in Paris before being apprehended by the city police. [2]

Robert says he intends to continue his career of conquering the world's highest office blocks, using no climbing equipment except for a small bag of chalk and a pair of climbing shoes. [16]

Cambridge IGCSE First Language English
Answers to coursebook questions

Daredevil French climber and urban sherpa Alain Robert added one of France's tallest office towers to his tally on Tuesday before scaling back down into the arms of the waiting police. [1]

The crowd which gathered to watch the man, who is sometimes called the French Daddy-long-legs or the Human Spider, may have unwittingly tipped off police to what was going on. [5]

Although Robert has courted arrest several times in the course of his urban climbing career, the French police are known to be a lot more sympathetic towards the local Spiderman than police in many other parts of the world. [7]

'It was a little more difficult than I'd expected because of the wind, because of the sun,' Robert told Reuters after his vertiginous conquest. 'Sometimes it was a bit slippery,' he said, adding that the windows had just been washed. [6]

Using his bare hands and dispensing with safety lines, Robert took about 90 minutes to reach the top of the headquarters of the oil corporation TotalFinaElf in the city's crowded La Défense business district. [3]

Robert was apprehended on Tuesday, but not charged. According to local media reports, the police even offered him orange juice. [8]

The law has not always been so good to Robert. In March, Chinese authorities refused him permission to climb the 88-storey Jinmau building in Shanghai, China's then-tallest building, He did so, once again wearing a Spiderman costume, and was later arrested and jailed for five days, before being expelled from China. [9]

In November last year, Singapore's police arrested Robert for attempting to scale the 280-metre Overseas Union Bank tower. And in April 1998, Parisian police arrested the stuntman after he climbed up the Egyptian obelisk in the Place de la Concorde and cheekily made a call on his cell phone from the top. [10]

A mountaineer by training, Robert's first urban feat took place in his hometown of Valence, when the then-12-year-old scampered up to enter his family's eighth-floor apartment after losing his keys. [14]

He was, however, given permission to climb the 200-metre high National Bank of Abu Dhabi, UAE, watched by about 100,000 spectators. [11]

Now aged 50, his conquests have included the Sydney Opera House, the Sears Towers, the Empire State building, the Eiffel Tower and what was then the world's highest skyscraper, the Petronas Twin Towers in Kuala Lumpur, Malaysia, where he was arrested for criminal trespass on the 60th floor. [15]

After climbing the New York Times Building in New York City on 5th June 2008, he unfurled a banner with a slogan about global warming that read 'Global warming kills more people than 9/11 every week.' [13]

On 28 March 2011, Robert climbed the tallest building in the world, the 828-metre Burj Khalifa tower in Dubai, taking just over six hours to complete the climb. [12]

However, he used a harness in accordance with safety procedure. [4]

7 **notoriety:** infamy, disrepute
apprehended: caught, arrested
conquering: overcoming, vanquishing
tally: score, total
unwittingly: unknowingly, unintentionally
courted: invited, encouraged
vertiginous: dizzying
dispensing with: doing/going without
charged: accused
feat: difficult achievement, rare accomplishment

8 Students' own answers.

9 **a, b and c** Students' own answers. Ensure that the layout and content of the interview transcripts reflect the information given in the Interviews box next to the task.

10 (Example answer)

At 09.38 on 25 April, I received an anonymous phone call informing me that a man could be seen climbing up the outside of the TotalFinaElf building in the La Défense business district of the city, which is France's tallest tower. I immediately drove a police vehicle to the scene, arriving at 10.05.

By this time the man, dressed in a Spiderman costume, was on his way down and had reached half way, about 100 metres up. I noted that he was not using any climbing equipment despite the building being made of glass and potentially slippery. A crowd had gathered to watch the event, and I assumed that the tip-off had come from one of them.

I recognised the figure to be Alain Robert, a 50-year-old French national known as the Human Spider, whom I had come across on a previous occasion in April 1998 when he scaled the Egyptian obelisk in the Place de la Concorde. I was aware that he had also previously climbed the Eiffel Tower.

At 10.24 Robert reached the ground, and I arrested him. He said he was thirsty so I offered him some orange juice. I informed him that his action was illegal and dangerous to himself and to people in the street below. He did not accept there was any danger to anyone, saying that he was a very experienced climber and had already climbed taller buildings than this one. He mentioned having climbed the National Bank of Abu Dhabi, with permission, and that his stunt had entertained 100 000 spectators. He also boasted that he had climbed the tallest building in the world, the Burj Khalifa tower in Dubai, in 2011, and said that, therefore, there was no need to make a fuss about his having scaled a building of less than a quarter of that height.

I decided not to charge him with the criminal offence of trespass, after he pointed out that the French police have always been sympathetic in the past, but warned him that next time he might not be treated so leniently.

C Transforming genres

1 **a–e** Students' own answers.

2 explained, informed, clarified, claimed, insisted, divulged, stated, told, specified, described, registered, reported, uttered, exclaimed, announced, intimated, responded, replied, answered

3 **(Example answer)**

   Yesterday two (a) <u>middle-aged, disguised</u> robbers failed in their (b) <u>ill-considered, bungling</u> attempt to stage a (c) <u>large-haul, daylight</u> robbery at a (d) <u>previously targeted central</u> bank. Wearing (e) <u>home-made, comic carnival-type</u> masks and waving (f) <u>genuine stolen</u> pistols, they threatened (g) <u>frightened, compliant</u> bank staff. Tellers handed over money, but one (h) <u>foolish, clumsy</u> robber dropped the (i) <u>specially reinforced, black canvas</u> bag. Cursing, he tore off the mask when he could not see where it was, in full view of the (j) <u>live, internal-security</u> camera. (k) <u>Amused, relieved</u> staff watched as the (l) <u>quick-response, armed</u> police burst into the bank and escorted the robbers away.

4 Students' own answers. Ensure that their news reports have a headline and sub-heading(s) and that they follow the stylistic points listed in the News Report Style box next to the task.

Unit 6

A Identify and analyse devices

1–4 Students' own answers.

5 Reading task.

6 a metaphors of speed and movement– *boiling, mounting, writhing*
colour – *sulphurous, ochre*
heat – *sweltering, boiling*
fear and pain – *terrible, boiling, sweltering, terrifying, black, sulphurous, writhing*

b (Example answer)
The unpleasant colours and the references to heat evoke being in hell, and the unnatural speed of the storm make it seem an unavoidable danger.

c (Example answer)
The penultimate shorter sentence and final short sentence have a dramatic and climactic effect, suggesting impending doom and conveying how exposed and vulnerable the observer is, as the only creature not yet protected from the storm.

7 Students' own answers. Ensure that their descriptions show choices of vocabulary and grammar as outlined in the Task Tip A6 next to the task.

8 Reading task.

9 a The town is unchanging, inhuman, filthy, noisy and smelly, and the working people's lives monotonous and governed by factory routine.

b *unnatural, black, chimneys, interminable, monotonously*

c Imagery includes: *the painted face of a savage; serpents of smoke trailed; like the head of an elephant in a state of melancholy madness.* These unnatural images convey a sense of threat and imprisonment by machines.

d Use of senses includes: *smoke and ashes; purple with ill-smelling dye; rattling and trembling.* Sounds and smells add to the unhealthy colours and disturbing sights to make the industrial environment seem totally polluted, unhealthy and indifferent to living creatures.

e The effect of the multiple repetitions (*It was a town, for ever and ever, like one another, all, same*), and the frequent use of *and*, is to emphasise the impossibility of change or escape from this 'town of machinery'', or of any expression of individuality by its occupants. All the sentences begin with *It*, stressing the dominance and impersonality of the town.

10 Reading task.

11 a The description starts with factual content and style, giving a list of statistics as if there is nothing unusual about the caves, and saying dismissively *and this is all, this is a Marabar cave.* This impression is continued by the list of numbers conveying that there are many caves, and that they are unvaried and indistinguishable.

b The short, impersonal opening sentence is minimalistic and uninspiring. The lists of numbers and repetitions of *again and again* and *nothing* emphasise the factual nature and apparent dullness of the caves, which are devoid of human or animal features. Repeated use of the tentative *or* shows that it is impossible to relate definitively to the caves. Finally, with the phrase *for they have one*, it is hinted that there might, after all, be something interesting about the caves because of their reputation. This is confirmed with the sudden switch to a different mode, with the use of direct speech and fanciful suggestions that words *can take root in the air* and that the surrounding land or the birds can talk and that they find the caves 'Extraordinary'. This is the word that remains in the reader's mind and which seems to cancel out all that has been implied previously about the caves.

Cambridge IGCSE First Language English — Answers to coursebook questions

c **(Example answer)**

A series of apparently featureless and unremarkable caves in Marabar have some effect and power over the local wildlife and human visitors, although it is not possible to say why this is, other than that they seem beyond nature.

B Describing an event

1 Reading task.

2 a The audience might include someone searching for information on the internet, possibly for a school project or piece of research. The title is the kind of question someone puts into a search engine.

   b This passage does not reveal the opinions or emotional reactions of the writer, whereas these are stated or can be inferred from the imagery, vocabulary and syntax of the previous three passages. The first passage gives an account of a particular occasion and event; the others describe a permanent state or process.

   c Stylistic features of the passage:

   Structure and length of most of the sentences: mainly short and simple; brackets are used to include extra information.

   How the sentences begin: with the subject of the sentence (noun) or a time adverbial

   Use of lists: to give details of the meals

   Use of numbers: to give the account accuracy and authority

   Use of time references: specific times give the account a morning-to-evening structure

3 and 4 Students' own answers.

5 Reading task.

6 Students' own answers.

C Adding the details

1 a, b and c

   Students' own answers. Ensure that their plan for the descriptive piece includes:
   - a suitable voice/viewpoint
   - an appropriate structure
   - ideas in a logical order
   - imagery, references to senses and at least one other descriptive device.

2 Reading task.

3

Content	Style
– meals, food, clothing, tasks, previous history, childhood, exercise, feelings, family, friends, colleagues, entertainment, the future, education	– first person – informative and factual (little figurative language) – mixed sentence types, but mostly simple or compound – everyday vocabulary – simple verbs (mostly monosyllabic) – varied sentence openings (different noun subjects) – clichés (e.g. *can't believe my luck*, *left me breathless*) – colloquialisms (e.g. *It's amazing*, *catch up with*, *works great*), contractions (*There's*, *I've*) – repetition (e.g. *miss*, *favourite*)

4 Students' own answers.

Unit 7

A Expanding notes

1 (Example answer)

One in 8000 people in the USA reaches the age of 100, and 90% of those are women. They are the fastest-growing sector of the population, with an increase of 8% per year, eight times higher than other age groups. 90% of those enjoy good health until they turn 90, and 15% of them are able to live independently.

Diet is apparently one of the keys to a long life, although there is a belief that optimism and consequential low physical stress levels are also contributors. A hereditary factor is evident in that the siblings of centenarians are four times more likely to live to at least the age of 90 than the rest of the population. Another characteristic of female centenarians is that they are three times more likely than those who lived to only 73 to have been over 40 when they gave birth.
[149 words]

2 Reading task.

3 Zeinab Badawi

1959	Born in Sudan. Her grandfather was a pioneer of women's education and her father was a newspaper editor and social reformer. [1]
1962	Family moved to London where her father worked for the BBC Arabic Service. [1]
1970	Attended Hornsey High School for Girls, London, taking A Levels in Russian, Latin and History. [2]
1978	Studied Philosophy, Politics and Economics at St Hilda's College, University of Oxford. [2]
1982	Broadcast journalist for Yorkshire Television. [3]
1988	Studied for MA in Middle East Politics and Anthropology at the School of Oriental and African Studies (SOAS), University of London. [3]
1988	First anchorperson to present the *ITV Morning News* television programme. [3]
1989	Co-presenter of *Channel Four News*. [3]
1998	Moved to BBC: hosted various news programmes including *Hard Talk*. [4]
2009	Interviewed Sudan's President Omar Al-Bashir, the first serving head of state to be charged with war crimes. [4]
2009	Named International Television Personality of the Year. [4]
2011	Appointed member of the Board of New College of the Humanities, London [4]

She has also:
– founded the African Medical Partnership Fund
– campaigned extensively for the rights of girls and women in traditional societies
– acted as Moderator of United Nations conferences
– acted as Adviser to the Foreign Policy Centre
– acted as a Council Member of the Overseas Development Institute. [5]

4 (Example answer)

Zeinab Badawi, born in Sudan in 1959 to a family involved with social reform, moved to London aged three when her father got a job with the BBC. She attended a London girls' high school, and after taking A Levels went to Oxford to study PPE in 1978. Her first job was with a TV company, and after doing an MA course at the University of London, she started presenting a morning TV show, followed by being made co-presenter of a Channel 4 news programme in 1989.

From 1998, Badawi hosted various news programmes for the BBC, which included interviewing Sudan's president in 2009, earning her the award of International Television Personality of the Year, followed two years later by a place on the board of the New College of the Humanities in London.

Other organisations she has been involved with during her career so far are the African Medical Partnership Fund, which she founded, the United Nations, the Foreign Policy Centre and the Overseas Development Institute, in addition to her continual campaign for the rights of women in undeveloped countries. [181 words]

5 Reading task.

6 a **inspiration:** source, stimulus
establishing: demonstrating, proving, earning his place, winning recognition
classics: outstanding of their kind, of the highest standing
blockbuster: hugely popular, very successful
perennial: permanent, enduring

b i *colourful, adventures*

ii *illustrious, distinguished*

7 a • Norwegian
• born in Wales
• born September 13, 1916
• went to boarding school
• was a writer, fighter pilot
• went to Africa, Greece, USA
• liked antiques, paintings, greyhounds
• married in 1953
• started writing children's books in 1960
• had five children
• titles of his books
• names of prizes he won
• worked in shed with yellow pencils
• died in Oxford November 23, 1990

b nationality, date and place of birth, secondary schooling, occupations, countries visited, partner, number of children, country of residence, interests, achievements, prizes, work methods, beliefs, passions, significant quotation, legacy, place and date of death

8 (Example answer)

The Norwegian Roald Dahl, who was born in Wales in 1916 and died in 1990, was a fighter pilot before becoming a prize-winning children's writer with a passion for antiques, art and dogs.

9 Sentence **d**: *Roald Dahl, who was born in 1916 in Wales of Norwegian descent, was a highly successful author of prize-winning children's fiction which inspired a love of reading.* This sentence has the most appropriate focus, includes the most relevant content, and gives a range of information.

10 and 11 Students' own answers.

12 (Example answers)
• Roald Dahl, who wanted his readers to love reading and be entertained by his books, knew what children like, as he had five children.
• Knowing what children like, since had had five of his own, Roald Dahl wanted them to be entertained by his books, as well as to love reading.
• Having five children, Roald Dahl, who knew what children like, wanted them to love reading whilst being entertained by his books.
• Roald Dahl, who knew what children like because he had five of his own, wanted children to be entertained by his books in order to love reading.

B Summary style

1 Reading task.

2 a An obituary informs readers of the recent death of a person usually a famous person, and pays tribute to the deceased.

Cambridge IGCSE First Language English — Answers to coursebook questions

- **b** You would find one in a newspaper, written by a journalist.
- **c** Like a biography, an obituary is a summary of the life story of a person, but it gives more than just factual detail: it emphasises the person's achievements and what was unique about them, and therefore has an evaluative element
- **d** Someone might read one if they have a particular interest in either the person or in the jobs they did throughout their career.

3   **epitaph:** words engraved on a tombstone
    foibles: eccentric characteristics
    endearing: attractive to the beholder
    syndicate: publisher who publishes material simultaneously in a number of newspapers, TV stations, etc.
    convention: official gathering of people who have a job or interest in common
    opted: chose

4   **a** *epitaph, retirement, support, remembered, endearing, constancy, misfortune, combat, syndicate, recalled, international, convention, remained, contract, compose, symphonies*

    b *epi* – upon; *re* – again; *sub/p* – under; *en* – within; *con/m* – with; *syn/m* – together; *inter* – among

    c Students' own answers.

5   Students' own answers.

6   *'Peanuts' creator Charles M. Schulz died on Saturday* **[a]**

    Schulz was 77, and died in his sleep **[a]**

    Schulz was born in St. Paul, Minnesota, USA on Nov. 26, 1922 **[a]**

    His wildly popular 'Peanuts' made its debut on Oct. 2, 1950. The troubles of the 'little round-headed kid' and his pals eventually ran in more than 2,600 newspapers, reaching millions of readers in 75 countries. His last strip, appearing in Feb. 13 Sunday editions, **[c]**

    Sergio Aragones, a Mad *magazine cartoonist and friend for more than 30 years, called Schulz 'a true cartoonist.' 'In a couple of centuries when people talk about American artists, he'll be the one of the very few remembered', Aragones said.* **[b]**

    'And when they talk about comic strips, probably his will be the only one ever mentioned.' **[b and c]**

    One of the most endearing qualities of 'Peanuts' was its constancy. **[c]**

    Over the years, the Peanuts gang became a part of American popular culture. **[c]**

    Schulz was drafted into the Army in 1943 and sent to the European theater of war, although he saw little combat. **[a]**

    After the war, he ... taught art and sold cartoons to The Saturday Evening Post. **[b]**

    His first feature, 'Li'l Folks', was developed for the St. Paul Pioneer Press *in 1947. In 1950, it was sold to a syndicate and the name changed to 'Peanuts', even though, he recalled later, he didn't much like the name.* **[c]**

    Although he remained largely a private person, the strip brought Schulz international fame. He won the Reuben Award, comic art's highest honor, in 1955 and 1964. In 1978, he was named International Cartoonist of the Year. **[b and c]**

    In his later years ... he frequently played hockey **[a]**

    He had had a clause in his contract dictating the strip had to end with his death. **[a, b** and **c]**

    'That's why I draw cartoons. It's my life.' **[a** and **b]**

7   (Example answer)

    Cartoonist Charles M. Schulz died in his sleep on Saturday, aged 77. The 'Peanuts' creator was born in Minnesota, USA on November 26th, 1922. Schulz was drafted into the Army in 1943 and sent to the war in Europe, but was not involved in much action. He enjoyed hockey, but cartoons were his life.

    After the war, he taught art and sold cartoons to *The Saturday Evening Post*. His first feature was developed for the *St. Paul Pioneer Press* in 1947 and sold to a syndicate and first published in 1950. Although originally called 'Li'l Folks', the name was changed to 'Peanuts', even though Schulz didn't like it.

    Although he liked his privacy, the strip made him internationally famous and brought him many awards, including International Cartoonist of the Year. The strip featuring the reassuringly predictable 'little round-headed kid' and his pals who became part of American popular culture appealed to millions of readers in 75 countries and more than 2,600 newspapers until the last one on February 13th this year, when the gang and its creator both expired. He had a contractual agreement that the strip would not be continued after his death.

His friend and fellow cartoonist, Sergio Aragones, said he was a 'true cartoonist' and he and his strip will be one of the few American artists and comic strips remembered for all time. [227 words]

8 Reading task.

9 a
- Captain Yu born 1986 in Sichuan
- Joined PLAAF in 2005
- Became China's first female fighter pilot in 2009
- Nicknamed 'golden peacock'
- Became member of Chinese Air Force aerobatics team in 2012
- Renowned as pioneer and hero
- Died 12th November 2016 in a collision during training

b The obituary expands the basic biographical facts, using full sentences, to include more precise and informative details. It also adds colourful details to make the subject seem more interesting and individual.

c The text is written in only four sentences; because they are complex structures each one contains multiple pieces of information without needing to repeat the subject or use more than one main verb in each. A range of clause sequences and types of connectives give variety.

C Comparing styles and purposes

1 Reading task.

2 **a and b** Students' own answers.

c Text A is newspaper article, designed to inform a broadsheet readership about a historical figure; Text B is a memoir, recording and justifying the events surrounding the murder of a historical figure.

3 a *infiltrated the imperial inner circle*: penetrated/gained access to the exclusive group of those ruling the empire

b *the power-vacuum left by Russia's crushing defeats*: the absence of authority created by the devastating blows against Russia

c *brought Rasputin almost supreme power alongside Alexandra*: gave Rasputin nearly equal maximum influence with Alexandra

d *were driving Russia to ruin*: were causing the destruction of Russia

e *whose version of the events surrounding Rasputin's death*: whose own account of the circumstances of Rasputin's demise

4 **(Example answer)**

The Tsar is irresponsible and unfit to govern as he has a weak character, doesn't want to be in the position of ruler, and will not face up to important concerns of national interest.

The Tsarina is controlling, severe, unwilling to listen to criticism, closely allied to Rasputin, and determined to get her own way.

5 a the character of Rasputin: *vice, carousing and passion*; *monster*; *his humour expanding*; *devoured the cakes*; *even merrier*; *inviolable*; *superhuman*; *glared*

These words and phrases make Rasputin seem to be self-indulgent and excessive in all his habits and behaviours, more animal than human, a deeply dangerous character and therefore unsympathetic to the reader. He is referred to as *the monk* to make clear how hypocritical he is.

- **b** the dramatic nature of his death: *a frightful scream*; *whirled and fell*; *amazing strength*; *sprang*; *wrenched*

  These words and phrases are strong, suggestive of powerfulness and pain; they add sound effects and violent movement to the description of the event and make clear that Rasputin was no ordinary human being. The scene is set at midnight, in dim light.

6 **a** *Hours slipped by*: This creates suspense because something should have happened immediately.

  b *seized with an insane dread*: This shows how much the conspirators feared their victim.

  c *his black, black eyes*: People don't have black eyes, and the repetition stresses the unnatural and evil nature of his glare.

  d *his removal and obliteration*: The need to eradicate all trace of Rasputin, even after death, conveys their hatred of him and what he represented.

  e *still and cold and – dead*: This phrase builds up by degrees to the climax of his finally being dead, reinforced by the dash.

7 **a** His background and position at court:

  Gregory Rasputin was born to lowly parents in Siberia on 10th January, 1869. Having become a wandering monk, in 1905 he insinuated himself into the Tsar's household as a mystic who could help their haemophiliac son and provide emotional support. When war broke out in 1914, he and the Tsarina jointly governed the state, injudiciously and corruptly, while Nicholas was away, and betrayed Russia in its war with Germany.

  b His character and behaviour:

  He charmed and deceived many people into believing him to be pious, though he relished his evil nature. His treachery, greed and taste for luxury made Prince Felix Yussoupov and some others despise him and plot his demise.

  c The circumstances and causes of his death:

  Poisoned cakes and wine had no effect on Rasputin, so he was then shot in the back. Although believed to be dead, he suddenly recovered and ran into the courtyard, where he was shot again. He was tied up, taken to the river and pushed through the ice. When the body was found three days later it was discovered that despite everything, the actual cause of death was drowning.

D Writing devices

1 (Example answer)

  a The vocabulary choices are mainly simple and monosyllabic, bordering on slang and cliché, such as *bad thing*, *good*, *great*, *nice friends*; they make the writer seem honest, friendly, unpretentious – and the teenager that she is. The sentence structures are mainly compound, with some simple sentences and non-sentences, but very few complex ones. This adds to the sense of the letter being uncontrived and a straightforward sharing of experience and emotion, rather than a considered and edited argument. The use of an ellipsis and unfinished sentence in the fourth paragraph strongly suggests the unplanned nature of the letter. Humour contributes to the overall casual impression, as in her satirical mockery of *take off our chains*.

  However, the use of double and triple structures and rhetoric, antithesis and repetition for effect reveal that it is deliberately written to be persuasive. In the context, her lively expression refutes the claims of her mother's detractors, proving that she is far from being the repressed and timid person they would expect her to be.

b

formal:	informal:
metaphor/quotation (*slings and arrows*); rhetorical question (*who says, what does it really mean*); double structures (*You feel it*); triple structures (*They don't...*)	fashionable expression (*But for real, feeble, so not true, I guess, pretty much do my own thing*); contractions (*you've, Daddy, Funny how*); idioms (*cracking up, busted, throw it back in my face*); colloquialisms (*Well, that's funny because..., Oh well, it doesn't matter, Here's why, At any rate...*); exaggeration (*a thousand times*); sentences beginning with *And*, *But* or *So*; use of dashes

The formal language is embedded in and disguised by colloquial expression to mitigate the effect of formality. The final section of the letter is the most formal part, as it builds up to its climax of vindicating her mother, and the single line final paragraph is a device to ensure the message of exoneration and gratitude stands out clearly.

c The mixture of registers reflects the paradoxical nature of the letter: it is addressed to a family member, yet is intended for publication to an international audience. It is touchingly intimate and personal but contributes a serious argument on the subject of child-rearing, which is of universal relevance because of the global reaction to her mother's published memoir. The mixture also reflects that the writer is an 18-year-old on the border between childhood and adulthood.

d *was no tea party*: wasn't easy
tunnel vision: ability to focus on only one limited objective/view
at 110 percent: giving more than the usual limit/maximum possible

e The use of direct speech helps convey the close relationship between daughter and mother – even including her pet name of *Soso* – and makes a point for her argument that her mother was actually gentle and understanding. It offers variety by including the lively teenage voices of her friends.

2 a Purpose and audience: desire to exonerate her mother among the readership of the newspaper, who know of the reputation of her mother and may have been critical of her; to express public gratitude to her mother; to reassure other students being made to work hard by their parents that it is worth it.

b Letter form: paradoxically both a personal form and yet published in an international newspaper; in this case, both formal and informal expression can be used; the first person form leads readers to expect sincerity/genuine feeling.

c 'Tiger Mom' is a metaphorical name for a fierce, authoritarian and uncompromising parent who puts pressure on their child to achieve success. This is what the world calls her mother. The writer also uses it as an affectionate term – she is a tiger cub.

d The writer addresses her mother as 'Tiger Mom' throughout because it shows the letter is a public document refuting the attacks that have been made on her mother. Calling her 'mother' would not have any distinct resonance or make clear what the issue is.

e The effect of the letter convinces us that she did not suffer as a child because of the examples of memories she gives, the humour she uses, and because she conveys how proud she is of what she has achieved. The quotations make it authentic and moving.

Unit 8

A Vocabulary choices in persuasive writing

1 Reading task.

2 **a** The adjectives *unspoilt, beautiful, lively, ideal, exotic, luxury, spectacular, private, fabulous, excellent, sophisticated, unique,* and *friendly* evoke associations with relaxation, pleasure and exclusivity, all the attributes of the high life.

  b The reader feels the desire to go to such a place and envies those who can.

  c The brochure is targeting those who are reasonably wealthy who feel they deserve a special treat or who need to get away from their everyday existence for a while. There is a focus on sport and dancing to appeal to the physically active; there are no facilities or activities suitable for children, so it is not targeted at families.

  d It is effective as persuasive writing in that it gives information about the facilities in a way that makes them sound attractive and comprehensive, but at the same time they are the things one expects to find and do on holiday.

3 **(Example answer)**

  Dear Sir/Madam

  My wife, two young children and I have just returned from a fortnight's holiday at the Hotel Paloma on Tamara, organised by your company. We were not satisfied with several aspects of the hotel and its location, and I feel strongly that various claims made in your brochure are misleading.

  The location is described in the brochure as being on 'unspoilt' coast, but this is not how we would describe it. The beaches may be private and sandy, but they are also completely covered in litter, some of it dangerous in the form of broken glass and discarded tin cans. Two swimming pools are advertised, but the smaller one had green slime on its walls and is a serious health hazard for young children. The riding which is offered 'nearby' turned out to be an hour's journey away on the other side of the island. Furthermore, the 'regular courtesy bus service' does not actually go there.

  As for the accommodation, the air conditioning worked only intermittently – and not at times one actually needed it – and the 'spectacular' view was of the rubbish bin area behind the hotel. There are indeed three ethnic food restaurants, but none of them caters for young children who want small portions of simple food, and this seems to be a basic expectation of any hotel wanting to attract families. The live music was much too 'live', i.e. loud, and went on far too late: we were unable to sleep before 2 a.m. throughout the two-week period we were there. The room service may have been 'friendly' but it was certainly not efficient: we had to wait for food to be brought on several occasions, once for more than an hour.

  In view of all the ways in which our holiday was less than satisfactory, I hope you will be able to offer a substantial refund of the cost of the accommodation. The children in particular were disappointed by the lack of facilities and catering for their age group. I look forward to receiving your reply at your earliest convenience.

  Yours faithfully [348 words]

4 **a** is rather dull and unsubtle; **b** is catchy, since it contains assonance and alliteration and evokes happiness by referring to smiling; **c** is long, lacking an image, and the diction is polysyllabic and unmemorable, the emphasis being on science. So **b** is probably the most persuasive.

5 **(Example answers)**

  a *slaughter*: suggests enormous number and brutality

  b *possess*: two-syllabled and less common word connotes control as well as ownership

  c *home*: more than just a house or a building; has connotations of warmth, comfort and company

  d *beautiful*: a more profound and rare quality than the fleeting or superficial *attractive*

e *unwillingly*: the negative reminds one of the absence of the positive, that this is happening against one's will, not just with a mild reluctance

f *adore*: a more unusual and therefore memorable usage than everyday love, and with connotations of worship of something divine or superior

g *phobia*: sounds like a more serious and incurable medical condition than just an ordinary and natural fear of something

h *sorrowful*: stronger, partly because polysyllabic, than the overused, mild word *sad*, and contains a strong idea of grief

6 a Words with strong positive connotations: *home*; *generous*; *traditional*; *savoury*; *fresh*; *feast*; *creamy*; *home-style*; *tender*; *succulent*; *flavoured*

b These adjectives are appetising either because they are directly related to positive taste experiences or because they are associated with old-fashioned home-cooking, which is generally believed to be more satisfying and genuine – more loving and caring – than the mass catering often provided in restaurants.

c Words typically used in menus: *local*; *premium*; *classic*; *distinctive*; *complemented by*; *served with*; *char-grilled*; *drizzled*; *seasonal*; *accompanied by*; *topped with*. These conjure the idea of elegance and luxury, and are more exotic than their everyday neutral synonyms: *cooked in/with*, *covered with*.

d The style of menus consists of noun phrases qualified by a string of adjectives and past participles. Full sentences are not used, there are no main verbs and grammar has been removed; the descriptions are a concentration of lexical items and the use of the passive *by*.

e Students' own answers.

7 a The first advert is more likely to be successful, as the vocabulary used has positive connotations, whereas that of the second advert focuses on negatives. *Unique* implies special and *antique* is a euphemism for old (*retro* is another adjective that would work here). Everyone loves a *bargain*, suggesting they are getting something more valuable than the price being asked, but *going cheap* has connotations of needing to get rid of something undesirable or past its sell-by date.

b and c Students' own answers.

8 a–c i *well built* is a euphemism for *large*, and sounds less critical because of the use of 'well', and because the phrase has positive connotations associated with houses.

ii *industrial action* means its exact opposite, which is *inaction* because of the staff being on strike, but *action* sounds more positive and politically acceptable.

iii *put to sleep* is a kinder way, especially when explaining to children, of referring to the *euthanasia* of a pet.

iv *somewhat eccentric* is an understatement for *odd*, and a less offensive way of describing strange behaviour.

v *a minor set-back* is the way in which a *quite serious defeat* is expressed in propaganda, where there must be no admission of failure or excuse for discouragement.

B Persuasive devices

1 Reading task.

2 (Example answers)

a It makes you feel virtuous; it's a way to get fit; you lose weight; you can chat at the same time; you'll live longer; it gets easier; you can go longer and faster; you can enjoy the scenery; it doesn't cost anything; you can do it anytime, anywhere.

b It makes you red-faced, sweaty and breathless; people tease you; there are cases of joggers dropping dead; it's boring; you have to follow a routine.

Cambridge IGCSE First Language English
Answers to coursebook questions

3 Students' own answers.

4 Students' own answers. Their flyers might include the following information.

Physical benefits:
- general fitness
- losing weight
- living longer

Mental benefits:
- positive thinking
- spending time with others
- spending time outdoors
- can be done anytime, anywhere
- it's free

The process of becoming a jogger:

i   In the gym, alternating walking and running, up to 20 mins.

ii   In the gym, continuous fast walking.

iii Outside fast walking, starting with six mins.

iv   A month later, 20 mins fast walking.

v   Slow running, 20 mins.

5 Students' own answers.

6 Reading task.

7

For	Against
- limited to relatively low speed - will reduce number of cars on the road as students can share - saves parents having to drive them - cost of school runs reduced by sharing - gives young people independence - more comfortable, warmer and dryer than a bicycle or motorcycle - better protected on the road than on a two-wheeled vehicle - enables young people to carry things safely	- age has never been so low, and doesn't make sense to reduce it now, when cars are faster, roads bigger, traffic systems more complicated, and volume of traffic much greater than in 1903 - young drivers show off and take risks; casualties in 16–17 age group high in other countries - number of accidents might increase because of inexperience and immaturity

8 (Example answers)

   a In the majority of countries, the minimum driving age is 18. It is as low as 16 in most of the USA and Canada, Nepal and the Philippines, and parts of Australia. It is 17 (or just under) in Israel, Malaysia, Fiji, New Zealand, UK and a few other European countries.

   b i Several island countries mentioned have a minimum age of 16. This implies that it is less dangerous to drive on an island, perhaps because the distances to be travelled are short, the number of vehicles or amount of traffic is small, or because there are no motorways.

© Cambridge University Press 2018

Unit 8 **Answers** 199

> **ii** Africa, Eastern Europe and some parts of Australia have a minimum age of 18. This may mean that these countries have a high accident rate generally or among young drivers, or that the maturity of young drivers in these countries is an issue. Most states in North America have a minimum age of 16, but the underpopulated areas have one very long, very straight interstate highway going through them with no traffic hazards so little likelihood of accidents. Farming communities need young people to be able to drive at an early age so that they can be be employed to drive farm vehicles and transport crops and animals.
>
> **c i** This suggests that young people try harder and drive more carefully when accompanied by a parent, perhaps because they fear their criticism or want to impress them.
>
> **ii** This suggests that the bigger and heavier the vehicle, the more driving skill, experience, physical strength, is needed.

9 Students' own answers. Ensure that their letters to the newspaper follow the conventions of a formal letter, and use both facts and inferences from the text.

C Evoking emotions

1 Reading task.

2 (Example answers)

  a *glinted cruelly in a thin shaft of sunlight that had suddenly slunk inside the darkened room*: shone threateningly in a narrow sunbeam that had swifty crept in

  Supine, his rotundity had spread into a flatness denying his huge bulk: lying down, his round shape had flattened out to disguise the large mass of his body

  where the Primus roared and her dreams were extinguished: where the stove burned fiercely and all the things she longed for evaporated

  b *stink* (a very strong word for an unpleasant smell, sounding shockingly disrespectful); *stone-grey* (evoking an unnatural colourlessness evocative of a cold, rigid, dead body); *pitilessly* (comparing the disease, the medical instruments and the behaviour of the narrator); *shudder* (strong involuntary physical movement of disgust and rejection); *blocking my throat* (his emotions seem to have become concrete and are suffocating him); *all the white hairs* (now representing age and physical deterioration and the loss of hope, which humans can do nothing to resist)

  c The message of the story is that one doesn't appreciate one's family and the suffering they go through until one realises how lucky one is to have loved ones and how terrible it would be to lose them. There are many possible quotations in the second half of the passage, but the strongest is the last: *for all the white hairs I was powerless to stop.*

3 (Example answer)

It was such a shock to see Viraf's father looking so ill and helpless. And the smell made it worse, the smell of medicines and death. He looked the colour of a corpse. I couldn't bear to look at the long needle in his arm. I shouldn't have been there, spying through the open door, and I couldn't wait to get away from the scene of horror. I needed to get out of the sickly darkness into the wholesome sunshine.

I remember when Viraf's father was a big man in robust health. What terrible thing has struck him down so suddenly?

And now I feel doubly terrible about how I have behaved towards my best friend, my neighbour, my cricket buddy. I should have stayed to play board games with him, to take his mind off what is happening in his home, to be a support to him, not have slunk away like a thief, a coward. I owe him an apology for mocking him for crying. He has every reason to cry, and I could not be as brave as he is being.

I am losing my Daddy, too, not quickly and obviously like Viraf, but slowly. He cannot win the battle against ageing, against his hair turning grey, against the fading of hope of ever getting another job. But I should be a kinder, more understanding and more grateful son. I should be willing to do whatever he needs of me. I feel he is disappointed in me; he doesn't talk to me, laugh with me, play with me as he used to. And I can't tell him how much I love him, how precious he and Mummy and Mamaiji are. They have all given up their dreams and youth to spend all day doing chores to raise me and to make my life pleasant. I am lucky to still have them all and I should appreciate them, and I will from now on. [326 words]

Cambridge IGCSE First Language English — Answers to coursebook questions

4 Reading task.

5 **(Example answers)**

a Q 1: How did you feel about leaving?
Q 2: Can you describe the journey?
Q 3: What happened to the rest of your family?
Q 4: What do you think should be done to help refugees?
Q 5: How should young refugees be supported?

b Pathos is evoked at the end of Section 2 by the references to not being able to find family members and having nothing but the clothes he was wearing when he left; by references to his younger sister in Section 3; distraught mother, death of child, so few people reaching the border in Section 4; not knowing about his family for many years in Section 5; homelessness in Section 6; living in fear in Section 7.

c Interviews are an oral genre even when written; not as concerned about accurate language/polished style so they can reflect the true/unmodified voice of the interviewee; they sound less professional/indirect/managed and so have more impact; there is no intermediary and the journalistic voice/interviewer is less intrusive/dominant; the interview gives a first-hand viewpoint throughout.

d Students' own answers.

6 Reading task.

7 **(Example answers)**

a A charity is an organisation that raises money from public donations and campaigns for a cause. The cause might be: against the abuse of animals and children; environmental and wildlife threats; homelessness; to support research into and treatment for specific diseases and illnesses; to support older people; to relieve famine; to free political prisoners.

b Amnesty International, UNICEF, Oxfam, Médicins Sans Frontières, World Wildlife Fund.

c Charities need to exist because governments cannot or will not support these causes, so, without public donations, the problems could not be tackled.

8 **(Example answer)**

Caught in the conflict, Struggling to survive, the burning heat, tightens its deadly grip, frightened and famished families. These phrases use violent vocabulary, metaphor or alliteration to convey danger and discomfort. Although they are clichés, they evoke pathos as an automatic reaction.

9 The purpose of the letter is to evoke pity for the plight of the sufferers and guilt in the reader for having a more comfortable existence.

a The material includes information about the setting and problems, and a case history to give authenticity and evoke pathos. It is easier to identify with an individual than with a mass.

b The content is a mixture of both fact and opinion. The verifiable information and the emotive language combine to produce maximum appeal and put pressure on the reader/potential donor.

c Statistics and numbers give credibility, make the charity seem to be fully aware of the exact situation, and cause a shock reaction in the reader that the scale of the problem is so huge.

10 **a and b** Students' own answers. The name of the charity is memorable because of its alliteration and symmetry, and because it is easy to say. The symbol is memorable because of its direct relation to the work of the charity.

c The simpler they are, the more likely it is that people will remember them. Many are a single word, formed by an acronym or a portmanteau. The most effective names relate to the aims (e.g. Shelter for a homeless charity, or Save the Children), but well-established charities can use initials instead of their full name and still be recognised (e.g. UNICEF, WWF). Alliteration and assonance facilitate memorability (e.g. War on Want, Greenpeace). The logo is as important as the name and should have a visual appeal because of its subject, or a pleasing design. Most logos are formed within a circle to make them neatly distinct and suitable for use on a variety of publicity materials, including badges. A distinctive shade of a bright colour, usually red, blue or green, is very important for immediate identification.

11 Students' own answers.

12 a The stages of the letter are: the situation; the individual story; the general suffering; further problems; the threat; the work of the charity; the appeal for money.

b The adjectives used are physical, graphic and harrowing – all designed to evoke pathos.

c The lists emphasise the problem and make it seem very urgent.

d This address immediately puts the reader in the position of aid-giver.

e The inclusive pronoun *we* and direct address to *you* make it hard to ignore the appeal, and *they* stresses how lucky the reader is not to be one of the victims. There is an assumption that the reader will want to help, established in the opening *We can't help but be moved*.

f Repetition is used to emphasise the key words *refugees*, *summer*, *fierce* and *struggling*, which sum up the situation even for a reader only skimming the text. Reiteration makes it more likely that the message will be received and acted upon.

g The word *family* is emotive and has universal appeal. The reader is positioned to identify and empathise with the refugees even though their situations are very different.

h The paragraphs are short, rather than being dense and off-putting. The sentences are mostly short and have either simple or compound structures. Some are non-sentences. The letter must be accessible even to readers with a limited vocabulary and low reading age in order to maximise its fund-raising potential.

i The tone is informal and confiding, and the style colloquial, as if the letter-writer is talking to a friend and can therefore count on their sympathy and support. Many of the sentences mimic speech by beginning with *But*.

13 a The phrases in bold on the left stand out, as does the centred text, as they are both bold and outside the main text blocks and normal letter format.

b The layout and graphic devices include the use of bold text, centring, italics, underlining, capitals (*Summer Survival Pack*), as well as the triple list in a column at the beginning.

14 and 15 Students' own answers.

Unit 9

A Engage your audience: tension and suspense

1 Reading task.

2 a setting: *waist-deep in the gras*, *like a piece of sheep's wool*; *gold light die*; *sleeping village*. The place is presented as rural and slow, and cut off from the world – as are its inhabitants. The narrator's mother is part of the setting, rooted in the village like an old, bent, gnarled tree.

b atmosphere: It is morning on a sunny day, and this creates a hopeful beginning for the journey. The words *bright*, *right*, *confident* and *good* are all very positive. He is young and fit, so we expect him to go far and discover a new life.

c mood: There is sadness as well as optimism. We can imagine what grief the lonely mother is feeling at the prospect of losing her son (perhaps her only son) and the long separation, although the narrator seems callously unaware of this. The narrator thinks he may never see her again. We worry about his youth, naivety and lack of both money and experience (he has never seen the sea); his being *soft at the edges* makes him vulnerable.

3 Students' own answers. Ensure that their autobiography plans cover the event they would describe in the first chapter, the setting and mood/atmosphere.

4 Reading task.

5 a Words and phrases that create an atmosphere of fear: *odd*, *impossible to identify*, *cautiously*, *hardly breathing*, *heavy*, *empty*, *moonlight*, *silence*, *seething*, *blanketing*, *musty*, *darkness*, *thick as felt*, *rigid*, *growling*, *tension*, *no idea what was beyond it*

b The physical response to fear manifested by the narrator and reflected in the dog convey that something unusual and disturbing is happening: the body tension reflects the mental tension. In addition, it is made clear that the noise is something strange because it is unidentifiable. The house is described as *musty* (damp), and *empty*: the narrator is the only human occupant and far from help. The word *blanketing* creates a sense of suffocation. The major factor in all horror stories is not knowing what the threat is, so that the maximum amount of suspense and fear is built up for the character and the reader.

c An old, remote and isolated house with passageways is a stereotypical setting for a horror story because of traditional associations with haunting and imprisonment. The character alone there will find it difficult to leave and no one would be able to come to the rescue. The heavy furniture and unmade beds add to the gloomy and derelict impression, and the darkness is only intensified by the reference to moonlight, also a stock feature of the Gothic genre. A locked door is a staple plot device, as whatever is behind it is both a mystery and a threat, otherwise the door would not be locked. It enables sounds to emerge from the hidden room which cannot be identified or investigated, creating suspense and terror.

d Dogs are known for their excellent senses of smell and hearing, and thus their ability to detect supernatural phenomena. Spider's tense, rigid body and growling signify that there is a malevolent presence behind the door, and that it is not just the character's imagination. The dog is unlikely to be able to protect the character, as she needs reassurance. The name of the dog, like the name of the house, plays on readers' fears and reinforces expectations that the outcome will not be a happy one.

e Triple structures and frontloading of main clauses with subordinate clauses and phrases (e.g. *Very cautiously, listening, hardly breathing, I ventured*) delays the information and creates tension. The last two sentences of the first paragraph, although long, have no main verb – they are not actually sentences. The fragmentation of the narration into short or non-sentences creates an atmosphere of fear and suggests an inability to think coherently. The final fragment, *Except the sound*, is the climax of anticipation of what lies beyond the locked door, and a reminder of the overpowering, terrifying sound.

6 Reading task.

7 a *trapped*, *heavy stick*, *darkness*, *loomed*, *swung*, *plunged blindly*, *wilderness of wire and iron*, *bodies*, *old iron bodies*, *caught*, *crashing*, *knife-edged*, *waste*, *grotesque shape of wire*, *barbed*, *tore*, *held him*, *death*, *Help me!*, *ripping*

b The semantic field is of sharp metal and blindness – *darkness*, *loomed*, *blindly* – so that injury is certain. The persona is outnumbered by the *bodies* of cars as well as having human adversaries to contend with. The connotations of *waste ground* are of a rough, lonely place of rusty, damaged and abandoned objects, a kind of graveyard for broken things. Many of the words denote weapons, and the verbs (*swung*, *tore*, *ripped*) relate to violent and destructive actions. The idea of injury is the dominant one, and the connotations of *trapped*, *caught* and *held* are of prisoners and victims in a context of war.

8
- narrator: First person is used in the first extract; third person in the second.
- atmosphere: Because of references to the feelings of anger and pain, as well as to wire, iron, knife and other metallic objects, within a setting of darkness, wasteland and wilderness, the atmosphere is hellishly ugly, brutal and terrifying.
- setting: The first is indoors, the second outdoors. Both are set at night.
- sense of a presence: In both passages the lack of definition of the threat is what creates the chilling effect; in the second passage, the car wrecks and barbed wire have been personified to turn them into an additional hostile presence, which can trap and hurt the protagonist.
- references to noise or silence: The first passage is about a noise and an eerie contrast between it and the otherwise stifling silence; the second is noisy, including *crashing*, *knocking* and *sobbing*, cries of pain and pleas for help, and the implied noises of contact with metal (e.g. *kicking* and *ripping*). The contrast with the word *voiceless* is therefore strongly conveyed: he needs noise to summon help, but can't manage it.
- use of paragraphing: Both extracts have two paragraphs and imply a passing of time, of a few minutes, between them.
- use of adjectives and adverbs: The second passage relies more on verbs and adverbs than adjectives, to create a sense of violent action; the point of the first passage is that nothing is happening, therefore the focus is on adjectives to create atmosphere.
- choice of verbs: The verbs in the first passage are those of perception and passive response, unlike the expansive movements of the second – of a man running and in fear of his life.
- sentence structure: The second passage consists of long sentences but they are almost all compound, formed with *and*, *but* or *so*. This gives the impression of lack of thought and continuous movement.
- pace (speed of events): Both passages cover a period of a few minutes, but the sense of the first is slow, because nothing really happens, while the second seems to move quickly, as though too much is happening, because of all the action verbs, and the absence of time adverbials.

9 Reading task.

10 (Example answers)

a The text speeds up at the paragraphs beginning: *But the snake …*; *What the snake did next …*; *Then wham …*; *Then at last …*. The rest is at a slower pace. The contrast of inaction with sudden swift movement creates drama and tension. The snake has the initiative for the first three pace changes, but the snake-catcher controls the final series of actions, reflecting that he has won the battle.

b It takes much longer to read than the actions would have taken in real time. This is because of the use of direct speech and the detailed description of the series of movements, which, although only taking *a hundredth of a second*, are extended using similes. This extended duration build up suspense.

c It would have lacked all the narrative devices that make it effective: pace, tension, suspense, drama, surprise, climax, dialogue, irony (in the way the snake-man talks to the snake) as well as the engagement of the reader through the evocation of a variety of emotions.

d Fast: short sentences (as in penultimate paragraph); speed adverbs (*abruptly*, *And now I saw*, *A moment later*); beginning sentences with *And* to continue the flow of the action; the onomatopoeic word *wham*; a series of present continuous verbs to suggest motion.

Slow: paragraph changes indicate small time lapses that extend the suspense; some sentences are slow and ponderous because of their monosyllabic or long vowels (*the air was heavy with death*); description and imagery slows the narrative pace, especially in Paragraph 4 (*motionless as a pillar of stone*); repetition (*Another minute ... and another ... and another*, *And still he waited*); ellipses, which symbolise the waiting; insertion of dialogue; questioning (*What happens next?*); and hypothetical outcomes (use of the conditional tense).

The sudden changes of pace and contrast between swift movement and stillness add to the effect of suspense and surprise; the reader is waiting to discover if and how the snake will be captured and cannot guess what it will do next. The winner of the battle will be the one who can move fastest, so speed is a major element in the passage.

e   The climax is the final confrontation between the protagonists, beginning with *Then wham* and ending with *Then at last*. The snake-catcher has already been struck on his boot (and the dog is dead) so the reader fears for him during the battle as he has only a stick and the snake has venom as its weapon.

f   Students' own answers.

g   The *stone dead* dog evokes fear for the snake-catcher, as it makes it clear that the situation is dangerous and the snake is lethal. Mentioning it at the end gives closure to the event and evokes a sense of pity for the victim, as well as reminding the reader that it could have been the children not the dog who were poisoned.

h   Double narration adds another level, so that the *I* is an internal observer, and although we know that the first person narrator was not killed by the snake, we do not know that the snake-catcher survived the incident, so the tension and suspense are genuine. It creates a double viewpoint that has a dramatic effect: the narrator can see what the snake-man cannot. It also allows a double level of use of dialogue, as there is a conversation taking place outside the room as well as the speech to the snake inside the room.

i   Students' own answers. In the course of the class discussion, ensure that no essential features are lost in their suggested cuts.

B Planning narratives

1   Questions the poem raises:
   - Who is the persona?
   - Is he addressing his real brothers or his neighbours?
   - In what sense is he 'giving back' the keys to his door?
   - What did he receive, and why was it more than he could give?
   - What has just happened to 'put out his lamp'?
   - What form did the 'summons' take?
   - Where is he going and how will he travel on his journey?

2–7   Students' own answers.

C Adapting a narrative

1   Students' own answers.

2   Reading task.

3   a   There is no plot as such, and minimal action: a woman gets on a train and talks to a man; the woman gets off; another man gets on. The force of the story is entirely due to the irony that both main characters are blind and neither of them knows that the other is.

   b   The setting is in a railway carriage, which functions as a stage. The story starts with one character in place, then another joins him. She then exits and another enters to take her place. This is the simple structure of the story – the entrances and exits into the carriage.

c The majority of the story is in the form of conversation. It is carefully written to deceive the girl and to be ambiguous about her own sense of sight. The viewpoint is that of the male narrator and we are as surprised as he is to learn at the end that she too is blind.

d The first sentence economically sets the scene, a train in India. The opening could be described as *in medias res*, since we are not told the name or age of the narrator, nor his reason for being on the train or where he is travelling to. This information turns out not to be relevant. The last sentence is poignant: he would presumably have had a different conversation with her had he known she was blind. He never gets to know about her hair, so will not be able to imagine her in future. Her beautiful eyes do not *have it* – that is, the ability to see. The newcomer is amazed that the man hadn't noticed that the girl was blind, not realising the reason. The man was attracted to her not by her prettiness, which he could not appreciate, but by her interesting personality. They enjoyed each other's company, and had more in common than they knew, but will never meet again, which makes it a sad ending to the story.

e The title is a pun on the expression 'The Ayes have it', which means those voting Yes have won the vote. In retrospect the implications are clear to the reader, but not before they have got to the end of the story.

4 and 5 Students' own answers.

Cambridge IGCSE First Language English — Answers to coursebook questions

Unit 10

A Stylistic choices

1   a   Reading task.

    b   Topic phrases: *changed the world*; *photographers are artists*; *preserve of the wealthy*; *became much more common*, *revolutionised this field*; *virtually no cost*; *within reach of everyone*; *rise of social media*; *new way of life*; *self-obsessed generation*.

2   (Example answers)

    a   The invention of photography changed the world because <u>it meant images could be recorded other than by painting</u>.

    b   The main reason photography spread in popularity was <u>the reduction of cost for colour</u>.

    c   Digital photography came about as a result of <u>spy satellite technological advances</u>.

    d   The main advantages of digital photography are <u>inexpensiveness and convenience</u>.

    e   The inventor of digital photography has regrets about his invention because <u>it has affected the way vast numbers of people live by making them extremely self-obsessed</u>.

3   The writer's views are not explicit, as this is an informative piece. However, the reader can infer that he has respect and admiration for photography as *an art form* which involves *considerable skill*, that s/he regrets that the reduction in costs allowed just anyone to be able to take an instant *snap*, and that digital photography was able to *win out* over use of film. The writer seems to lament that mobile phones make it possible for *virtually anyone* to become a photographer, and there is implied criticism that it has become an *obsession* that has led young people – who wish to render every *aspect of their lives public* – into '*extreme danger*' and *excesses*.

4   Students' own answers.

5   Reading task.

6   • suppositions the writer has made about the audience: that everyone owns a dishwasher; that everyone lives in a family; that everyone wants their dishes to sparkle; that everyone works (*had a busy day*); that we are impressed by what scientific experts tell us.
    • effective vocabulary: the pun of *crystal clear* (and *solution*); the associations of transparency, cleanliness, preciousness, attractiveness; the alliteration of the brand name; the assonance of *squeaky clean*; the positive connotations of *sparkling* with stars, joy, bright colour and light; the negative connotations of *shocking*, *problems*, *grime* (a stronger word than dirt), *unpleasant odours* (stronger than smells); the references to *experts' research*.
    • range of emotions: guilt towards your family for not keeping the dishes clean; guilt towards your dishwasher for not looking after it properly (it is presented as a member of the family that looks after you); guilt for allowing your house to smell; fear of *the tell-tale sign* of inadequacy which will happen *over time*, if you don't take action.
    • persuasive devices: statistics (although 54% isn't a very high proportion); lists (the breadth of knowledge and attention to detail); superlatives (*one of the greatest inventions*); addresses the reader as *you* to target and include; repetition and use of capitals (*Crystal Clear Dishwasher Cleaner*); the rhetorical question of the second sentence; the semantic field contrast between *good* and *thorough*, between *fresh* and *clean* and *shining*; the negative diction of *Bad*, *cloudy*, *unsatisfactory* and *smelly*.
    • combined effect of language and images: that there is something wrong with you if you don't immediately go out to buy this dishwasher cleaner, so that *you can say goodbye* to your problems and conform to the ideal of kitchen cleanliness and family devotion.

B Summary practice

1   Reading task.

2   a   **surreal:** freakish, abnormal
        bizarre: strange, weird, outlandish

conventional: typical, normal, usual

embarked on: commenced, set about

regime: authorities, system of control

painstakingly: meticulously, diligently, carefully

evasive: dodging, sidestepping, vague

elicit: obtain, acquire

custody: detention

declined: refused, turned down

dare-devil: risk taker, thrill-seeker

sheepishly: shyly, humbly, wryly

  b   <u>family and friends back home were grilled</u>: family and friends were subjected to interrogation; <u>an extraordinary volte-face</u>: an unexpected u-turn, a surprising change of mind; <u>plain sailing</u>: easy progress, straightforward

3   *Mikhail's mad invention* sounds like a children's story.

Do-it-yourself submarine is probably the best; it arouses interest because it is so unusual. It may be better than the actual title, which assumes a knowledge of the collocation 'one man and his dog', and not everyone will immediately realise that *sub* is short for *submarine*.

Pedal power has alliteration and balance but implies a bicycle and is not precise or engaging enough.

KGB arrest spy suspect sounds like a news report headline and gives a misleading time perspective, putting the focus in the wrong place.

Seasick sailor's secret sounds clever, with alliteration and assonance, but is misleading as he isn't really a sailor and it is no longer a secret.

4   a   Words and phrases that show the writer thinks Puchkov's achievement is strange but impressive: *rank as one of the more bizarre*; *submarine looks particularly out of place*; *eccentric device, whereas*; *managed to sail hundreds of miles.*

    b   The phrase *arrived to arrest me* evokes sympathy for Puchkov; *'accomplices'* in inverted commas mocks the KGB. With the phrases *he was held in custody for a week*; and *family and friends back home were grilled*, the implication is that the KGB, working for what the writer calls a *regime*, behaved in a ruthless and unnecessarily heavy-handed fashion, and then completely changed its mind. By saying *Leningrad as it was then known*, the writer suggests that he prefers the town's original, historical and more romantic name of St Petersburg.

5   a   Hyphens, which link two or three words without spaces in between, are used to <u>form compound nouns and adjectives acting as one word</u>.

    b   Hyphens are also used at the end of a line of writing to show that a word <u>has been split because of lack of space on the line</u>.

    c   Dashes, which are twice the width of hyphens and which have spaces before and after them, are used either singly to <u>add an afterthought or dramatic extra piece of information</u> or as a pair to <u>create a parenthesis</u>.

    d   Brackets are always used in pairs, and they show that <u>the material between them could be removed from the sentence grammatically and that the content is not essential to the text</u>.

    e   Colons indicate that <u>a list, definition or further explanation is being introduced</u>.

    f   Semicolons perform the role of <u>full stops, and their job is to separate sentences, but they imply that the ideas on each side are closely connected</u>.

6   a   its dimensions: The submarine is five metres by one metre, with a height of 1.2 metres.

    b   its movement: The submarine can travel up to ten metres below the surface and cover a distance of between 300 and 400 km.

    c   its power: The submarine's weight of 1.8 tonnes allows it to reach a maximum speed of 8 kph.

Cambridge IGCSE First Language English
Answers to coursebook questions

7 **(Example answer)**

Puchkov grew up in Ryazan, a town southeast of Moscow, where he became a factory worker after leaving the army at the age of 40. During this time, he spent six years secretly building his submarine, which he launched in 1987. He was arrested by the KGB but later sent to Leningrad for marine studies. He still sails between May and October each year, when not working part-time in a glass factory. He is interested in designing and building vehicles. Despite being a dare-devil, Puchkov is modest, patient and secretive, even with his closest friends and family. He chose independence over a secure job in the navy.

C Looking at vocabulary

1 Reading task.

2 **icon:** representation, symbol
plethora: excess
conquered: defeated, vanquished, subjugated
heinous: abominable
abode: dwelling place
deities: gods
consequently: therefore
plunder: loot
phenomena: unusual occurrences

3 **(Example answer)**

[1] mention
[2] suggest
[3] say
[4] observe
[5] state
[6] claim
[7] declare
[8] maintain
[9] assert
[10] insist

4 **(Example answer)**

The passage is factual, objective, informative writing, full of technical vocabulary, names and statistics. The effect of the content and the formal, passive structures, (e.g. *It is generally believed to be*), is that expert knowledge is being conveyed authoritatively and without bias. The emotive language of *heinous* and *concern* is used within references to the stated or implied views of others, and does not express the view of the writer.

5 Reading task.

6 **(Example answers)**

   a *had occult knowledge through which they wrought miracles*: knew mystical practices that enabled them to produce inexplicable creations

   b *remains an enigma*: is still a mystery

   c *reduced soil erosion*: cut down on the loss of topsoil

   d *it is strategically located and readily defended*: it is in an effective military position and easily protected

   e *The manicured lawns provide a battery*: The well-trimmed grassy areas offer rest and recovery of energy

7

	Text 1	Text 2
content	undeveloped separate points, statistics, includes theories, evaluative	developed aspects of one topic, factual and objective
vocabulary	non-technical, names	technical terms, sophisticated, academic
syntax and sentence type	mainly compound and some simple	mainly complex, use of passive, range of punctuation
purpose and audience	general tourism; entertaining as well as informative; people focus	purely informative for educated or specialist audience; place focus
overall effect	accessible information; persuasive	dense, dull; anti-tourist

8   Reading task.

9   (Example answers)

   a   The narrator is a woman from Egypt called Madiha. She speaks Arabic, French and English, admires the explorer Bingham, is enthusiastic about South American culture and an idealist (can beinferred). She intends to employ Eduard as a guide.

   b   The guide is a Ukrainian refugee called Eduard who works as a guide at Machu Picchu. He speaks Russian, Spanish and English, has a striking appearance with a large build, and is middle-aged [can be inferred].

   c   Hiram Bingham was the American university lecturer believed to have discovered Machu Picchu in 1911. He had strong convictions and was very determined [can be inferred].

   d   The people who used to visit Machu Picchu were committed, fit and hardy, willing to climb, carry baggage and sleep in tents. They enjoyed the challenge of exploring out-of-the-way places.

   e   The people who now visit Machu Picchu like comfort and to be able to travel easily and quickly; they are not seeking a mystical experience and enlightenment, but just want to say that they have been to fashionable tourist destinations.

10   (Example answers)

   a   *a great bear of a man*: The metaphor expresses Eduard's huge size and also his clothing, and implies that he is at home in the environment of the Andes.

   b   '*Fancy a coffee*?': The reduced form of the question and the choice of verb are colloquial, modern and friendly.

   c   *literally and metaphorically*: The binary phrase intensifies the point being made.

   d   '*follow the Inca trail*': The single inverted commas draw attention to this being a much-used phrase and fashionable ambition.

   e   *the first visitor for 300 years*: The dash introduces an additional piece of information dramatically.

11   • use of character: two characters make dialogue possible and can convey different personalities and viewpoints.

   • use of dialogue: gives variety of voice and form and enables colloquialisms and humour to be used.

   • type of vocabulary: tends to be a mixture of everyday conversational vocabulary and informative language, including proper names and dates.

   • sentence structures: varied, but tend to be shorter and simpler than that used in a guide book or other informative writing, and more informal (e.g. dashes).

   • voice and viewpoint: the narrator has a cheerful and enthusiastic tone and attitude; the guide is passionate but somewhat stern and critical, with a cynical view of modern travellers.

   • Content: contains opinion, description and personal details to dilute and make more accessible the presentation of the historical and geographical material.

Unit 11

A Writing convincing non-fiction

1 Students' own answers.

2 Reading task.

3 Text A is more restrained, more focused on the event, and more convincing than Text B.

   a the different content:
   - Text A has a sensational quotation from a victim but otherwise refers to officials and doesn't use quotations; it forecasts rain.
   - Text B contains several long quotations, one including a metaphor, but no victim interview; it forecasts a change in wind direction; it refers to the Prime Minister and the death of a pilot, and gives more detail about the evacuation procedure. There is more reference to actual or potential deaths in Text B.

   b the different style:
   - Text A is more succinct and also uses less exaggeration and fewer intensifying adverbs.
   - Text B increases the statistics to 15 helicopters, and *more than* 200 firefighters and *at least 11 houses*.

   c the different headline:
   - Text A uses alliteration and is a snappy headline, dramatically claiming that people actively fled.
   - Text B is considerably longer and includes redundant words (*New Zealand*, 'bush', *more than*); it uses the passive but more official term *evacuation*; there is the dramatic time element of it lasting four days.

4 a

	Facts	Opinions
Text A	- 11 houses destroyed - State of emergency declared - 1000 people evacuated - Approx. 30 firefighters - 12+ helicopters - 2000+ hectares affected - 450 homes evacuated - Cause unknown/under investigation	- Should burn itself out - Rain should help put out fire
Text B	- 100+ evacuated - State of emergency declared - 4th day of fire - 1800+ hectares affected - Minimum 11 houses destroyed - Wind made fire uncontrollable - PM cancelled engagements - 15 helicopters and aircraft despatched - 15 is maximum safe number - 200+ firefighters involved - Helicopter pilot died	- Fire is like a monster - Worst fire ever seen in the area - Situation very serious - Huge job - Wind could make it worse - Lower temperatures could slow progress

   b Text A is the more accurate report, although Text B appears to contain more news.

   c Text B is the more sensational report.

Cambridge IGCSE First Language English — **Answers to coursebook questions**

5   a   content differences: not a headline but an argument title; moves immediately away from fire to general comments on climate change; more than half the article is in speech; only one source but this is quoted five times

   b   style differences: news reporting is prolix (unnecessarily wordy) instead of concise, e.g. *so odd and weird* is tautologous, *more and more* is redundancy, present perfect tense is wordy; modern idioms (*down stream*, *insane*); first and last lines – beginning with elision dots for dramatic purpose – repeated to reinforce the message

   c   aim differences: not to inform but to argue a personal cause and stir up sense of fear; the fire is only the 'hook' or excuse for the message

6   Students' own answers. Ensure that their blogs express their own reactions and views and follow the guidelines in Task Tip A6 next to the question.

B Adopting a position

1   Reading task.

2   **(Example answers)**

   a   *Feng Shui* is an ancient Chinese philosophy relating to spaces, which has become accepted by interior designers in the West.

   b   It is based on the theory that there needs to be a balancing of opposing forces to create harmony in a place. It uses a special compass to determine the blend of the eight areas of life experience and the five Taoist natural elements.

   c   *Ch'i* is a positive flow of life forces; *sha* is a harmful and negative energy.

   d   Students' own answers.

3   Students' own answers.

4   Students' own answers.

5   Reading task.

6   a   Commas are the most common form of parenthesis.

   b   Brackets create the strongest separation of extra material from the main idea and are the least often used nowadays.

   c   Dashes are the least formal and most sensational of the three methods and are less likely to occur in older writing.

7   **(Example answers)**

   a   Possible titles: Does teenspeak limit life chances?; *Yeah*, *no* and *but* rule, OK; Are 800 words enough?; Simple and short may not be sweet; Electronic media in the firing line again

   b   • some teenagers use only 800 words per day

      • they risk being unemployable

      • they use repetitive, short, simple (texting) words

      • this reduces their ability to express themselves

      • teenagers communicate mainly through electronic devices

      • need to understand that formal language is a life skill

      • 16-year-olds have actual vocabulary of 40 000 words, but use only a tiny fraction of them

      • 1000 words is the minimum for meaningful communication

      • parents should limit babies to half an hour of TV per day

      • conversation is necessary to expand vocabulary

c   Teenagers are limiting themselves to such a narrow range of vocabulary that they are reducing the likelihood of academic success and getting a job.

8   **a, b and c** Students' own answers.

C Analysing an argument

1   **a**   genres of writing: informative article; review; report; advert; discursive article.

   b   personal view of writer on this topic: not in favour of current drones, as associates them with 'geeks' and thinks they're *clunky*; a better version will take too long to develop (*years away*) and cost too much (*thousands of dollars*); thinks they are a passing *fad* and that they are dangerous because of the stupidity or evil intentions of those who fly them; new restrictions will finish them off.

   c, d and e Students' own answers.

2   **a**   Sandy believes children should be constantly praised and never punished by adults, as this damages their confidence and causes them to underachieve in later life and have unfulfilling relationships. Kim believes that only through discipline, hard work and competition can a child acquire realistic goals and be prepared to become a successful and respectful member of society.

   b and c Students' own answers.

3   (Example answers)

   a   *Water has many uses*: pedestrian, unengaging

   b   *As with most questions, there are two sides to be considered*: general, vague

   c   *Nobody who has a television could have not been horrified by the recent events*: tortuous, unclear

   d   *Many factors affect how we live today*: obvious, uninteresting

   e   *I feel very very strongly about this topic*: personal, overstated, gives away viewpoint too soon

4   Students' own answers.

5   **a**   words/phrases that continue the argument in the same direction: *moreover, in addition, consequently, what is more, therefore*

   b   words/phrases that indicate a change to another viewpoint: *however, nevertheless, on the other hand, on the contrary*

6   (Example answer)

   [1] not distributed fairly

   [2] responsible for greed and envy

   [3] gives people false values

   [4] rich people often unhappy

   [5] can destroy relationships

   [6] cause of most crimes

   [7] connected to politics – causes corruption

   [8] reason for wars

7 and 8   Students' own answers.

9   **a**   Reading task.

b In the class discussion, students may note that newspapers have editorials to influence the readers' views on national and international news events and topical political and social issues, and to make readers feel that their newspaper represents their own attitudes to the world.

10 a words that evoke strong emotion: *horrific, disaster*

b words that have dramatic effect: *relentlessly, dramatic, ice-cool, horrific death, sinking, hero, miracle, disaster, certain catastrophe, slammed, wrestled, split-second*

c unusual word order for emphasis: *Not for nothing was he rapidly dubbed*

d alliteration for impact: *ice-cool reflexes and professional skill, Not for nothing*

e extremes, absolutes and negatives for tension: *vast, extremely, at all, outstanding, rare and extreme, many hundreds, most perfect … ever, only seconds, Nothing, no airfield, no power and no altitude*

f words that steer the reader's response: *relentlessly drive down, unwise observers, dramatic evidence, difference between life and horrific death, no amount of fancy electronics*

11 Students' own answers. Ensure that their plans reflect some of the features in the list in Task Tip C11.

Cambridge IGCSE First Language English — Answers to coursebook questions

Unit 12

A Dialogue in narratives

1 Reading task.

2 **a** Allegorical features: The characters have no names or physical descriptions; they are complementary genders and ages to represent human types; the dialogue is balanced throughout, as if they are making parallel moves, mirroring the game they are playing; there is no description or setting; the focus is the philosophies they are expressing; there is no conclusion to the game or the story, symbolising that life is always ongoing and one doesn't get to hear the end of the story.

   b Students' own answers.

   c We learn that they have similar voices but different viewpoints. They are both reflective and wise. They could represent ancient and modern as stereotypes, but with the twist that the young character surprises and teaches the older character.

   d The use of dialogue contributes a dramatic element, as if the game is being played on stage and tension is created as we wait to see how the characters will respond to each other in what is in effect a kind of argument.

   e Dialogue is likely to be effective in a narrative at the end, to provide a punchline or neat conclusion, or at moments of high tension in the action, either to cause delay and therefore suspense, or to explain the significance of what is happening. In this case, the dialogue is a device for indicating time jumps and the difference of opinion of the two protagonists.

3 Answers can be found in Task Tip A3 next to the task in the coursebook.

4 Students' own answers.

5 Possible verbs to use instead of *said*: shouted, muttered, screamed, exclaimed, murmured, whispered, stuttered, lisped, stammered, bragged, faltered, raged, moaned, complained, demanded, ordered, whimpered

6 Discussion task.

7 Reading task.

8 (Example answer)

'It is a bad idea to steal the chemicals from the school science laboratory,' pointed out Diwan to his friend Sanjeet, who was busy hiding packets of them in his school bag.

'No one will notice they are missing and we can have some fun with them after school,' responded Sanjeet.

'What are they for?'

'I plan to mix them together and set fire to them to make some spectacular smells, colours and noises.'

Diwan warned, 'If you don't know what you are doing, chemicals can be very dangerous, especially when mixed together. It isn't worth the risk of injury or of being caught for stealing.'

Sanjeet shouted, 'You are no fun, Diwan. You are much too timid and boring. If you aren't going to join in then I will find someone else to hang out with, today and every day.'

B Viewpoint and character

1 Reading task.

2 **a** The fairy tale is *Little Red Riding Hood*. The moral is that children will be punished if they do not obey their parents.

   b Text B is more sympathetic to the main character, because it includes her emotions. Text A stresses her disobedience rather than her fear.

c The sympathy has been created by saying that the girl is *young* and *doesn't want to go*, she is *frightened* and *unsuspecting*, the forest is *dangerous*, the wolf is *large* and *evil*, that he *tricks* her and that she is *terrified*.

3 Students' own answers.

4 Reading task.

5 a A case can be made for empathising with either character. The dentist inflicts unnecessary pain, enjoys having power, and achieves nothing; the mayor is overbearing, ungrateful and has possibly caused deaths. Both are victims and both are bullies.

b Students' own answers.

6 Listening task.

7 The writer responds to rather than initiates the conversation and its topics. He speaks Standard English, as befits his social status and occupation. Some of his answers are monosyllabic, as if he is the weaker partner in the dialogue, despite apparently enjoying a higher social status as a car owner and writer.

The hitch-hiker dominates the conversation by talking more, asking questions and being provocative. He speaks colloquially (refers to the car as *she*), in a forthright, emphatic way, using simple words and repetitions. He has a regional accent, omitting the final *g* and initial *h* of words. His use of idioms (e.g. *a tidy packet* and *crummy*), and abbreviations (e.g. *OK* and *ads*), and grammatical errors, such as *them that spend*, give the impression is that he is poorly educated.

8 (Example answers)

Hitch-hiker:
- *asked*: probed
- *said*: stated
- *said*: continued
- *answered*: declared
- *asked*: quizzed
- *said*: asserted
- *said*: demanded.

Writer:
- *said*: offered
- *asked*: enquired
- *told*: replied to.

9 Students' own answers.

C Use dialogue effectively

1 Reading task.

2 a Her mental disturbance is revealed in the lack of paragraphing, simple and non-sentences, sudden topic changes, excessive talk about the wallpaper, use of exclamations, and repetitive use of certain words (e.g. nervous). These are all the characteristics of a child; she identifies with children and seems to be regressing to a state of helpless dependency.

b Her husband has been conveyed as controlling and uncaring by his comment on the draught, his refusal to let her change rooms, his hourly over-medication, his patronising speech (*my dear*), the rules she must obey, his being more conscious of the length of the rental agreement than the need to make her surroundings comfortable. He is a hard-headed, pragmatic man, scientifically-trained, who has no sympathy for his artistic wife's imagination and *fancies*.

Cambridge IGCSE First Language English — Answers to coursebook questions

c   The story is in the form of a diary, so we feel she is being open and honest as she is writing to herself. We see her viewpoint and hear her first-person voice. We know how frightened she is of her husband. She would like to write openly but it is forbidden. She has to go along with her doctor/husband's diagnosis of her condition, but neither she, nor the reader, knows if it is a correct one. The windows to her prison are barred, and there is also a gate at the top of the stairs. She is desperate to go and visit the garden.

d   She is a naive narrator and therefore tells the reader things she does not realise the significance of. She is now a mother but is being treated as a naughty child, locked in her *atrocious nursery* as a punishment. She feels guilty about being a burden, yet it was her husband's decision to take away her baby, give him to a nurse, and lock up his wife. We know that he is not at all *careful and loving*, as she claims. She claims her case is *not serious* when it obviously is. He may think, in his callous way, that his treatment and her incarceration will do her good, but they are in fact doing her great harm.

e   The plot seems to be tending towards the total breakdown of the narrator, who will become increasingly obsessed with the wallpaper (see the novella's title) and start trying to free herself from her prison, of its tormenting *deadly depressing* effect on her. The children who previously inhabited the room had already stripped off some of the paper. There is a foreshadowing reference to *ghostliness* and her believing there is *something strange* in the house, so this will be developed. There is also a reference to suicide. The atmosphere, imagery and all other indications are against there being a positive resolution to this story.

3   a   the short sentences: The genre is a hidden diary and the short sentences are almost in note form; they make the persona sound secretive, naive, childlike, unable to develop a thought.

   b   the short paragraphs: One-sentence paragraphs make the text structure disjointed and unfocused, suggesting that the narrator is rambling incoherently, is disorganised mentally and unable to stay on one topic or link ideas.

   c   the sentence structures: Many sentences start the same way, many are simple or start with *And* or *But*, and there is no attempt at stylistic variation, which mirrors the idea of imprisonment and routine; they give the impression that the narrator is not used to expressing herself. Many of the compound sentences start with a positive utterance which is then negated by *but* or *and yet*, which has the effect of her contradicting herself or being contradicted by her husband. The overall effect of the sentence structures is one of confusion, negation and deprivation. *I* is used to begin a sentence less often than *He* or *It*, which accentuates the lack of self-worth and significance in the household of the narrator. There is a sudden and unexpected contrast in language when the wallpaper is described, which conveys how surprisingly strongly she feels about it and demands reader sympathy.

   d   the exclamations: These contrast with the lack of exuberance and emptiness of feeling in the passage – it's as if they are a kind of release for the narrator. They are juxtaposed with John's mode of expression to allow the reader to infer the vast difference in temperament and how much he disapproves of her displaying emotion.

   e   the imagery: The recurring images are of locks, bars and gates, and windows that must not be opened – all symbolic of the narrator being trapped in the house and in her mind by her husband. She is not allowed access to her baby and has nothing to do; *dull* and *nervous* are much-used words to convey the monotony of her days and surroundings, and the mental anguish this is causing. She has been deprived of the sight of the pretty roses in the garden and the lively chintz material downstairs, and has instead been confined to the ugly *sprawling flamboyant patterns* of the sickly yellow wallpaper, representing her unhealthy existence and impending breakdown.

4   Reading task.

5   **(Example answers)**

   a   The use of direct speech makes him seem to be a confident character. Similar to the opening scene of a play, a character arrives in a new location and is trying to attract attention and assert his presence. He seems to be a confident character, used to taking charge. He has to repeat himself, which suggests there is something wrong and things will not go according to plan. At this point he has the upper hand which warns of an ironic reversal of roles later in the story when he will become the listener not the speaker.

b The signalman's lack of response suggests there is something amiss. It adds dramatic tension to the scene. It begins the story with an atmosphere of abnormality and indicates to the reader that something odd is about to happen.

c The narrator is high up, looking down into a *steep cutting* and *deep trench* with a depressing and forbidding air. He has to descend into a different world, a darker and more constricted space, which may change his role and perceptions. It is ominous that he has to make a *zig-zag descent*, with connotations of risk, near to the *entrance to a black tunnel*. The *glow of an angry sunset* suggests that all is not well or peaceful, which is reinforced by there being only a *strip of sky* visible. It is a *solitary* place, far from help, and it is typical of ghost or horror stories to begin as the sun is setting and darkness is approaching. It is a place with *so little sunlight*, and much is made of it being below the normal world.

d We can infer that the narrator is used to being in control by the way he addresses strangers in an imperious manner and expects to be answered.

e The signalman is described as acting in a strange, confused manner. We expect to learn that he has recently had an unusual and disorientating experience, which has left him afraid to carry out his job. He is described as acting *out of reluctance or compulsion* and as *foreshortened*, which suggests that he is not in control of the situation and may well become a victim.

f The atmosphere is *dismal* and chilly, as if the story is set in darkness and damp. The senses of sight, sound, smell and touch have been used. There is an *earthy deadly smell* and *much cold wind*. We associate a *dungeon* with imprisonment. The words that contribute to this effect include: *shadowed*, *precipitate*, *clammy*, *oozier*, *wetter*, *dripping-wet*, *jagged*, *crooked*, *gloomy*, *gloomier*, *black*, *lonesome*.

g In addition to the foreboding created by the setting, the passage drops hints that the signalman is behaving in a peculiar and worrying way that foreshadows later developments. The narrator refers to *something remarkable in his manner*, and states that *he seemed to regard me with fixed attention*. He also says that *His attitude was one of such expectation and watchfulness*, and that he had a *singular air of reluctance or compulsion*. The pragmatic narrator admits that *there was something in the man that daunted me*. All of this builds the suspense.

h The train makes such a noise that the characters are drowned out. It is a *violent pulsation* and *an oncoming rush* that forces the characters to stand back, and the narrator comments that is seemed *as though it had force to draw me down*. The cutting was made for the train, and the train asserts its presence and disregard of human life, like a rushing mechanical monster bearing down on anything in its way. It foreshadows that a later event will include a train.

i The narrator feels as if he has *left the natural world*: this indicates that he has entered a strange and sinister world that is in the earth. The signalman will be the focus of whatever strange event will occur. He is already obviously disturbed: this has something to do with the words being called out to him by the visitor, because he does not reply to them, as if he doesn't believe that the visitor is real.

j The power of the story comes from our not knowing why the signalman is behaving so oddly and our seeing him only from the viewpoint of the first-person narrator. The only information we can learn is from the narrator's questioning of the signalman. Because the narrator is presented as practical, sensible and sceptical, providing a contrast to the signalman's odd behaviour, it will be all the more frightening if the narrator should later admit that he was wrong and the signalman was right.

6 Students' own answers.

Unit 13

A Fluency and clear speech

1 Students' own answers.

2 (Example answer)

The 'rules' of cricket
- Two teams play in the game. One team take its turn to score while the other team acts as fielders. One of the players bowls the ball to the batter.
- The aim is for the fielding team to get 'out', in turn, each of the 11 players in the team that is batting.
- The batting team scores by making runs between the two wickets while the ball is in play after the batter has hit the ball.
- The teams then swap places and repeat.
- The winning team is the one that scores the highest total of runs during their two innings (their two turns at batting) each.

3 Students' own answers.

4 Reading task.

5 (Example answers)
- idioms and colloquialisms: *Once upon a time*; *kids*; *way back*; *Actually*; *I guess a whole new dimension*; *What they don't get is that*
- fashionable expressions: *tech-savvy*; *geeks*; *clunky*
- contractions: *that's how*; *parents can't see and don't know*
- use of *you* and *I*: *I hope you can hear*; *you can imagine*
- monosyllabic vocabulary: *kids*; *geeks*
- starting sentences with coordinating connective: *So that's what playing games*; *But the key point is*; *And it is truly creative*
- acronyms: *'MMO' games*
- afterthoughts signified by dashes: *– or rather, not the invention|: mostly older people – ; is that many – most –*
- asides: *(if it ever was!)*; *(because they don't ask!)*; *think of the Sims*
- exclamations: *if it ever was!*; *they don't ask!*
- non-sentences: *Tomorrow, who knows?*
- simple grammatical structures: *At least, that's how parents interpret it*
- active rather than passive verbs: most of the verbs used in the extract

6 (Example answer)
- Do you believe that nowadays children learn more from their games than they did in previous times when they played with toys?
- Would you agree that playing on a form of computer technology is likely to reduce the amount of time children spend outdoors or on any form of physical exercise?
- Do you think that earning points for violence and *systematic slaughter*, even in a game, is a good message to be sending young people?
- Do you think the majority of people would agree with you that computer gaming is *fundamentally harmless*?

Cambridge IGCSE First Language English — Answers to coursebook questions

- Would you like to see adults and parents taking more interest in what children are playing on screen?
- If the type of games boys and girls play is very different, it is really true that computer gaming is reducing gender stereotyping?
- How do you foresee computer games developing in the future?

7   a   *Erm … I'm not really sure what I'm going to talk about, but my favourite pastime is probably fishing … I think*: unplanned, uncommitted

     b   *I am a leading expert in computer graphics, so listen and I'll tell you all about the subject, at length and in great detail*: long and dull

     c   *Sub-atomic particles can be subsumed into hadrons and leptons, but spin and sense are fundamental criteria for any hierarchical categorisation matrix construct*: incomprehensible, over-technical

     d   *Before I start, I need to explain my life history and how I came to be involved in recycling*: irrelevant and unfocused

     e   *I'm sure you feel the same way as I do about spiders. I mean, they're just really spooky, right?* subjective and too informal

8

Do	Don't
plan	go into unnecessary detail
rehearse	use jargon
speak fairly slowly and clearly	repeat yourself
use intonation	use distracting body language
use precise and varied vocabulary	use overlong and over complex sentences
vary sentence structures and lengths	use a lot of colloquial terms
get the length of the talk right	spend too long on the introduction
end strongly	

9   (Example answer)

- How long have I had this hobby? [2]
- What is its exact definition? [1]
- What equipment/environment is necessary? [7]
- What memorable/successful/disastrous moments have occurred? [9]
- What kind of people share my hobby/ how common is it? [5]
- How do I see my future with regard to this hobby? [10]
- What caused me to take up this hobby? [3]
- What is its physical/emotional appeal? [4]
- What are its difficulties and drawbacks? [8]
- How do my family/friends regard my hobby? [6]

10–13   Students' own answers.

B Appropriate dialogue

1–3 Students' own answers.

4

Formal	Informal
precise vocabulary	colloquial expressions
terminology	incomplete sentences
mature vocabulary	everyday vocabulary
longer words	contractions
complex sentences	shorter words
longer utterances	simple or compound sentences
passive verbs	shorter speeches
	active verbs

5 Speaking task.

C Interviews

1–3 Speaking tasks.

Unit 14

A Distinguishing facts and opinions

1 Students' own answers.

2 Listening task.

3 (Example answer)

Facts	Opinions
obsession is a form of mental illness	Health is a commodity
We all want to be healthy	we've all become more health conscious
health is not beauty and fitness	health is no longer something everyone is born with
The outer person is not a direct reflection of the inner person	It is something you can have more of
If life were that simple, medical diagnosis would be an awful lot easier	you have to buy a tracksuit
lots of supremely fit people […] are psychologically deranged	health is not a purely physical state
a lot of quite seriously disabled people […] are bright, happy …	in any society except his own, Attila the Hun would have been regarded as a psychopath
Compulsive slimming and exercising are a form of obsession	health is a terribly difficult word to define. It is nevertheless important to do so
the criteria for physical and mental health are a matter of opinion	Arguably, this says it all
a tribe in the Amazon rainforest […] regards you as unwell if you don't have pale, circular patches	'psychological health is the ability to love and to work'
unless we know what health is we don't know what to aim for	It's an easy thing to aim for and at the same time very difficult to arrive at
Enshrined in the constitution of the World Health Organization is this statement	There are […] occasional moments in everyone's life when you experience, simultaneously, a great love for those around you and also a great sense of personal fulfilment
	These fleeting moments are very hard to achieve, but they constitute a more worthwhile aim in life than trying to look like a supermodel.

4 Students' own answers.

B Expressing and supporting opinions

1 Listening task.

2–4 Speaking tasks.

C Public speaking

1 and 2 Students' own answers.

3 inclusive pronouns: use of we and you throughout and humble avoidance of 'I'

double/binary phrases: *prosperity… peace*; *prosperity and freedom*; *skill or vision*; *less… but no less…*; *conflict and discord*; *data and statistics*; *faithful to… true to…*; *violence and hatred*; *too costly… too many*; *of who we are and how far we have travelled*; *honesty and hard work*; *courage and fair play*; *tolerance and curiosity*; *loyalty and patriotism*

emotive abstract nouns/military archaisms: *prosperity*; *freedom*; *happiness*; *progress*; *peace*; *dignity*; *hope*; *virtue*; *America*; *carried forth*; *let us brave once more…*; *huddled by dying campfires*; *stained with blood*

alliteration: *old friends and former foes*; *prosperous*; *powerful*

repeated structures: *So it has been… So it must be*; *On this day…*; *the time has come…*; *God bless…*; *generation to generation*;

triples/rule of three: are *real…are serious… are many*; *houses… jobs…businesses*; the risktakers, the doers, the makers; *all our equal*; *all are free*; *and all deserve*; *struggled and sacrificed and worked*; *birth or wealth or faction*

sustained metaphors *journey; battle; winter*

short, simple and compound sentences:/categorical statements: *These things are true.*

direct speech and quotation

4–6 Students' own answers.

7 Speaking task.

Acknowledgements

The authors and publishers acknowledge the following sources of copyright material and are grateful for the permissions granted. While every effort has been made, it has not always been possible to identify the sources of all the material used, or to trace all copyright holders. If any omissions are brought to our notice, we will be happy to include the appropriate acknowledgements on reprinting.

Unit 1 'Time' by Allen Curnow, used with the permission of Auckland University Press on behalf of author; Unit 2 Adapted from 'Monty's method' by Harvey McGavin in the TES, September, 2001; Unit 3 'A Boarder's View' by Donald McGregor in *The Alternative Old Pocklington Bulletin* by permission of the author; Unit 5 excerpt from *Boy* by Roald Dahl used with the permission of David Higham Associates © 1984 published by Jonathan Cape Ltd and Puffin Book Ltd; Unit 5 excerpt from 'The Rose-Beetle Man' in *My family and Other Animals* by Gerald Durrell, used with the permission of Curtis Brown Group Ltd on behalf of the Estate of Gerald Durrell, copyright © Gerald Durrell 1956; Unit 6 'Games at Twilight' from *Games at Twilight and Other Stories* by Anita Desai, Published by Anvil Press Poetry, 1990, used with the permission of Rogers, Coleridge & White Ltd., 20 Powis Mews, London W11 1JN, Copyright © Anita Desai; 'Hide and Seek' by Vernon Scannell, used with the permission of The Estate of Vernon Scannell; Unit 7 'The End of the Party' by Graham Greene, published in 1929, used with the permission of David Higham Associates; Unit 8 Extract from *Lord of the Flies* by William Golding, published by Faber and Faber Ltd., copyright 1954, renewed © 1982 by William Gerald Golding used with the permission of Faber & Faber Ltd.& G. P. Putnam's Sons, an imprint of Penguin Publishing Group, a division of Penguin Random House LLC.; Unit 8 *The Woman in Black* by Susan Hill, adapted and used with the permission of Sheil Land Associates Ltd., published by Vintage, © Susan Hill 1983; Unit 9 'Jim Thompson's House', James H.W. Thompson Foundation; Unit 10 Excerpt from 'Relative values: Amaral Samacumbi and his brother', Luis, The Sunday Times: 24.02.2008, with permission from News Licensing; Unit 10 Extract from *Things Fall Apart* by Chinua Achebe, used with the permission of Penguin Random House UK, © Penguin Classics, 2001; Unit 11 'Cousteau and his incredible Trojan shark' by Matthew Campbell, The Sunday Times: 02.10.2005, adapted and used with the permission of News Licensing; Unit 12 'Too Bad' by Dorothy Parker, abridged extract, copyright 1923, renewed © 1951 by Dorothy Parker, *The Portable Dorothy Parker* by Dorothy Parker, edited by Marion Meade. Used with the permission of Gerald Duckworth Ltd & Viking Books, an imprint of Penguin Publishing Group, a division of Penguin Random House LLC; Unit 12 'Suffering in Silence' from 'The Way Up To Heaven' in *Kiss Kiss* by Roald Dahl, Penguin, 2011, used with the permission of David Higham Associates; Unit 13 'Fur and against' by A.A Gill, The Times, adapted & used with the permission of News Licensing; Unit 13 Extract from www.furisdead.com used by permission of PETA; Unit 15 'Well done class, you learnt zilch' by Chris Woodhead, The Sunday Times, 15.04. 2007, adapted and used with the permission of News Licensing; Unit 16 *Native Speaker* by Chang-Rae Lee, used with the permission of Granta Books and Riverhead Books, an imprint of Penguin Group (USA) Inc. © 1995 Chang-Rae Lee; Unit 16 'Hello, class, I'm the 16-year-old head' by Dean Nelson, Sunday Times, 29.06.2008, adapted and used with the permission of News Licensing; Unit 18 'There will come soft rains' by Ray Bradbury, Published in Harper Voyager, 1995 used with the permission of Don Congdon Associates Inc.; Unit 19 *Rebecca* by Daphne Du Maurier, Virago, 2003, used with the permission of Curtis Brown, UK; Unit 20 'Portrait of a city: Tokyo' by Andrew Miller, published in High Life Magazine, British Airways, Sept 2008, used with the permission of United Agents Ltd.; Unit 20 'Chinatown, Kuala Lumpur: A Walking Tour and Long Lunch' by Revati Victor, adapted and used with the permission of the author; Unit 20 'Temple of Heaven' from Beijing tour guide, used with the permission of Wanderstories; Unit 21 'The final choice' published in *Touching the Void* by Joe Simpson, used with the permission of Penguin Random House, UK and Harper Collins, USA. Copyright © 1989 by Joe Simpson; Unit 22 *A Horse and Two Goats* by R. K. Narayan, abridged, used with the permission of Wallace Literary Agency, New York copyright © 1970 by R. K. Narayan; Unit 23 *The Wall* by William Sansom, published in The Vanguard Press, 1945, used with the permission of Greene& Heaton © William Samsom; Unit 23 *The Go-Between* by L P Hartley (Hamish Hamilton 1953, Penguin Books 1958, 1997, 2000) Copyright © 1953 by L.P. Hartley, Penguin Books 1997, 2000 editions Copyright © Douglas Brooks-Davies 1997. Reproduced with permission of Penguin Books Ltd., UK; Unit 24 'The Pedestrian' by Ray Bradbury from *The Golden Apples of the Sun*, Avon Books, 2008 © 1951 by the Fortnightly Publishing Company, renewed 1971 by Ray Bradbury used with the permission of Don Congdon Associates Inc.

Thanks to the following for permission to reproduce images:
Cover image: AleksandarNakic/Getty Images; Unit 1 Classen Rafael/Getty Images; Adam Burton/Getty Images; Unit 2 Image courtesy of Monty and Pat Roberts Inc., photo by Christopher Dyke; Unit 3 Peter Dazeley/Getty Images; Unit 4 Hero Images/Getty Images; Funstock/Getty Images; Unit 5 THEPALMER/Getty Images; AttaBoyLuther/Getty Images; Unit 7 Taiyou Nomachi/Getty Images; Unit 8 Pierre-Yves Babelon/Getty Images; Andy Catlin/Getty Images; Edsongrandisoli/Getty Images; Unit 9 Paul Williams/Alamy Stock Photo; Unit 10 Uriel Sinai/Getty Images; Unit 11 Stephen Frink/Getty Images; Bettmann/Getty Images; Unit 12 JENasir/Getty Images; Unit 13 Lillisphotography/Getty Images; Unit 14 Kertlis/Getty Images; PashaIgnatov/Getty Images; Unit 15 Pavliha/Getty Images; Unit 16 Kantapat Phutthamkul/Getty Images; Anna Henly/Getty Images; Unit 17 H. Armstrong Roberts/Getty Images; Fine Art Images/Getty Images; 'L.H.O.O.Q' © Association Marcel Duchamp/ADAGP, Paris and DACS, London 2017; MalcolmFreeman.Com/Alamy Stock Photo; © Udronotto aka Marco Pece; Rui Vieira/PA Archive/PA Images; Walter Bennett/Getty Images; Unit 18 Martin Garnham/Alamy Stock Photo; Paul Seheult/Getty Images; Ben Pipe/Getty Images; Miguel Navarro/Getty Images; Hisham Ibrahim/Getty Images; Jayme Thornton/Getty Images; Daniel Schoenen/Getty Images; I. Glory/Alamy Stock Photo; Unit 19 Melinda Moore/Getty Images; Unit 20 20.1 SeanPavonePhoto/Getty Images; Jayk7/Getty Images; Manfred Gottschalk/Getty Images; Unit 21 StockFinland/Getty Images.

Thanks to the following for permission to reproduce texts within the Progression Checks:
'It is dormant, right?' Stephen Bleach, Sunday Times, June 2012, used by permissions of News Licensing; 'An amazing eight seconds' from the website of the American Astronomical Society (http://aas.org) used with permission of the American Astronomical Society and TracelQuest International (www.travelquesttours.com); 'Heroic rats' is based on information from www.apopo.org and used with permission; 'Mexican Mariachi Music from 'Nuestra Herencia': How a Chicago Schools Mariachi Group Landed a Latin Grammy Nomination' by Kristina Pugs, October 2017 NBC News www.nbc.com; 'Jim Thompson's House', James H.W. Thompson Foundation; 'On your bike: the best and the worst of city cycle schemes' by Patrick Collinson 25 Feb 2017, copyright Guardian News & Media Ltd 2018; 'Hot in the City'by Francesca Angelini - Dabbawalas in Mumbai, Sunday Times Magazine, November 2017 used by permission of News Licensing; 'Lost in evolution'by James Gillespie for the Sunday Times, December 2011, used by permission of News Licensing.

Cambridge IGCSE First Language English